# Continuity & change

Casuistry & Chance

# Continuity and change

Personnel and administration
of the Church in England 1500–1642

Edited by Rosemary O'Day & Felicity Heal

Leicester University Press
1976

First published in 1976 by Leicester University Press
Distributed in North America by Humanities Press Inc., New Jersey

Copyright © Leicester University Press 1976

Designed by Arthur Lockwood
Set in Monotype Baskerville
Printed in Great Britain by Western Printing Services Ltd, Bristol
Bound by G. & J. Kitcat Ltd, London
ISBN 0 7185 1138 7


The publication of this book has been assisted
by a grant from the Twenty-Seven Foundation

To all students of Reformation history

# Contents

7

Contents

# 𝕿𝖍𝖊 𝕮𝖔𝖚𝖗𝖙𝖘 𝕮𝖍𝖗𝖎𝖘𝖙𝖎𝖆𝖓

# Preface

The editors and contributors thank the following for their help and advice in the preparation of this volume: the staffs of the undermentioned libraries and record offices: British Museum; Bodleian Library (Dr M. Barratt); Borthwick Institute of Historical Research, York; Cambridge University Library (Mrs D. M. Owen); Cheshire County Record Office; University of Durham Library; Guildhall, London; Inner Temple Library; Lambeth Palace Library; Lichfield Joint Record Office (Miss Jane Isaac); Lincoln Record Office; Norfolk and Norwich Record Office; Northampton Record Office; Prior's Kitchen, Durham (Pat Mussett); Public Record Office; West Sussex County and Chichester Diocesan Record Office. We express our appreciation of the co-operation and help extended to us by the Secretary to the Press, Mr Peter Boulton, and by Professor G. H. Martin of the University of Leicester. We also thank the Twenty-Seven Foundation for a grant towards the cost of publication.

Spelling in quotations cited in the volume has been modernized. References to manuscripts contained in the British Museum have been cited as B.M., MSS. for the convenience of the reader, despite the recent retitling of the Library and Manuscripts Room as the British Library. The editors wish to thank Dr W. J. Sheils for his kindness in up-dating references to manuscripts in the possession of the Borthwick Institute of Historical Research, York.

Rosemary O'Day and Felicity Heal

January 1975

# Abbreviations

### Journals

| | |
|---|---|
| A.H.R. | *Agricultural History Review* |
| B.I.H.R. | *Bulletin of the Institute of Historical Research* |
| C.Q.R. | *Church Quarterly Review* |
| E.H.R. | *English Historical Review* |
| Ec.H.R. | *Economic History Review* |
| H.J. | *Historical Journal* |
| H.T. | *History Today* |
| J.B.S. | *Journal of British Studies* |
| J.E.H. | *Journal of Ecclesiastical History* |
| P. & P. | *Past and Present* |
| T.R.H.S. | *Transactions of the Royal Historical Society* |

### Other works

| | |
|---|---|
| A.P.C. | *Acts of the Privy Council* |
| C.J. | *Commons Journals* |
| C.P.R. | *Calendar of Patent Rolls* |
| C.S.P.D. | *Calendar of State Papers Domestic* |
| C.Y.S. | Canterbury and York Society |
| D.N.B. | *Dictionary of National Biography* |
| Foster | J. Foster, *Alumni Oxoniensis* (Oxford, 1891–2) |
| H.M.C. | Historical Manuscripts Commission |
| L.P. | *Letters and Papers Henry VIII* |
| S.R. | *Statutes of the Realm* |
| V.C.H. | *Victoria County History* |
| V.E. | *Valor Ecclesiasticus* |
| Venn | J. and J. A. Venn, *Alumni Cantabrigienses* (Cambridge, 1922–7) |

### Libraries and Record Offices

| | |
|---|---|
| B.M. | British Library, British Museum |
| Bodleian | Bodleian Library, Oxford |

# Abbreviations

| | |
|---|---|
| Borthwick I.H.R. | Borthwick Institute of Historical Research, York |
| C.U.L. | Cambridge University Library |
| C.C.R.O. | Cheshire County Record Office |
| C.R.O. | West Sussex County and Chichester Diocesan Record Office |
| D.W.L. | Doctor Williams' Library, London |
| E.D.R. | Ely Diocesan Records |
| G.C.L. | Gloucester City Library |
| G.L.MS. | Guildhall London Manuscript |
| I.T.L. | Inner Temple Library |
| L.C.L. | Lichfield Chapter Library (now subsumed into L.J.R.O.) |
| L.P.L. | Lambeth Palace Library |
| L.J.R.O. | Lichfield Joint Record Office |
| L.R.O. | Lincoln Record Office |
| N.L.W. | National Library of Wales |
| N.R.O. | Northamptonshire Record Office |
| P.D.R. | Peterborough Diocesan Records |
| P.R.O. | Public Record Office |
| S.C.R.O. | Stafford County Record Office |

# Introduction

The historiography of the English Church in the century of the Reformation is already rich and diverse. The subject of this great religious change has raised strong passions among historians but also has produced some of the most powerful and convincing of descriptive writings, from the work of Bishop Burnet in the seventeenth century to that of Frere and Gairdner at the beginning of our own. This flood of writings has shown no signs of diminution during this century and, as the range of specialist research upon particular aspects of the Reformation has increased, more convincing general interpretations of the period have emerged. The present generation of scholars owes an especial debt to the work of A. G. Dickens, Patrick Collinson and Christopher Hill. Their works and others in the last 15 years have made accessible to scholars and students of the Tudor and Stuart period a whole range of fresh evidence and new ideas, and have in their turn stimulated further research into various aspects of the Reformation story.

The present volume is intended to show something of this new research and of the preoccupations of the younger generation of specialists in this field. Too much valuable work is still submerged in unpublished theses or hidden in local history publications which are not always readily available to those interested in the Reformation. The contributions are also intended to reflect the shared concerns of a particular group of young scholars, which have been furthered by the meetings of a Reformation history colloquium as well as by informal contacts. The major common ground between us has been an interest in using the local records of the Church as a basis for research. Until the last war little serious attention had been given to diocesan and other local ecclesiastical records by sixteenth- and early-seventeenth-century historians. This neglect reflected both inadequate cataloguing and often inadequate access to these archives and also a rather fixed belief among scholars that most of the significant evidence about the Church was to be found in the works of the English divines and the records of the central government. Noticeably, the historian's concept of what is *significant* has now changed. The essays in this volume demonstrate how important it is to base an understanding of the Church upon local records and other specialist sources, while not neglecting the crucial evidence available from traditional sources.

The use of local evidence has proved a basis upon which new common interests and concerns have emerged among Reformation scholars. One of these provides the theme for the volume: the study of the administration and personnel of the Church and the relationship between its internal organization and the wider problems of society. Institutional history has been out of fashion in ecclesiastical studies and much of the best recent research on the period has been strongly biased towards an examination of the impact of Protestantism upon society. Since the early years of the century, when Frere and Kennedy edited the *Visitation Articles and Inductions* and Usher wrote his important work on *The Reconstruction of the English Church*, few analyses of the institutions of the Church have been produced. Such detailed labour has all too often been left to medievalists. Yet were the institutions of the Church in the early modern period identical to those of the medieval Church? A study of the Reformation without a sympathetic understanding of the theoretical and practical functioning of the Church is a poor study indeed. Two works in particular have demonstrated this truth to Tudor and Stuart historians and have helped to stimulate the research comprised in this set of essays. B. L. Woodcock's detailed examination of the Canterbury diocesan courts in *Medieval Ecclesiastical Courts in the Diocese of Canterbury* (1952) showed how much could be drawn from the apparently arid record of judicial proceedings and his example has been followed for various other dioceses, including Norwich, Lincoln, York and Chichester. Even more influential has been Christopher Hill's book on *Economic Problems of the Church from Archbishop Whitgift to the Long Parliament* (1956), a book which combines an understanding of the organization of the Church with a new analysis of the relationship between that body and lay society. Hill's emphasis upon the economic aspects of the

Church opened a different field of study, and several of the essays in this volume reflect this interest in economic organization and the tensions within the fabric of the post-Reformation Church while applying to them a new type of evidence.

Above all it must be stressed that while the essays presented here stem from a common inspiration there has been no attempt whatsoever to make the individual contributions conform to a common interpretation of the Reformation or of aspects of organizational development. The discerning reader will note several divergences of opinion, for example, concerning the effectiveness of Church discipline.

2

The theme of continuity and change in the English Church provides a link between essays covering a wide diversity of subjects. The features which most distinguished the post-Reformation Tudor Church from its Continental reformed neighbours were those institutional structures which were a relic of the Catholic past: bishops and the ecclesiastical hierarchy beneath them; church courts administering the old canon law and also seeking to govern; and cathedrals staffed in the traditional way by prebendaries. Such a system had all the external appearance of continuity with the past and it was little wonder that the Puritans under Elizabeth lamented that the Church was 'but halfly reformed'. The crown saw the ecclesiastical hierarchy as an essential, or at least useful, bulwark against any radical alteration of the social and religious framework. Under Edward VI and Elizabeth the doctrinal attitudes of the establishment moved in close harmony with the Continental Reformation, and the 'popish' elements in the Church's structure were often underemphasized. Yet the Puritans were right to fear that the old organization could be employed for ends inimical to Calvinist theology, as well as Calvinist ritual. The spread of Arminian ideas under James I and their official acceptance under Charles I led to a reinvigoration of the old institutions and their employment for a partisan attack upon the religious views held by a large section of the English community. This general outline of continuity and tension is well known: the essays here try to probe beneath this external structure and they ask whether there was a true and effective continuity in administration and personnel in the pattern of the medieval Church or whether we must, after the Reformation, consider the surviving institutions as being altered fundamentally from within.

This volume makes no claim to cover this theme exhaustively over this long period. The essays are strictly insular. This is justified by the sharp separation in institutional structure between the English and the Continental reformed churches but it perforce ignores the similarity of the problems facing all the Protestant churches. These included the need to provide an educated, articulate ministry; the difficulties entailed in handling minority groups resolutely opposed to the established Church; and the need to establish discipline without the support and protection of Rome. Within the English Church the topics covered are limited both by the nature of the research being done in the area and by the editors' belief that certain topics demand immediate attention. The organization, jurisdiction and authority of the church courts have been given a prominent place, since it was through the courts that the ecclesiastical hierarchy most frequently came into contact with the rest of society and since it was through the courts that the policy of the Church had to be made operational and the dioceses administered. Also crucial in the relationship between Church and laity are the parish clergy. The quality of the clergy on the eve of the Reformation has already been examined elsewhere, and Dr O'Day's essay suggests what material is available and what interpretations are possible for the later sixteenth and early seventeenth centuries. Outside the parishes the most important personnel were the bishops on the one hand and the administrative officials of the dioceses on the other. Almost all the essays consider either explicitly or implicitly the effectiveness of the bishops in controlling and disciplining their sees during this disturbed century. The relationship between the bishop and his delegates who administered the diocese and organized the courts, and so put into effect the wishes of the hierarchy and crown, also receives attention. The editors have attempted to achieve a balance between essays which discuss the events in one particular diocese or locality and those which consider a general problem such as the jurisdiction of the church courts, the collection of clerical taxation or the control of clerical recruitment. It is hoped that the specialist studies also throw light on these broader issues. Both the approaches – specialist study by theme and by area – are crucial to a deeper understanding of the Church and of the Reformation.

Each of the essays has its own technical and source problems which are discussed in the appropriate place. It may be useful, however, to comment briefly upon some of the difficulties regularly encountered by those using ecclesiastical archives. Many of these difficulties arise from the poor state of preservation of diocesan, capitular and archidiaconal records. It is now rare to have to conduct research in chilly corners of cathedrals or medieval upper rooms, since the Church authorities have generously loaned most of their manuscripts to county record offices or libraries. The process of cataloguing has also proceeded apace, although in some cases it is still incomplete and overall only a limited number of published lists are available. This volume contains one particularly important example of the value of good cataloguing: Dr Kitching's article on the Prerogative Court of Canterbury has only been made possible by his own sorting of the scattered materials in the Public Record Office. While other treasures of this sort may still remain to be un-earthed, it is clear that the main problem of the ecclesiastical archives is that so much evidence has been lost for ever. The preservation of manuscripts varies greatly from diocese to diocese and from jurisdiction to jurisdiction. Many of the rich, well-organized dioceses such as Canterbury, Durham and London retain most of their formal records for the sixteenth and early seventeenth centuries. At the other extreme only a few manu-scripts survive from the Welsh sees, and even a see such as Ely has large gaps in its archive. Such uneven distribution of the surviving documentation of the Church makes truly comparative study of the English and Welsh sees difficult, if not impossible. Among the lesser jurisdictions cathedral chapters have often fared well, because of the continuity and stability of their organization, while archidiaconal records are rarely as good as those of the bishops. At the heart of the administration of the English Church, the loss of most of the records of the Court of

Arches and of the High Commission creates an irreparable gap.

The records of the various ecclesiastical bodies also change in character over the period. Episcopal registers and the act books of deans and chapters are often the only full manuscripts to survive for the early sixteenth century, although fortunate dioceses such as Canterbury, London, Lincoln and Chichester retain records of visitation and the activities of the courts. Most of the losses in other sees and jurisdictions must be attributed to time and mismanagement, but they may reflect also a less systematic approach to contemporary record-keeping outside the crucial episcopal register. In the later sixteenth century the register declined in importance in most dioceses, to be replaced by a variety of specialist records of institution, sequestration, licensing and so on. Court records survive far more uniformly and regularly from the Elizabethan period onwards, although deposition records are often lost, and various ancillary documents such as precedent books and correspondence survive sporadically. In this later period the main gaps occur in the economic records of the bishoprics and chapters: the obligation to keep such systematic accounts was never so strong as in the spiritual jurisdiction of the see and only after the Restoration can the financial affairs of the leaders of the Church be reconstructed in considerable detail.

3

The twin themes of continuity and change pervade most areas of the post-Reformation Church. Only where wholly new institutions were established, as in the new dioceses, or in cathedrals changed from monastic to secular government, is it difficult to find *direct* continuity with the early sixteenth century, and even here change was often more apparent than real. In ecclesiastical jurisdiction, the administration of the canon law through the complex system of church courts, the twin forces are well displayed. By the time of the Reformation the general pattern of the courts had been fixed for several centuries. Yet the system was neither rigid nor unchanging: the various jurisdictions still competed for business – archiepiscopal courts such as the Prerogative Court of Canterbury were still defining their jurisdiction in the early sixteenth century and in some dioceses the bishop's court of audience was beginning to play a more important part in the settling of cases. There were considerable organizational differences in the courts of various dioceses. To take but one example, in some sees the judicial powers of the archdeacons had been severely curtailed by agreement, whereas a few archdeacons, such as those of Richmond in the diocese of York, exercised virtually episcopal powers in their own territory. Thus it is not easy to produce a neat 'medieval model' of the functions and powers of the courts or to contrast such a one with a model for the post-Reformation period. However, some generalizations can be made. The medieval courts operated in an atmosphere in which the right of the Church to regulate all aspects of religious and moral behaviour was rarely questioned, and in which the purely spiritual sanctions of suspension and excommunication were still viewed with some dread, partly because the Church was still able to ensure that these sanctions had social and economic repercussions. Most of the normal activities of the church courts were tolerated by the crown, although direct appeal to Rome for the settlement of disputes was always a sensitive issue.

Within this very general framework the early Tudor decades saw a variety of changes, demonstrating that the courts were open to a number of direct influences. Dr Houlbrooke shows that the attitude of the crown could be important within the kingdom as well as in the matter of external appeals to Rome. Under Edward IV a charter of ecclesiastical liberties allowed the courts to flourish and probably to increase their business with little interference from the laity. Under Henry VII, however, in that period often popularly seen as the Indian summer of the medieval church, the weapon of *praemunire* was revived by the secular courts, with official support. The result was restrictions placed upon the operation of ecclesiastical jurisdiction, and something of a clerical backlash when the old king died. It is the behaviour and activity of the church courts under Henry VIII that provides an even more interesting background to the Reformation disturbances. In recent years research has shown that the old image derived from the 1532 *Commons' Supplication against the Ordinaries* of corrupt and inefficient church courts is inaccurate and partial.

Dr Lander's work on Chichester corroborates and strengthens the view that in fact the church courts in the 1520s were unusually efficient and that a bishop such as Sherburne of Chichester could breathe new life and vigour into these old institutions. Fragmentary evidence from Lincoln, Norwich, Coventry and Lichfield and Ely suggests that in the 20 years before the Reformation Parliament a number of bishops were taking a close personal interest in the administration of justice in their sees and that, even when they were not personally involved, their deputies were managing to despatch the most ordinary cases with speed and efficiency. The well-known persecution of the Lollards both at the beginning of Henry's reign and again during the period of More's ascendancy as chancellor reveals in another sense the determination of the bishops to use their judicial authority effectively.

This new drive to search out heretics, which was probably one of the main reasons for lay hatred of the courts under Henry VIII, can be related also to the broader concerns of some of the pre-Reformation bishops. Dr Lander shows that office causes, cases involving the discipline of laity and clergy, grew rapidly at Chichester. This is somewhat surprising as an increase in court business is more normally associated with the profitable instance causes between parties or with testamentary disputes. These causes remained important in the 1520s – indeed much of the tension between Wolsey as legate and the diocesan bishops arose because of the former's attempt to extend the range of his testamentary activity. Yet evidence from Lincoln and from Ely supports Dr Lander's contention that the bishops were interested in enforcing discipline through their courts and that they were particularly concerned with the behaviour and standards of the clergy.[1] Bishops Smith and Atwater at Lincoln kept a tight check on non-residents through their courts, as did Nicholas West at Ely. This concern for the clergy extended beyond the activities of the church courts to the positive commitment which many of the early-sixteenth-century bishops had to clerical education, which in turn owed much to the humanist ideals of Fisher's generation of bishops.

The state of at least some of the church courts in the 1520s would suggest that this, rather than the reign of Henry VII, was the Indian summer of the old order. Yet the courts already faced a crisis, created by the steady hostility towards their activities of a small but influential section of the laity, and greatly stimulated by the Hunne affair. With the Reformation Parliament the power of the old system was gravely threatened and, indeed, it must have appeared both to external observers and to many church-men virtually to be destroyed. The status of the courts themselves and of the law that they administered was in doubt for much of the century, as no Tudor monarch would sanction a re-codi-fication of the ecclesiastical law. The intervention of Cromwell as vicegerent in the 1530s, and the drastic changes in religious policy in the following two decades, also weakened the courts and led to a decline in business. This decline was reversed under Elizabeth: by the end of the sixteenth century the volume of business transacted in most courts was greater than it had been in the lively era before the Reformation. The survival and re-vival of the courts in these difficult years owed something to conscious government policy and something to the sheer inertia of institutions. More significantly it reflected the continuing usefulness of the courts, to the bishops and higher clergy as a means of imposing discipline and uniformity, and to the laity as a place for the settlement of disputes.

The jurisdiction of the church courts was eroded by the decisions of the crown, and in the later sixteenth century by the encroachments of the secular courts through the issue of writs of prohibition. The main threat to the courts and to the power which the bishops exercised through them came from below, from the growing contempt of many of the laity for ecclesiastical authority. The articulate minority of lawyers and gentry in the Reformation Parliament had already expressed this contempt and it was only a matter of time before they were echoed by large numbers of the less educated. In Dr Houlbrooke's vivid phrase, the ecclesiastical jurisdiction appeared like a house 'shifted from its foundations by heavy bombing'. A decline in respect for ecclesiastical sanctions can be seen very clearly in dioceses such as Norwich and Chichester: far more cases were left unfinished or were unduly protracted because one or more parties failed to appear; the penalty of public penance was rarely exacted. Neither suspension nor excommunication held the same terror that once

they had and, especially in urban and highly mobile com-
munities, large numbers of the excommunicate made no attempt
to be reconciled to the Church. The social and economic dis-
abilities incurred appear to have been few. To this disregard,
stemming from indifference, was added in the Elizabethan
period disregard arising from conviction, as both recusants and
Puritans resisted the will of the bishops.

The question of the decline of the church courts in the post-
Reformation period raises specific problems. On the one hand,
particularly in the immediate post-Reformation years, there was
often organizational failure: particular dioceses had corrupt and
inefficient courts or bishops who supervised their court officials
inadequately. The famous Elizabethan example of corruption is
the consistory court of Gloucester, presided over by a grasping
and dishonest chancellor who was subject to little or no control
by his diocesan.[2] None of the dioceses studied specifically in this
volume quite plumb the depths that Gloucester did but both
Chester and Peterborough are shown to have been deficient
because their bishops never had the resources or ability to establish a viable court system under their direct control. It is true,
however, that on occasion a consistory court could be run
efficiently when the bishop displayed little interest and even
when the chancellor was absentee but conscientious. On the
other hand, there was the more fundamental failure of the courts
to retain the respect and obedience of a majority of the laity. Mr
Hill has suggested that the sanction of excommunication lost its
effectiveness not because of the contempt into which the Church
fell in the 1530s but because it was an anachronism in a new
economic situation. Is this so? Whatever the conclusion on this
point, it is certainly true that even when strong bishops under the
Tudors, or efficient Arminians such as Neile under the Stuarts,
succeeded in tightening the control of the courts over diocesan
administration, they could not reverse the crucial changes in the
religious and social situation which made the courts irrelevant to
the indifferent and anathema to a small body of convinced and
often articulate recusants or Puritans. Only when the courts had
some particular use and value to lay society, as Dr Kitching
demonstrates that the Prerogative Court of Canterbury did in
probate business and as was true in instance litigation, did they

continue to wield the same effective power over the lay world both before and after the Reformation.

One would like to know why certain pre-Reformation bishops were so energetically engaging in the business of correction in the pre-Reformation period and whether their very zeal in purging the Church of its corruption eventually acted to the detriment of the Church's authority over the laity. Later churchmen were well aware of the danger of exposing in public the frailties of the Church's ministers and officers. Did men like Sherburne awaken in the laity contempt for their priests and dislike for the un-accustomed efficiency and wide-ranging jurisdiction of the courts spiritual in disciplining the laity? It has been hazarded occasion-ally that it was the increased effectiveness and rigorousness of the church courts in their approach to discipline and conformity after the Reformation, assisted by the visitation system, which roused hostility among the laity, just as it was disagreement with the views of the hierarchy on doctrine, ceremonial and church organization which caused groups of laymen and clerics to dis-regard the courts' injunctions. Certainly the courts now touched upon the lives of more of the laity than previously. Moreover, there is much to be said for the view that a system intent upon the enforcement of religious conformity was doomed to failure when faced with groups who were equally intent upon nonconformity and totally unwilling to submit to a law with which they dis-agreed fundamentally. The issue of consent was crucial to the continued authority of the church courts over the laity and clergy.

It was not then simply a matter of inefficient organization and administration. Corruption of church officials did not necessarily render a court ineffective in administering a particular policy. Technically the system was still capable of resuscitation when an individual bishop was determined enough and able enough to grasp control and inaugurate reforms. There are many examples of Elizabethan and early Stuart bishops who invigorated their diocesan administrations in much the same way as Sherburne, Atwater and Longland. Yet to increase the authority of the courts the bishop required a large measure of consent from those whom he was attempting to govern. Despite Arminian views and opposition to the Puritan wing, Neile appears to have achieved co-operation with lay and clerical groups. The courts Christian could still prove a highly effective means of correcting and disciplining the ministers and officials of the Church; of guarding church property and fabric; and of ensuring that the clergy could protect their tithing rights. As Dr Sheils has shown, this apparent effectiveness could be undermined, in certain instances, by strong lay support for clerical nonconformity. Essentially, however, what is really at issue after the Reformation is whether the courts still can control the laity effectively. On the whole it appears true that the Reformation undermined the general authority of the Church as a body (and not simply the courts) over the average Englishman. It was normally within the power of the post-Reformation bishops to keep their own house in order and little more.

The church courts and the whole administrative system of the English Church were controlled by the episcopate. In practice it is often difficult to gauge how much real influence the bishop exerted in his see. The problem is especially acute in the early sixteenth century when absentee bishops were not uncommon and when the administration of a see such as Worcester had to function for several generations without any direct support from its nominal head.[3] Episcopal intervention was crucial when unusual decisions had to be taken or difficult cases decided. Dr Lander demonstrates the importance of episcopal initiative in the reorganization of the Chichester courts, although even Sherburne, having chosen good deputies, delegated to them most of the routine execution of his new policy. The use of the audience court in a number of dioceses or the procedure whereby the bishop merely sat in consistory to hear important causes provided an opportunity for the bishop to decide difficult cases personally, although even heresy cases were often heard by the chancellor. The perambulations of the bishop about his diocese – conducting primary visitations in person, preaching, or merely leading a peripatetic existence between his various manors – no doubt strengthened the administration and created tenuous links between the parochial clergy and the hierarchy. More study of the pre-Reformation generation of bishops is needed to establish whether Sherburne typified the general attitude of the pre-Reformation episcopate.

Far fewer of the later Tudor and Stuart bishops were non-resident. All were required by the government to take an active part in enforcing religious conformity within their sees. They were also burdened with other duties, such as the closer supervision of tax collection, which proved onerous and caused friction in their relations with central government. These duties were imposed upon them at a time which was not favourable to the exercise of authority by the Church. The bishops laboured under peculiar difficulties: their lands and revenues were subject to demands from the crown and aristocracy; the poorer sees no longer had the financial resources to sustain an adequate administration or to exercise enough patronage to retain the support of the local gentry. The new bishoprics, given barely adequate revenues at the *beginning* of a period of inflation, were never able to provide outstanding leadership or to ensure that religious conformity which the crown required. Economic weakness haunted a see such as Chester throughout the Tudor period. Even when the Laudian bishop was able by vigorous action to strengthen episcopal finances, he did so at the expense of other aspects of administration and at the cost of alienating some sections of the laity.

Financial weakness and preoccupation with secular tasks prevented some of the bishops from acting effectively in the control and discipline of their dioceses. Another source of weakness was the relationship between the bishop and his deputies, especially when the bishop had little administrative experience or interest. A distinction has sometimes been made between those bishops trained in canon and civil law and those who were theologians, with the corollary that the latter have been noted as less competent administrators. Yet despite the loss of training in the canon law after the Reformation there were always men on the episcopal bench with administrative flair, who controlled the activities of their deputies, and who displayed interest in administration. The best example cited in this study is that of Bishop Neile, but there were others, such as Richard Cox, John Whitgift or Thomas Morton. It is true, however, that many of the theologian bishops, particularly those first-generation Elizabethan bishops, were less concerned with administration than with the preaching of the Protestant message and the recruitment of vocationally suitable clergy. Since few had previous experience of senior office, they were tempted to allow deputies to undertake all the regular administration of the diocese, although men like Thomas Bentham of Lichfield became deeply involved in the business of correction.[4] The classic example of administrative weakness was Bishop Parkhurst of Norwich, who allowed an entrenched group of administrators to dominate the diocese and to lead him into substantial debts with the crown.[5] While Parkhurst is an extreme case, the difficulties which he encountered exemplify the conflicting demands placed upon the bishops after the Reformation, and the inadequacy of some of the new type of church leader in face of them.

Below the bishops the key diocesan figures were the chancellor, the registrar and the other officials of the consistory court. These men suffered a change of role less sharp than did the bishops as a result of the Reformation: administrative processes continued in much the same way, although, of course, the canon lawyers were gradually replaced by those trained in civil law. The chancellor has not been accorded specific attention in this volume but his central importance in the smooth running of a diocese cannot be too much emphasized. The bishops placed great stress upon the value of a good chancellor: Bishop Bird of Chester emasculated the finances of both estates and administration in order to tempt George Wilmesley to the North. The chancellor frequently supplied continuity in diocesan administration: for example, John Rokeby, chancellor of York, ruled in the diocese for over 30 years until 1572, and gave to the courts during those disturbed years a reputation for honesty and efficiency that was rare indeed in Tudor England.[6] Where the chancellor was weak, or his position contested, the rest of the administration was likely to be inadequate: the nepotic policy of the bishops of Peterborough did nothing to strengthen them in their struggle with local Puritans. Alternatively, the chancellor could be unsatisfactory because he was too closely identified with the interests of the administration, and therefore liable to oppose rather than further the bishop's work. The diocesan administrations of the period show, Dr O'Day suggests, many of the features of the Weberian bureaucratic model, especially in their attempts to become self-perpetuating and to elevate their importance.

Dr O'Day's article on the office of registrar stresses a different aspect of diocesan administration, the influence which could be exerted by the secretariat. The registrar's office actually grew in power and influence as it managed an increased volume of business. Although the registrar did not have the same close personal relationship with the bishop as a secretary would have done, there are obvious parallels between the growing importance of this office and that of the Tudor secretaries of state. The growing complexity of the ecclesiastical bureaucracy as a whole is probably a reflection of changes occurring in secular government, as well as of the peculiar circumstances of the Church. There was the same tendency for offices to become the monopoly of a particular family or group and for the bishops thereby to lose effective control over their administrations. Vigorous bishops sought to counteract this movement by purchasing back hereditary offices when they were for sale or by creating new positions, such as that of episcopal secretary which became prominent in the early seventeenth century.

The administrative personnel formed the group least subject to change both during and after the Reformation, although they changed slowly in response to new social pressures. The clergy with cure of souls, or with responsibilities for teaching or preaching, were forced to be more directly aware of the new demands and conditions of the era. It is usual to think of the parochial clergy as responding only very slowly to change and of the Protestant ideal of a learned cleric as having a late and uneven influence in the parishes themselves. Dr O'Day's survey of the changing educational qualifications of the clergy confirms the general impression that changes were only gradually felt in the parishes but stresses that change in the standard of recruits was swift indeed when under way. By the second decade of the seventeenth century most clerical recruits had studied at one of the universities. This had been the goal of the Protestant hierarchy, as well as of the Puritans, from at least the beginning of Elizabeth's reign, but it could only be accomplished when the attitudes of those lay groups who supplied candidates for the ministry had been adjusted to accept the need for learned clergy. This shift of attitude occurred during Elizabeth's reign but it took a generation for these new forces to produce sufficient 'new' clergy to people the parishes. Only in exceptional circumstances, given the slow turnover of personnel and the additional complications of the patronage system, could the transformation in the parishes themselves be swift. Dr Marcombe supplies a very vivid example of the swift transition from the old to the new order in the cathedral of Durham. The new foundation of the dean and chapter, which unlike the new sees was well endowed, quickly came to occupy a different place in the diocese from that of the old priory. The essential differences were that the new chapter was closely involved in the life of the diocese and was active in preaching and, under Elizabeth, in making the cathedral a centre of Protestantism in an area still largely Catholic in sympathy. The dean and chapter had one other advantage over the priory and, indeed, over most of the parochial clergy whether old or new: the prebendaries were drawn from a higher social class than their predecessors. The confidence which their position gave them enabled them to withstand demands by the gentry for their estates and to uphold the general influence of the cathedral in the diocese. The lowly social status of many of the bishops had already been a subject of comment for several generations before the Reformation, but it was the intensely status-conscious world of the later sixteenth century that chose to make an issue of the origins of the clergy in general. Even then the question of social origin was normally raised only when the authority of the Church was in question: as Mr Foster points out, the Arminians were subject to more sneers about their dubious origins than any other generation since the Reformation.

When the essays which comprise this volume are evaluated as a whole, the theme of change in the post-Reformation churches emerges more clearly than that of continuity. Change has often, in this context, to be equated with decline: decline in the influence which the Church exerted over society; decline in the effective power of the courts; decline of episcopal influence owing to poverty and exclusion from central political power. Yet change was also a matter of building anew; of improving the existing institutions of the Church; of strengthening it from within to meet changed social conditions and religious demands. This is seen most clearly in the new dioceses and secular cathedrals of the Tudor period and studies presented here throw fresh light on the difficulties, successes and failures of these changed administrative units. In a broader sense there was a major change and revival among the parochial and other clergy who were the main representatives of the Church; over several generations the clergy was made to conform to the Protestant concept of an educated group whose primary function was the instruction of the laity. Even the Laudian revival, while denying the supremacy of preaching, still emphasized that the ministry must be educated in order to influence the laity. The Laudian revival also witnessed a resuscitation of those institutions which had been weakened by the Reformation, especially the church courts. The revival failed, in large measure because it was employed to further narrow, partisan and generally unpopular religious policies, but the fact that it was accomplished by using the existing organization and framework of the English Church itself suggests that contemporaries believed the institution still to be viable. The Laudians thought in terms of a continuity with the pre-Reformation Church, a continuity disrupted by the excesses of Calvinism. They therefore sought to make the old Church a powerful influence in society. The essays in this volume would suggest that such an aim was anachronistic and doomed to failure; that while the Church could do much to set its own house in order, this 'house' was now of limited compass. The Church's influence over the whole of society was now of a different order. In the century before the English Revolution it was the preaching and moral guidance of the Church which were most valued by the laity. It required the trauma of the Civil War to revive in the ruling classes as a whole an appreciation of the value of a strong institutional Church as a means of providing social stability.

# Personnel

Personnel

# 1

## The function of a bishop:
## the career of Richard Neile, 1562–1640

### Andrew Foster

A Bishop is a minister of God, unto whom with permanent continuance there is given not only power of administering the Word and Sacraments, which power other Presbyters have, but also a further power to ordain ecclesiastical persons and a power of chiefty in government over Presbyters as well as Laymen a power to be by way of jurisdiction a Pastor even to Pastors themselves.[1]

So wrote Richard Hooker, the great Anglican apologist of the 1590s. For him a bishop was first and foremost a minister responsible for the spiritual wellbeing of his flock. There were other duties, however, which required skills distinct from that of preaching God's word. A bishop might be required to write in defence of his Church; he would certainly need to exercise sound judgment in his selection of men for clerical and lay positions within that Church; he would need to be capable of administering the Church and its estates soundly and efficiently. As a spokesman for the Christian viewpoint, a bishop might be called upon for advice in Parliament and sometimes in the Privy Council. In the law courts, wisdom, learning and wide expertise would be in demand. He might well demonstrate his pastoral concern through acts of charity and endowment. Some of these roles are less integral to the function of a bishop than others; frequently the emphasis has been varied.

Hooker realized that the authority of the bishops was presently under attack and provided in their defence the notion of the 'apostolic succession', a concept which had caused much controversy when preached by Richard Bancroft in February 1588/9. The opening blast of the Martin Marprelate tracts, the *Epistle*, declared that 'those that are petty popes and petty anti-christs ought not to be maintained in any Christian commonwealth'.[2] The bishops were seen as 'intolerable withstanders of reformation'.[3] Given this divergence of views on episcopacy in the 1580s one may well ask, what functions were regarded as essential to a bishop in the late sixteenth and early seventeenth centuries? What elements of change and continuity can be discerned?

One impact of the Reformation was to undermine episcopacy; it was unavoidable when so much anti-clericalism was expressed and the 'priesthood of all believers' was stressed. Between 1558 and 1562 many of the returned exiles had grave doubts about accepting bishoprics. 'It was with the most progressive of intentions that the emigré bishops assumed their burdens.'[4] But the moderate Protestant reformers who received the posts were in the event prepared to obey their new Constantine in the hope of gaining significant concessions later.[5] The ambiguous attitude of Elizabeth to her Church was yet to be brought into the open. The works of Foxe and Jewel played on the memories of past suffering, stressed the virtues in Elizabeth's settlement, and effectively stifled more radical ideas of theology and church organization for the present. Nevertheless, the new bishops were quite clear that the primary duty of their office was that of preaching God's word.

If the reformers had doubts, the queen also did nothing to show that she had a high regard for episcopacy. Elizabeth rarely adopted a bishop as an intimate counsellor. She is thought to have worked reasonably well with Parker and later with Whitgift, her 'little black husband'. Nevertheless, these people were scarcely as close to her as Andrewes, Neile, Mountague and Williams were to James I, or Laud to Charles I. While recent writings have tended to prove that Elizabeth did not 'plunder' the Church's wealth to the same extent as her predecessors, she certainly did nothing to aid the financial state of the Church. It may well be true that her reasons for keeping Bristol, Ely,

Exeter and Oxford vacant for long periods were other than mercenary, yet her record must compare unfavourably with that of the early Stuarts. Under their rule only Ely, Salisbury and Winchester were vacant for more than one year. The writings of Phyllis Hembry, Claire Cross and, more recently, Felicity Heal have shown that the Act of Exchanges of 1559 typified the crown's attitude to the episcopate at this juncture: Cecil may have wished to reorganize the financial basis of the bishoprics; the crown merely seized the opportunity to reap financial rewards.[6]

The weakness of the bishops was brought out in December 1566 when Parker and other leading clerics petitioned the queen to allow a bill before Parliament to enforce subscription to the 39 articles.[7] The queen was unsympathetic and such a bill did not become an Act of Parliament until 1571, by which time it was patently obvious that the bishops needed greater power to discipline their clergy than that given them by their suspect status. Yet the queen did not hesitate to interfere in the government of the Church. In August 1561 she barred wives from cathedral closes and colleges.[8] In 1564/5 Elizabeth finally made her position in the vestiarian controversy reasonably clear, ordering Parker to take a firm line and accusing him of laxity in his 'sufferance of sundry varieties and novelties, not only in opinions but in external ceremonies and rites there is crept into the church by some few persons'.[9]

In this search for a *raison d'être*, the new bishops were not always innocent victims. They had families to provide for and their own positions to maintain. Many were accused of impoverishing their sees and nepotism was common – charges which many had once levied at pre-Reformation, Catholic bishops. Even the more idealistic bishops, faced with great difficulties and the temptation to abuse their power, were taking on the attitudes of a conservative establishment.

The demands from the godly for further reformation increased in intensity as the reign progressed. Despite setbacks they still expected the bishops to implement their programmes and when Edmund Grindal became Archbishop of Canterbury in 1576 it seemed that their prayers had been answered. Grindal favoured moderate reform and, in particular, sponsored the prophesyings which fulfilled an educational role and also promised to strengthen the Church pastorally and administratively. The queen's conservative fears were aroused and she ordered suppression of the meetings; when Grindal protested in December 1576 he was suspended from office.[10] Determined to see her own view of the Church prevail, Elizabeth alienated a larger section of public opinion than before. 'In the later 'seventies, the substance of power in the church passed from the progressive bishops of the *Zurich Letters* (Leicester's bishops?) and into the hands of a new generation who were glad to adopt as their own the queen's view that the status quo must be strictly and equally maintained against both papists and puritans.'[11] With this new generation of bishops – men like Freke, Aylmer, Piers, and, above all, Whitgift – came a more positive approach to the administrative problems of the Church. Greater stress was laid upon conformity to the 39 articles. The queen seemed more interested in the work of these bishops and more prepared to support them. Although these people were exercising power in the Church long before Grindal's death, the election of Whitgift in September 1583 may certainly be regarded as 'a decisive climacteric' in the history of the reformed Church.[12] Subscription to the three articles was now demanded of all and the power of the High Commission was brought to bear on the activities of dissidents.

Yet the queen still did not hold her bishops in high regard. Her attitude, or rather that of her government, to Whitgift was ambivalent. He may have had Hatton's support, yet Burghley in July 1584 openly compared the activities of the High Commission with the Spanish Inquisition and advised the prelate to seek a more tolerant and less troublesome approach towards nonconformists.[13] Enforcement of the rubric was always sporadic and rarely permanent. In certain areas, where recusancy was rife, Puritans received lenient treatment. Consequently, even within the ranks of the increasingly radical Puritan opposition there were still those who had faith in bishops as agents of reform. The elaborate surveys undertaken by the Puritans in 1584-5 were still aimed initially at bringing the queen and her bishops to appreciate matters of which they were supposedly unaware. What followed, however, was that the radicalism of the Puritans in Parliament, the tactless writings of Marprelate, and the relentless propaganda of Whitgift and Bancroft ensured that the queen resisted their pleas to the end.

The last years of the reign saw little Puritan influence at Court and a relatively smooth passage for the work of Whitgift and Bancroft. Even to the last, however, the queen refused to lend definition to her concept of the Church. In November 1595 she ordered Whitgift to withdraw the nine Lambeth articles calling for an end to religious controversy in Cambridge. Even at the height of his power, the archbishop could not rely upon crown support. It was the same with administrative reform. He and Bancroft managed to strengthen the ecclesiastical courts and the visitation procedures for diocesan discipline of the clergy, but were unable to pursue thoroughgoing economic reforms.

Upon the accession of James I in 1603 there was a lull in activity while Puritans and bishops alike waited for the new monarch to declare his views. Both groups had high hopes. Historians have shown that the bishops were far from happy when James summoned the Hampton Court conference, but the skilful propaganda of Bancroft ensured that some of the Puritan proposals failed to materialize.[14] Meanwhile the king took on the mantle of defender of the Church's revenues when in 1604 a statute was passed forbidding alienation of ecclesiastical property, even to the crown, and calling for leases for years rather than lives.

The work of William Lamont has shown that during James I's reign the bishops made every effort to prove their usefulness to the crown.[15] Furthermore, James was the type of king who was prepared to accept notions of the *jure divino* status of bishops precisely because he believed in that of the monarch. Thus in a practical sense the position of the bishops changed for the better in the seventeenth century. They were still subject to crown interference, but at last they had a monarch who was aware of the need to support them in matters of administrative reform. The view that he allowed 'worldly, courtly, talented place-hunters'[16] to gain access to the episcopal bench neglects to mention that James allowed Bancroft a chance to strengthen the Church and also that bishops had considerable influence under James. Some of the bench were 'courtier prelates', but those in positions of influence were often conscientious men – the

37

Puritan privy councillor, James Mountague, who kept a Protestant foreign policy alive under James; George Abbot, the conscientious objector in the Essex divorce case; Lancelot Andrewes, privy councillor and eloquent preacher; Richard Neile, trained as an administrator in the school of the Cecils and Richard Bancroft. Whatever one may say of the venial nature of some of the Jacobean bishops, they had greater freedom to manoeuvre under James and some of them utilized good access to a reasonably helpful king to effect long-overdue reforms in the Church.

Although under Bancroft the drive for conformity continued, the reign of James still saw a relatively quiet period for the Church. Successive Parliaments lamented the fate of the 'silenced brethren', but the number of ministers deprived was quite small.[17] Enforcement was patchy and dependent upon the whims of particular bishops. The diary of Richard Rogers reveals that he was frequently suspended and then restored.[18] In Abbot and Mountague the Puritans had champions comparable to men like Grindal; champions who were assured of more power at Court than Grindal ever had.

The presbyterian party, crushed under Bancroft, had now reverted to seeking reform in the Church from within. The bishops and the crown seemed prepared to implement long-overdue reforms. At last there seemed to be general agreement as to the *raison d'être* of the episcopate. The bishops had been freed from overmuch royal interference; their economic position had been stabilized; they were accorded a privileged place at the royal council table. Moreover, James seemed to favour good preachers. But what led to a renewal of fears about episcopacy was the rise within the Church of the Arminian movement whose early representatives were Overall, Andrewes, Buckeridge and Neile.

Arminianism, a rejection of the harsher aspects of Calvinist thought, particularly on the question of predestination, involved greater stress on the sacraments and upon the history of the 'visible' Church in the form which it took in England. There was a now almost definitive stress upon the apostolic succession of bishops.[19] The progress of the group under James was slow but assured, once they had captured the royal favourite Buckingham through the ministrations of William Laud. Charles defended their position from the moment of his accession and the movement grew from strength to strength. Archbishop Abbot's position had been weakened in 1621 by the Act of Manslaughter, which was used against him in 1627; in 1630, the last of the influential Calvinists at court, the third earl of Pembroke, died. Fears of clerical supremacy were aroused again when fears of royal supremacy were also aroused, especially because the Arminians were using their close connection with the crown to advocate new ceremonial policies and to take the Church dangerously near to the old Roman position.[20]

In a sermon preached at the consecration of the bishop of Carlisle in December 1626, John Cosin took up an aggressive position as regards the nature and function of episcopacy.[21] He started off by stressing comparisons between the role of Christ on earth and that of bishops. He proceeded to the usual point that preachers derived their power to preach from bishops and made an interesting aside: 'I come not here to preach down preaching; but this I wonder at, that preaching now-a-days should be counted our only office, as if we had nothing else to do, and an office independent too, as if we were all bishops when we preach'.[22] The stress upon the Church as an institution was coming to the fore, and with the swing of the theological pendulum back towards Rome came a revival of interest in functions other than the preaching which the reformers of the 1560s had stressed. Discipline was necessary in Christianity; Cosin claimed that religion should not be a commodity brought and sold according to taste – an obvious reference to Puritan laymen who resisted the dictates of the clergy. The activities of the Laudians during the 1630s illustrate this new emphasis. Much greater care was now taken in administration and there was a higher degree of central control. Reports were demanded of the bishops; orders concerning leasing policies were meant to be obeyed; palaces were either rebuilt or newly constructed; an impressive church restoration campaign was begun, symbolized by the renewed interest in the repair of St Paul's after 1631.

The reforms were long overdue but, because they were implemented by the Arminians in a partisan manner, there were many who hated the programme. Early in 1633 Laud crushed the

independent attempts of the feoffees for impropriations to improve
the economic position of the clergy. The work of interested laymen was discouraged. There was considerable interference even
with churches in good structural order: pews were hacked into
order and altars were moved to the east end. Conformity to
many new doctrinal requirements was demanded of clerics and
laymen alike. All this was not without well-documented opposition. In the works of William Prynne the bishops were
compared with the devil, Jewish high priests, and Antichrist.[23]

When the bishops finally had the status and the support of the
crown to perform their duties as pastors and administrators well,
they and their Church were regarded by many as the very em-
bodiment of Antichrist. What light does a study of the career of
Richard Neile throw on the trends discussed above? How far can
Neile be said to demonstrate an Arminian concept of episcopacy?

Richard Neile was born, the son of a tallow-chandler, in 1562.
His early career was furthered by the patronage of the Cecil
family and then of Bancroft, who saw in him an orthodox
administrator who would be useful to the Church. Possibly
through Bancroft's influence, Neile became dean of Westminster
in 1605. Personal friendship with the king, however, secured him
the sees of Rochester (1608), Coventry and Lichfield (1610),
Lincoln (1614), and Durham (1617). That friendship also enabled
him to become the natural leader of the proto-Arminian party to
which he gravitated while still at Cambridge.[24] Close to the king,
Neile promoted the fortunes of that group despite the hostility of
James towards Continental Arminianism. He also became known
as a strong disciplinarian with firm ideas about the bishop's role
as a leader of his clergy. But he could also be an indulgent
'father' and was certainly a loyal patron to his chaplains. In
James's Parliaments Neile showed himself a firm believer in the
divine right of kings. He also displayed a passionate attachment
to the Church of England as an institution. In keeping with the
policy pursued by Robert Cecil of practical toleration towards
certain groups of Catholics, Neile became their defender in
Parliament.[25] Given his practical approach, his experience of
the recusancy problem at Lichfield and Coventry, and his

leanings towards greater ceremonial in the Church, his stance is not surprising.

A man of 63, Neile took a back seat role in the accession of Charles I, leaving the Arminian leadership firmly with his old chaplain, William Laud. He was still a mainstay of the party, however, and in 1627 he and Laud became privy councillors, and in the following year Neile became bishop of Winchester. In the Parliament of 1628–9 Neile and Laud were singled out as leaders of the innovators in religion. In 1632 Neile reached the pinnacle of his career as archbishop of York. He proceeded to play a prominent part in the government of Thorough. Neile was a churchman whose great administrative skills were put to good use in the 1630s, but in support of a monarchy and a Church which were sadly lacking in popular appeal. By whom would Neile have been considered a godly bishop? What role did he envisage a bishop should play?

Richard Neile was not, and did not consider himself to be, a good preacher. Prynne maintained that 'He seldom or never preached himself, and therefore could not endure frequent preaching in others'.[26] Neile himself adopted a jocular vein on the subject of his own abilities: he apparently once stopped a teacher from flogging a boy on the grounds that corporal punishment had not done Neile any good. But to say that he was neither an intellectual nor an eloquent preacher is not to accept the scurrilous stories of Alexander Leighton or Arthur Wilson that Neile entertained the king with dirty jokes during sermon time to keep him from concentrating on theology.[27] Neither did Neile completely neglect the function of preaching. He preached more often than his critics suggest. Moreover, as Heylin noted, he was conscientious in keeping about him very able chaplains.

Did Neile seriously restrict preaching within his dioceses? He was careful to ensure that only Arminians were granted licences to preach. Certainly the Arminians were shifting the emphasis to the sacraments and away from the 'vital rage for utterance'.[28] One of the doctrinal aspects of the administrative reforms of the 1630s was the reliance upon more set, written services which allowed less room for Puritan innovations. The greater elaboration of consecration services was another grievance, as with the case of White's consecration as bishop of Carlisle in 1626. In relation to churches, men like Sir Henry Slingsby felt it was wrong that they 'must attribute a sanctity to the very walls and stones of the church'.[29]

In the early days of James, Neile may have suffered by comparison with Andrewes and Donne as a preacher, but in the Laudian church of the 1630s the need for such individuals was less clear. The work of the Laudian intellectuals was directed towards short treatises on specific points of theology or church organization. Sermons and books were printed for mass consumption on subjects such as allegiance to the king, sabbath day observance, the position of the altar, and various points of ceremonial. Although Neile was no intellectual, he played a great part in these activities. There is no doubt that he gave practical encouragement to many writers and dedications abound from such Arminian intellectuals as Thomas Jackson and Francis White. One of the more controversial books of the period was Cosin's *A Collection of Private Devotions*, a manual of prayers for court ladies. In 1624 Neile was instrumental in gaining the publication of Richard Mountague's book, *A New Gag For An Old Goose*. Both Cosin and Mountague submitted much of their early work to Neile for his judgment. In 1628 Prynne asked who were the leaders of the Arminian faction: Parliament named Neile and Laud.[30] By the time Prynne wrote *A Quench-Coale* in 1636/7 he was sure that Neile and Laud were the men behind the group of intellectuals he attacked.

With little relevance to the Church was Neile's earlier patronage of Edward Topsell, the popularizer of zoology. His major works were dedicated to Neile.[31] It illustrates the practical nature of Neile's patronage that in the case of Topsell this took the form of doubling his income as curate of St Botolph's Aldersgate, in Neile's gift as dean of Westminster.

Neile was a natural committee man; his administrative flair and some slight legal training ensured that he frequently sat on parliamentary and royal commissions. It is not surprising to find that Neile's sole publication should be an account of the work of a commission set up in 1622, which he headed, to look into the Spalato affair.[32] Despite this book, it is still true that Neile was no intellectual. A sound theologian and no more, it was his other qualities which drew people to him for patronage. For the

Arminians he was an influential patron, a careful administrator whose concern for the Church earned their admiration and respect, a man whose practical support did much to further their cause.

In caring for his clergy a bishop had several duties: he had to ensure their careful selection, supervise their preaching and pastoral activities, and care for their personal economic and spiritual needs. Neile appears to have been a popular bishop because he heeded these requirements. Intense pride in the Church as an institution made Neile ready to defend passionately the interests of the clergy. In the 1610 Parliament Neile drew vividly upon personal experience to attack inexperienced idealists like Abbot over what constituted a living wage for a cleric

> I myself when I came from a reader into a curate, when I had paid all duties forth of my living, my means were so small as if it had not pleased God to send me a good master I could not have told what to have done, for a living of 100 marks per annum a soldier that trails a pike shall eat more hot meat and have contenteder hours than he, and better it were to enjoy an annuity of £20 per annum and diet in a gentleman's house than a benefice of £80. I am sorry to live to hear it said 100 marks is a fitting living for a preacher of God's word.[33]

That attitude remained with Neile throughout his long career. In the 1620s, when involved in collecting loans for the king or for the Palatinate, he took personal care to see that wherever possible the poorer clergy were untaxed. On his promotion to York in 1632, 'being advertised by some of his officers how he might levy a tenth upon his clergy, as well as his late predecessor had done, he answered he would in no case attempt any such matter: for he was come to benefit, not to charge his clergy'.[34]

Although there are many examples of Neile being strict with nonconformist clergy, he was often very careful to respect their problems and misgivings. He seems to have possessed the ability to persuade men of the correctness of his own views. Neile has the dubious distinction of being the man responsible for the last burning of a heretic in England – Edward Wightman in 1612 – but this was not before Neile had conducted endless conferences

43

in an effort to save him. More successfully, Neile is said to have
converted Thomas Jackson from a Calvinist to an Arminian
position. Lenient with Catholics, Neile seems to have persuaded
many to Anglicanism. Neile's approach was so cautious and
tolerant at York in the 1630s that Prynne later claimed that this
was because the archbishop was out of favour at Court.[35] In his
history of New England, Cotton Mather wrote of the suspension
of Ezekial Rogers of Rowley in 1635, but noted that the archbishop 'who suspended him, shew'd him so much respect, as to
let him enjoy the profits of his living, two years after the suspension'.[36] In 1635 Neile reported to the king that there was
resistance to the Book of Sports in his diocese, but that he had
given the ministers concerned time to peruse copies of the bishop
of Ely's text on the subject before they took action which would
force him to discipline them.[37] The cooling-off period appears to
have done the trick. There seems to be some justice in Neile's
self-appraisal of 1636/7: 'I never deprived any man; but have
endeavoured their reformation with meekness, and patience.'[38]

The bishop had a vested interest in maintaining the ecclesiastical hierarchy. That involved careful selection of men for the
senior positions within the Church – of those who would be their
eventual successors. Bishops of all views encouraged others of
like persuasion by employing them as chaplains and secretaries
and by exercising shrewd use of available patronage of livings.
One sure way of commanding loyalty in the administration of a
diocese had always been to employ relatives. Thus at the core
of Neile's entourage from the outset of his career was his half-
brother, Robert Newell. He rose to be archdeacon of Buckingham
in 1614 and thereafter remained in Lincoln diocese. Richard
Neile's brother, William, accompanied him in the early days of
his career as household steward; he was not an educated man
and he was never over-promoted by his brother. On the other
hand, William's clever son, John, reaped much profit from his
uncle's position in the 1630s when he was given prebends at
Southwell, Ripon and York, eventually ending his days after
the Restoration as dean of Ripon. Others did well by marrying
into the family. Gabriel Clarke married William's daughter,
Mildred, and once he had proved his merit he rose to become
archdeacon of Durham. Despite all this, Neile did not noticeably

over-promote the interests of his family to the detriment of the Church.

Neile himself was the product of one of the most highly organized court factions of his day – the alliance formed between Richard Bancroft and Robert Cecil from the late 1590s until 1610. Neile became a lynchpin in that alliance when he gained the influential position of Clerk of the Closet in 1603. When Neile finally relinquished that position in 1632, its importance was appreciated by Laud who passed it on to Juxon 'that I might have one that I might trust near his Majesty, if I grow weak or infirm'.[39] But not until Neile became bishop of Durham in 1617 did he have power to do more than aid members of his own family and Laud. Arthur Kautz drew attention to the failure of the Elizabethan bishops to rationalize the procedure for selecting bishops.[40] As host of 'Durham College', the headquarters of the Arminian party, Neile did much to provide an answer to the problem. Four of his chaplains became bishops either before or after the Restoration and Neile was also successful in furthering the careers of the best-known Arminian intellectuals.[41]

How did Neile come to make such use of the existing system of patronage? Durham was one of the richest and most powerful sees in the land. He was now in a position to promote chaplains and others to livings and to house them, either in palaces in the North, or in his London house in the Strand. Through his old friendships with established Arminians like Andrewes, Buckeridge, Overall and Howson he was able to ensure that Durham House became a meeting-place where his new protegés could have access to people of influence. A minor favourite with the king, he could also ensure that they entered Court circles quickly. Neile seems to have selected able men with unerring accuracy and to have inspired them to loyalty by his own steadfast nature. Richard Mountague had little need to remind John Cosin to be loyal to Neile because 'every man is not my Lord of Durham, who is sure and fast and immoveable where he taketh'.[42] So it was that, aided by fortune which saw more deaths in the Durham dean and chapter than in any decade since the Reformation,[43] the second-generation Arminians came to settle in the diocese of Durham or with Neile in London.[44]

45

These men were soon deployed in strategic positions. Gabriel Clarke became archdeacon of Durham. Francis Burgoyne was given the archdeaconry of Northumberland. The dean and chapter was packed with Neile men from places where he had served – two illustrious examples were Augustine Lindsell from Lincoln and John Cosin from Norwich. Thomas Jackson took up the living of Newcastle, was aided in his writings by the group, and in 1630 was elevated to the mastership of Corpus Christi College, Oxford. When he moved to Winchester, Neile took under his wing Benjamin Laney, who later became Master of Pembroke College, Cambridge. When he was at York, men such as Yeldard Alvey and Barnabus Barlow were garnered. Some men travelled with Neile from diocese to diocese, as did Eleazor Duncon from Durham to Winchester to York. By the 1630s Neile men were in key positions in most dioceses of the land and also in the colleges of the universities. The success of the group is perhaps attributable to its close-knit family nature; thus Lindsell in his will thanked Neile for taking him into his family almost in the literal sense; legacies went to Neile, his wife and son, and old and new members of the 'family' – Laud, Buckeridge, Newell, Birkhead, Cosin, Burgoyne and Neile's secretary, Edward Liveley.[45]

There was nothing novel in a bishop promoting the interests of his chaplains. Other bishops of notably different views showed similar concern for their clergy; but Neile was extremely thorough, and the influence of 'Durham College' was noted by contemporaries and led to the attack upon Neile and Laud as leaders of the Arminian faction in the 1628–9 Parliament. More important still, the organization of the team involved close connections with lawyers and lay officials and thus helped Neile tighten his grip upon the life of his dioceses. In its dependence upon relatives, upon tried and trusted clerics and laymen, and upon 'his' men as opposed to the local gentry, the team overcame problems raised by corrupt court officials and by an administrative machinery which was not directly responsible to the bishops. This was personal, centralized government with a vengeance and one in which, if Prynne is to be believed, 'arch-deacons, chancellors, registers, apparitors, household chaplaines, secretaries, and private informers', played the key supporting roles.[46]

Brian Levack's *The Civil Lawyers in England, 1603–1641* has underlined the close relations between the civil lawyers and the bishops in Jacobean England and has also noted that this association amongst others led to the lawyers being tainted with popery.[47] But although Levack points out that both John Lambe and Sir Nathaniel Brent served Laud well, he is unable to draw firm conclusions as to the political and religious sympathies of the civilians. Examination of Neile's career shows that he was able to mobilize lawyers in his team to act far more positively than Levack suggests. Neile took the initiative in locating like-minded lawyers willing to work for administrative reform; as an honorary member of Gray's Inn and Doctors' Commons he mingled with the best lawyers of the day. While dean of Westminster he employed Sir Henry Hobart as legal adviser. At Durham he consulted strange bedfellows, Sir James Whitelocke and Sir Henry Yelverton. While at Durham he also sought the advice of the Hutton family. He came to know many lawyers because of his travels and seems to have got on well with diocesan chancellors even when they were not his own appointees. He formed useful friendships in London so that even when away from the capital he was served by good lawyers: Dr Eden, professor of civil law at Gresham College and master of Chancery after 1625, and Thomas Mottershed, registrar of the High Commission of the southern province, proved particularly valuable. Mottershed's son, Edward, became a lynchpin in Neile's York administration as official, first of the East Riding, and then of the Nottingham archdeaconry. Where existing archidiaconal officials were unreliable, they were eased out of office.

Neile's care in the selection of men is perhaps best exemplified by the career of William Easdall. This latter served his 'apprenticeship' with Neile at Westminster and then followed him as personal secretary to the dioceses of Rochester, Lichfield and Coventry, and Lincoln, until Easdall became official of Buckingham in 1616. Thereafter he rose to become commissary of the Exchequer and Prerogative Court at York in 1624. He rejoined Neile to become chancellor of Durham in 1628, but by that time his career was clearly tied to York because he became a chancellor there in 1624. In 1632, however, the partnership was renewed and a catalogue of their joint success in the administration of the diocese of York forms a substantial part of Ronald Marchant's works.[48] In 1640 Easdall acted as godfather to Neile's grandson, Richard – a human touch in a working relationship which extended over 25 years.

Neile's careful selection of able subordinates released him from many of the routine tasks which faced a bishop and enabled him to concentrate on more important matters. Yet his personal control was always present. He checked the accounts, ordered surveys, and kept strict records of all reforms and business transactions. This attitude produced the *Dean's Book* at Westminster: a catalogue of his work in increasing the revenues, improving the leases, and restoring the property.[49] Long before the king ordered that leases be for years and not lives, Neile was implementing that policy. When stricter orders were issued in 1634 he was faithful in carrying them out. With great tact he contested the crown's presentation to certain livings, usually winning his case. Following land surveys, he frequently improved his property and he was shrewd in the way he financed such operations. When at York, Neile ran a land drainage scheme in Nottinghamshire with an eye to increasing the see's revenues in the long term.

Within his dioceses Neile supervised long overdue building operations. He was the first dean of Westminster to make any major structural repairs or alterations since the foundation of the collegiate cathedral in 1560.[50] During the five years that he was dean, £1,128 was spent on such work, and on the school and its extension at Chiswick. Heylin noted that Neile spent huge sums repairing the episcopal palaces at Rochester and Lincoln. In 1637 Neile wrote of his own repairs at Southwell and Bishopthorpe: 'These two houses at my first coming to them, I found very ruinous; and have been at a great charge in repairing to them'.[51] Isaac Basire, commenting upon John Cosin's architectural work at Durham, at Cosin's funeral service in 1672, was forced to point out that: 'in this he was a good imitator of his great patron Bishop Neile, who in less than ten years did bestow upon the same . . . about seven thousand pounds, for indeed he was "Vir Architectonicus".'[52]

Neile was not only concerned with external repairs. The new emphasis on ceremonial stressed the position of the altar at the east end of the church, the adequate decoration of the altar,

altar rails, a proper font, uniform pews, and an organ. Everywhere he went Neile paid attention to these points. He regarded it as part of his function to see that his cathedrals were kept decently.

In the 1630s the campaign for church restoration was carried a stage further. Neile approached the problem of decayed churches cautiously, well aware of the problem of non-cooperation on the part of churchwardens. One of the triumphs of his first visitation in York in 1632–3 was the extent to which it was an accurate picture of the problems he faced. It was accurate because Neile succeeded in tightening up the presentment system and caught people unawares with his deceptively moderate visitation articles. In the diocese of Chester 309 churches were found to be in need of structural repair (roughly 69 per cent of the churches in the visitation); in the diocese of York only 32 per cent were thus presented. During his archiepiscopate, Neile used the Chancery Court as an administrative tool, to compensate for the decline of the High Commission. Commissioners from the Chancery Court viewed churches within the diocese of York and produced startling results. They took on cases referred from the visitation courts, but also, significantly, picked up many cases which had been concealed at the visitation, notably in the puritan areas of the diocese. Forty-three per cent of the churches dealt with in the Chancery Court, 1633–40, had not been cited in either the 1633 or 1636 visitation. Approximately 355 churches in York diocese, 309 in Chester diocese, and 200 in peculiars and the archdeaconry of Nottingham were ordered to undertake repair work as part of Neile's campaign; many others conducted repairs voluntarily. Others may have preached more eloquently, but Neile was one of the few to ensure that places of worship were in adequate physical repair.[53]

In his role in central government, Neile gave Puritans ground for discontent. In 1614 he ran into trouble with the Commons for an over-aggressive defence of the king's prerogative on the issue of impositions; thereafter he was regarded as an over-zealous royalist and crypto-papist. In 1621 he defended the right of clerics to sit on commissions of the peace; he wanted Parliament for practical purposes to make distinctions in recusancy proceedings between lay Catholics and priests and between Jesuits and secular priests, hence 'their fingers did itch at him in the lower house'.[54] To some extent the unpopularity of the bishops in Parliament was caused by the king. Whereas Elizabeth had ensured that her privy councillors dominated the proceedings and had relied on her bishops for block voting, James was less astute and his defenders were more often exposed individually to attack. However, there was more to it than that; the Arminians were hated because Parliament saw enormous changes being wrought in the Church as a result of the bishops' increasing influence over the king. After 1625 the Arminians had a king who thoroughly believed in their programme for the Church of England, and their opponents had no quarter at Court. The Commons were alarmed in 1628 because Neile and Laud had recently been made privy councillors, and allocated a role in the decision-making processes of central government. Opponents were prosecuted in the Court of Star Chamber. In October 1629 a proclamation ordering repair work in churches exemplified greater royal support and showed that Neile and Laud were prestigious royal officials as well as bishops. Ecclesiastical issues took on the attributes of matters of state: the case of St Gregory's altar was referred to the Privy Council; the feoffees were disbanded in 1633.

The Church seemed to be impinging too much on civil society. Neile had long supported such a role for the Church. At Durham there had been complaints of increased clerical representation on commissions of the peace. Although Neile groomed and used lawyers like Easdall, he ensured that much power remained in clerical hands; at York, for example, Wickham, Hodson, and Stanhope were extremely powerful in some courts. There was a concerted attempt to curb the power of antagonistic city corporations in the 1630s. In 1636 the Privy Council withdrew York's new city charter because it was said to infringe upon the powers of the dean and chapter at York Minster. In 1637 the presence of the mayor and corporation at cathedral services was ordered in various cities as an example to the population. The Arminians employed ceremonial, not sermons, as their propaganda; if they could force city councils to attend services in High Church cathedrals they would stand a chance of commanding greater obedience in those cities where aldermen protected Puritans.

In some respects the bishops performed their role in central government for the general good. Bishops sat on the commissions handling money for the Palatinate and releasing prisoners of war. The commission set up for the repair of St Paul's in 1631 was timely, if slow and often ineffective. The Laudians have a creditable record for their concern for the poor; in 1631 Neile sat on the new poor law commission. Some might argue that clerical control of the treasury brought integrity under the unimpeachable supervision of Juxon. The problem was that even when the bishops were acting for the best, they carried out their work in a high-handed manner and from a suspect theological standpoint. It was ironical that when a close link between Church and state was finally achieved, the able bishops found it impossible to create a strong and united 'popular' Church because they had alienated a large body of public opinion.

While the bishops in general were strongly involved in social and charitable work, Neile's other commitments gave him little time for such activity. No schools, scholarships or poor houses were founded in his name. Yet he was responsible for many acts of public charity. The records of Westminster are full of his payments of money to the poor and for the relief of plague victims. He was concerned for the situation of the poor clergy. He helped many to fellowships at St John's, Cambridge, having great influence in that university until the 1620s. A 'good John's man', he persuaded that college to accept bequests from John Williams, including the setting up of new fellowships in 1623 when the fellows were quibbling about the meaning of the statutes.[55] Neile improved the food at Westminster School, and more significantly, he sent some scholars to Cambridge at his own expense in remembrance of his furtherance through a Lady Mildred Cecil scholarship.

Neile was an able organizer and administrator. He sought administrative reforms so that the Church could regain the wealth and power lost since the Reformation. As part of that power, however, he also sought conformity to a concept of Anglicanism which many found difficult to accept. Whereas many would not have objected to the reforms in themselves (indeed many of them were supported by moderate Calvinists such as Bishop Morton of Lichfield), they found Neile's methods in implementing them tainted with a theology which they labelled abusively 'Arminian'. The teams of chaplains and lawyers which he used to extend his personal control were regarded as 'ushers in of popery'.[56] Arminian theology and over-zealous support of the royal prerogative threw other activities of the bishops into disrepute. They were accused of giving bad counsel to the king in church matters and their concern for the poor was thought to be too paternalistic. The attacks upon the bishops often concentrated upon their low social origins, their lack of concern for preaching, and their intellectual shortcomings; the wheel had come full circle since the attacks upon Catholic prelates of the 1520s and 1530s.

What changes in attitude towards the bishops had brought about this situation? Firstly, the crown, since the accession of James I, gave the bishops greater power than before, and James's reluctance to interfere in the Church facilitated the rise of the Arminian party. That group associated itself with the interests of Buckingham and Charles and its power grew accordingly in the next reign. Secondly, the pressing problems of the Church called for swift and decisive action which the now influential bishops took in an authoritarian manner. Disciplinary problems were met with extensive use of the ecclesiastical courts and by restrictions upon preaching and lectures, by the take-over of key positions in the Church by loyal and trained personnel, and by the use of censorship. The Church as an institution was seen to require uniformity and hence a bishop to exercise these powers. The anarchy of Elizabeth's reign was being transformed into the authoritarian, albeit paternalistic, stance of the seventeenth-century bishops. Thirdly, however, came a subtle shift in attitude which was facilitated by the support of the crown and by the ways in which the Arminians carried out their reforms. Neile and the Arminians took upon themselves a pre-Reformation function – that of defining the Church's doctrine without reference to crown, Parliament or public opinion. The convocation of 1640 saw the apogee of this movement with the publication of 17 canons which were extremely innovatory in character. Able men were trained by the Arminian bishops in such a way that they operated like teams in the dissemination of Arminian ideas in the ecclesiastical courts and from the pulpits. In 'Durham

College' one can see the archetype of this system. In Neile one sees the pride of the Arminians in the Church as an institution, but it was no longer the loose-knit, ill-defined Church of Elizabeth, but rather one with a clear hierarchy, planned personnel recruitment and training, and rigidly defined modes of worship – all of which embodied an unpopular theology. Gone was the preacher-bishop who had close links and conference with clergy and congregations alike; in his place was now a rigorous and conscientious 'leader'.

The Arminians did strengthen the Church as an institution, but there is irony in the fact that when the Church did command more power and respect than at any time since the Reformation, it also commanded more fear and hatred and was more exclusive. There are a number of problems at the root of this discussion: the primary function of the bishop is to be a preacher, yet if the Church is to survive as an institution on earth, other more worldly abilities must be called into play. A balance was not achieved during this period. Under Elizabeth the bishops were weak and after the initial fervour of the Reformation their preaching was strictly circumscribed. When the bishops gained more influence at Court it became possible for them to have a more effective voice in the councils of state and also to implement long-needed reforms. That it was beyond them was due to a more essential effect of the Reformation – that their authority as such was undermined. The bishops had been unseated as automatic counsellors of state; their return to such a position in the 1630s was unacceptable. No matter how capable they were as administrators, their ability to reform the Church had been severely curtailed by the Reformation. Land transactions during the post-Reformation period had made it impossible for the bishops to settle the problem of impropriations in the Church's favour. Selection of clergy, as is demonstrated in chapter 2 below, was as much in the hands of lay patrons as of the bishops.[57] In their attempts to re-endow the bishops with some of these powers, Charles and the Laudians underlined differences in attitude towards the episcopate which had emerged since the Reformation. How much attitudes had changed they learnt in 1641. Arminians like Neile had cogently redefined the duties of a bishop; their failure to fulfil them resulted from these changes and this basic hostility.

## Arminianism

The word 'Arminian' was used originally to describe a follower of the Dutch theologian Jacobus Arminius. The latter attempted to modify Calvinist thought on divine grace. The original Arminians remained within the Dutch Presbyterian Church but became associated politically with republican, anti-centralist groups in the United Provinces. In England in the 1590s a similar questioning of Calvinist orthodoxy had taken place but, largely because of differences in church organization, this became associated with a 'High Church' group within the Church of England. By the time the word 'Arminian' came to be applied in England it was as a form of abuse expressing rather vague fears of a group of theologians who, by their emphasis upon the sacraments, ceremonial, and the *jure divino* status of bishops, seemed to be taking the Church back towards Rome. The English Arminians' reliance upon the support of the crown, and, in its turn, the support which they lent to theories of the divine right of kings, linked them very firmly with a totally different political threat from that which Arminianism had posed in the United Provinces. The identification of Arminian ideas with episcopacy and ceremonial in England only served to increase the speed with which Arminianism in general was regarded as a pernicious doctrine leading only to Rome and Antichrist.

# 2
## The reformation of the ministry, 1558–1642

## Rosemary O'Day

The Reformation in England undermined the clerical position. Now that the priest was no longer necessary as a mediator between the individual soul and God, a new *raison d'être* had to be sought either consciously or unconsciously. This was to be found in the pastoral function of the reformed ministry. Basically, this involved a change in emphasis. Catholicism had stressed the sacrificial function of the priest in offering the mass. Put simply, the emphasis was on the office and not on the man. Some even maintained that the efficacy of the sacraments was in no way dependent upon the merit of the priest in his everyday life, although this did not imply a licence for clergy to live wicked or worldly lives. The reformed view was that the minister should offer individual and loving care and advice to each member of his congregation as well as administer a fatherly discipline. Clearly the clergy of the established Church could not successfully claim that they were fulfilling this duty as long as they were ignorant, ill-educated men. The life, training and vocational dedication of the clergyman became all-important. Not all accepted that the Reformation implied a radical change in the nature of the ministry – the queen, for example, seems to have clung to something akin to the Catholic idea of priesthood, both because of her innate conservatism and because of her fear of political reprisals. For a large part of Elizabeth's reign, however, the ecclesiastical hierarchy did accept, if in a modified form, the ideal of a worthy, preaching, pastoral ministry, and even with the advent of Whitgift there was an espousal for rather different reasons of the cause of a graduate ministry.

Historians have done much to document the profound transformation of the established clergy during the late sixteenth and early seventeenth centuries. There is no reason to dispute the prevailing view that the clergy of the 1630s were a far cry from the mass of ignorant, vocationally unsuitable men who formed the clerical group in the late 1550s and early 1560s. Less attention has been given to the reasons for this change. Were the efforts of the hierarchy to re-form the ministry according to this new *raison d'être* wholly or partially responsible? What were the other possible influences on the nature of clerical education, recruitment and placement?

There had long been attempts to regulate entry into the ministry although there is some evidence that examination of candidates for orders were either far from rigorous or had been allowed to lapse in the later Middle Ages. Restriction of entry to the suitable was difficult at the beginning of Elizabeth's reign because the rate of recruitment among such men was poor at a time when many livings were completely unserved. The reasons for this state of affairs were many but it is possible to distinguish some of the most important. The decline in the overall number of clerical recruits has been dated from the reign of Edward.[1] This may have been attributable to the apparently higher standards of admission enforced during that reign. Probably, however, it was as much due to the unsettled state of affairs and to the contempt in which the ministry seems generally to have been held. In addition there were fewer opportunities for advancement within the Church now and the Pluralities Act of 1529 had considerably reduced a cleric's chances of raking together a comfortable living. The reign of Edward not only witnessed the dissolution of many collegiate foundations but also the removal of high civil office from the grasp of the ambitious ecclesiastic. The deprivation of married clergy during Mary's reign made many reluctant to enter the Church. Despite Elizabeth's own antagonism to a married clergy, this deterrent was effectively removed at her accession, but the general insecurity which had surrounded the profession for 30 years past remained.

This insecurity was largely expressed in financial terms. As late as 1585 Archbishop Whitgift was to complain that there were scarcely 600 livings (out of well over 9,000 in the country) capable of supporting a learned minister.[2] Livings were generally poorly endowed, although the incomplete contemporary surveys which survive do suggest that in many cases income was rising and probably keeping pace with or exceeding a like rise in the cost of living. Many clergymen had additional sources of income, either from the patron or impropriator, and many employed legal or illegal means to stretch or supplement their resources – teaching, preaching, trading or practising a craft being the most common means.[3] Moreover, the clergyman could protect his income either by legal action or adroit management. One must balance these possibilities against two considerations. Firstly, a clergyman might lose a considerable proportion of his income in tax – either tenths or payments of a clerical subsidy – and his presentation to a living involved him in heavy expense, both in securing his presentation and in paying his first fruits to the crown.[4] Secondly, there were many rules restricting his occupational activities and, at a time when many livings offered little more than subsistence prospects in themselves, such rules proved a definite barrier to recruitment among the able.[5]

Moreover, there were excellent and sure prospects for the educated man in alternative employment. Contemporaries such as William Day, provost of Eton, bewailed the fact that it was the legal profession which was reaping the benefits of university education; some recommended the implementation of a quota system for the professions which would drive at least some able men into the ranks of the parochial clergy.[6]

Thus in 1558 many were aware that the ministry was not attractive to most educated men as a career and that the existence of lucrative opportunities in other fields confirmed the position of the Church as the preserve of uneducated and sometimes vocationally unsuitable men. Most of the new bishops wished to encourage recruitment of conscientious pastors and to remodel parochial and diocesan organization on reformed lines. Their very consciousness of the importance of the pastoral role led to fresh difficulties. Between 10 and 15 per cent of livings were void at Elizabeth's accession and certain populous areas, such as the

archdeaconries of Canterbury and London, had vacancies in as
many as one-third of their parishes.[7] The shortage of curates and
other assistants was probably yet more acute. An unusually high
death rate prevailing between about 1556 and 1560 accounted
for many of these vacancies, although deprivations for non-
subscription and resignations for religious and political reasons
also took their toll.[8]

Initially the new bishops resorted to mass ordinations to fill
the vacant cures, acting on the principle that an ignorant pastor
was better than no pastor. For example, 167 deacons were admitted in London diocese between 28 December 1559 and 24
March 1561.[9] Similarly, in the first eight months of his episcopate
Matthew Parker, or persons commissioned by him, ordained 233
men in the diocese of Canterbury.[10] Even at this stage there was
some attempt to regulate entry but when it is appreciated, for
example, that Archdeacon Mullins acted as sole examiner in
London diocese and that examinations normally took place on a
single day prior to ordination, it is evident that the examinations
can scarcely have been searching.[11] The 'Interpretations of the
Bishops', recognizing the acute shortage of clergy, agreed that
candidates without knowledge of Latin should be admitted to
deacon's orders provided that they were supported by good
character references. The bishops stipulated that such men should
not proceed to the priesthood until they had served a 'good time
of experience' as deacon.[12]

A note of caution must be introduced here. Few bishops were
appointed or resident within their sees during the period 1559–60
and fewer still held *mass* ordinations. Ordinations held at Ely in
1560 were not noticeably large and that at Worcester in early
1561 involved only nine men. Archbishop Parker was ordaining
'men to serve in all parts of England' – a matter of expedience
as the mass ordinations held in a few major centres were not
large enough to flood the market.[13]

The policy of mass and almost indiscrimate ordination was
intended to be temporary only. Matthew Parker was faced with
a perplexing problem: in an attempt to meet the recognized
pastoral needs of the nation many men totally unfitted for the
pastoral role were being admitted to livings – what had been
conceived as a temporary expedient would have serious long-

term consequences for the standard of pastoral care in England and Wales. In August 1560 Parker felt impelled to write to Grindal, bishop of London, and other bishops of the southern province, advising them to raise the standards of admission and to avoid ordaining those of base occupation or non-clerical background.[14] Having met the exigencies of the moment, it was now time to curb the flow of uneducated recruits.

It is significant that at this very time Parker was wedded to an alternative scheme for the provision of adequate pastoral care until such time as well-trained clergy could be recruited. This scheme involved the employment of readers or lectors, usually laymen, empowered to read the prayerbook services but not to administer the sacraments. Such a band of auxiliaries was undoubtedly needed in Parker's own diocese where fewer than half the parishes had a resident incumbent in 1559. Indeed, Parker fully intended the readers to have some status, envisaging something akin to an ordination ceremony. He saw the 'order' of lectors as more than a temporary expedient: they would be used not only in parishes devoid of clergy but also as assistants to incumbents and to curates. He evolved an elaborate scheme in which the pluralist rector or vicar would supervise and ride a circuit of parishes, each of which was to be served by a resident curate or lector. Seventy-one lectors served in Canterbury diocese alone between December 1559 and 1562; in the latter year the experiment was abandoned. After this the appointment of lectors was left to the discretion of individual bishops and they were employed on an *ad hoc* basis, never again forming part of a coherent scheme.[15]

The advantages attached to employing lectors to serve parishes instead of permitting the ordination and consequent institution of inadequately educated clerics are obvious. The lector had no freehold right to the living which he served or its income; on admission he was required to swear 'to give place upon convenient warning ... if any learned minister' were presented to the benefice by its rightful patron. Although a lay reader was but a poor substitute for a *good* clerical pastor, presumably having no vocation and treating the post as a supplementary source of income, at the very least he was easily removable and fully answerable to the bishop for his actions. When the number of adequate recruits to the ministry swelled, the readers could be dispensed with and, because they did not belong to the 'profession', the hierarchy was in no sense responsible for their future employment. Why then was the experiment abortive? Certainly the shortage of educated clerics was not thus short-lived. Perhaps the chief reason lay in the fact that to be well organized the scheme depended upon the ability of a bishop to refuse legal institution to unlearned ministers, reserving their places for removable lectors. Unfortunately, the bishops were empowered to reject presentees to benefices under extreme circumstances only – the patron's rights were so well protected at common law. Had co-operation between the bishops and patrons been possible, the scheme might successfully have stretched the Church's manpower resources and could have meant that the entire income of a group of parishes (forming the circuit) could be redistributed between one learned, resident incumbent and his resident assistants, ensuring adequate support for the educated man and providing an incentive for such men to enter the Church. As things were, however, the whole scheme was unworkable because patrons were exceedingly jealous of their rights. Patronage rights in lay hands were to prove the stumbling block for this scheme as they were for plans to redistribute impropriate tithes or to pursue a policy of rigorous examination at institution or ordination. It may be also that the clergy themselves raised an outcry at the professional implications of the scheme. There was certainly feeling that deprived clergy and private chaplains, who had refused the oath of supremacy, should be employed as temporary curates in preference to laymen during this time of shortage.[16]

Parker's directive to Grindal should be viewed, therefore, as one aspect of the archbishop's plan to control recruitment and to provide incentives for university men to serve at parochial level. There are some signs that the instruction was taken seriously. Grindal's own ordinations were considerably reduced in size. At Ely the examiners were careful to inquire into the age and background of the candidates. Richard Skynner's case, for instance, was referred to the bishop because Skynner was 66. Henry Funston, earlier made lector in Norwich diocese, seems to have been rejected because of a combination of age (60) and poor knowledge of the scriptures and Latin. Even so, older men continued to be admitted to orders until the supply of young, university-trained recruits improved.[17]

By the 1570s, however, Bishop Parkhurst of Norwich was making an interesting declaration of ordination policy which echoed Parker's earlier sentiments: that there was no longer any necessity for ordaining mature men who had not been specifically set apart for the ministry from youth and that, therefore, the bishops should abide by the canons which they themselves had approved.[18] Parkhurst rejected at least one such candidate on these grounds. The Ely ordination lists from 1560–80 suggest that where a non-graduate was concerned, the issue of clerical background was often crucial to his success.

Despite all these efforts, in the 1580s and 1590s, however, both the educational qualifications and the vocational aptitude of the beneficed clergy almost everywhere were still deplorable. In part this reflects the fact that improved recruitment took time to show itself at parochial level, owing to a generally low rate of mobility and turnover, as well as to the barriers raised by the patronage system.[19] On the other hand, initial recruitment outside the university ordination centres and London showed only a gradual improvement.[20] Between 1560 and 1570 only one of 282 ordinands at Chester was noted as a graduate; recruitment was by no means wholly graduate in this diocese in the 1590s.[21] Contemporary comment and, more specifically, Puritan surveys make it clear that a large number of both graduate and non-graduate clergy were unable or unwilling to fulfil their pastoral functions satisfactorily.

When examining the attempts of the hierarchy to re-form the ministry during the period 1558–1642 one is bound to distinguish two linked interests. Firstly, the concern that the clergy be a graduate profession. This involved an appreciation of the need for university expansion and the encouragement of theological study at the universities as well as of the need for financial and other incentives within the professional structure itself. Secondly, there was a movement to ensure the vocational suitability of ministers which ran hand in hand with a call for more congregational participation in the choice of pastor and more clerical supervision of the exercise of ecclesiastical patronage.

One or two examples must suffice to demonstrate the major characteristics of these policies. Later the question of why university recruitment accelerated to such a great extent will receive some further consideration, but it is necessary to establish here that both hierarchy and crown were concerned to foster this expansion and to direct the products of both universities into the Church. As early as 1566 John Oxenbridge had blamed the universities for not replenishing their numbers after the reign of Mary.[22] As the Ely ordination lists indicate, those graduates who were produced right at the beginning of Elizabeth's reign were destined for immediate preferment outside the realm of parochial responsibility, becoming archdeacons, canons, bishops' chaplains, masters of colleges, fellows and masters of hospitals.[23] There were attempts to control and correct the situation. David Marcombe has noted that the prebendaries of the cathedrals of the new foundation were required to fulfil a pastoral function. Moreover, the crown saw the need for provision of financial incentives for the study of theology at the universities, and for an increase in the value of benefices. In 1560 Elizabeth instructed her Lord Keeper to make available to theology students the income from crown prebends assessed at less than £20 per annum, thus creating in effect a sizeable number of theology scholarships.[24] Although Elizabeth is well known as despoiler of the Church's revenues, this plan of hers for the encouragement of theological studies at a time when they were in decline at the universities was probably no less important for the redirection of graduates into the Church than was James I's ambitious but abortive project for the reclamation by the Church of tithes in the hands of the universities. Despite the claims of historians that Oxford and Cambridge were becoming increasingly secular educational institutions, there is much contrary evidence that in fact their role as seminaries was being emphasized and encouraged as never before.[25] It is true that the universities did provide a general education for young gentlemen but to stress this aspect of their character is to effect a serious distortion. Elizabeth and her successors intervened as often as they did in university affairs because they saw the clergy as upholders of the political and religious establishment and were duly concerned that the clergy should be educated into conformity so that they, in their turn, might ensure the political docility of the laity. That the undergraduate syllabus at the universities was non-theological is true, however.

Many members of the episcopate, including Whitgift, Laud, Grindal, Sandys and Morton, actively sought to encourage the education of future clerics at the universities as well as to recruit men directly from them. Bishop Morton of Coventry and Lichfield, for instance, was in the 1620s and 1630s instrumental in the establishment of scholarships for boys from Shrewsbury school to study at St John's, Cambridge.[26] Such endowments, although important, could effect only piecemeal improvements and there are signs of a more concerted effort to educate the clergy – an effort which aped but lagged behind developments in the Continental reformed churches, and which was initiated by ardent laymen in the first place. Thus both Sidney Sussex and Emmanuel colleges at Cambridge were founded with the express purpose of providing a learned and Protestant ministry. In the statutes of Emmanuel (1585) is to be found an admonition to members of the college 'that in establishing this college we have set before us this one aim, of rendering as many persons as possible fit for the sacred ministry of the word and the sacraments; so that from this seminary the Church of England might have men whom it may call forth to instruct the people and undertake the duty of pastors'.[27] The achievement of this end was not to be left to chance; a truly vocational training, within the terms of reference of contemporaries, was envisaged. It is significant that by 1617 Emmanuel boasted 200 undergraduates – more than any other Cambridge college except Trinity.[28] The college expanded somewhat in the ensuing period and even managed to hold its own during the Civil War and the unsettled years which followed it. Earlier endowments with a clerical complexion, such as St John's, Christ's, and Gonville and Caius at Cambridge, had their seminarial function emphasized and reinforced during the early modern period.

The intention in founding and encouraging Protestant seminaries was specifically to produce preaching ministers. There was a deep Puritan conviction that the clergy required specific training and skills to be able to instruct the people. As already indicated, one must not be misled by the word vocational into believing that the training planned was practical – the course was still essentially an academic one. There was also a deeply held belief that the office involved was a ministerial rather than a priestly one.

Elizabethan and early Stuart England witnessed attempts at the diocesan level to control the placement of ministers as well as to provide 'in-service' training for the less well qualified. Extremely well known are the associations of the clergy within a region into prophesyings, exercises and classes, all of which had a specifically educational and professional function. Less well known are the continual attempts to devise satisfactory methods of controlling the admission of men into livings. One of these means in constant use was the ancient device of ordination examination. There are sufficient examples from throughout the period to indicate that bishops often did examine conscientiously and, when the supply position allowed, did restrict entry into the profession when the men presenting themselves were blatantly unsuitable on grounds of education, knowledge of the scriptures or background.[29] Several bishops tried to extend this means of control by granting conditional approval to certain men, who had to perform set study tasks and produce certificates of their satisfactory completion. Such methods were also employed by many bishops prior to institution and there are classic examples from both Lincoln and Norwich to illustrate that bishops would reject candidates even at this late stage.[30] In some cases conscientious patrons would formally examine their clients. The most notable example is that of the Lord Keeper. It is true that his patronage was so extensive that he could not exercise stringent personal control over its distribution but it is also evident that an examination system was adhered to and that, at least under Egerton, some men were presented on condition that they provide sermons for their congregations.[31]

These attempts to control clerical recruitment made use of long-established methods – they worked within the existing framework of the patronage system. At best the bishops could hope to control the type of man eligible for patronage and to veto the presentation of specific individuals. Used freely, such powers could have achieved much, but there is considerable evidence to suggest that bishops were only free, or only felt themselves to be free, to use these methods infrequently and then in exceptional circumstances. Various schemes were drawn up which strove to modify or even radically alter the patronage structure through which the bishops were forced to work. In the 1570s, for example, Thomas Lever, archdeacon of Coventry, drew up some detailed 'notes for some reformacon of the mynistrye and mynisters' to be observed until the promulgation of official rules.[32] The notes constituted an integrated plan for the admission of men to the priesthood and to benefices and for supervision of their ministry once they were ensconced in livings. Lever reiterated the rule that no man should be ordained without a cure or without the proven ability to preach God's word and administer the sacraments. His concern, however, was not so much with the physical maintenance of the newly ordained as with the establishment of a truly pastoral ministry. The 'office' of a priest to him implied responsibility for a congregation and not simply initiation into a mystery or even entry into a professional group – here were to be no barristers who never practised, no teachers who never taught. The examination of ordinands and presentees envisaged was not to be a test of knowledge but an attempt to enforce pastoral standards. Lever was deeply conscious of the scandalous way in which many patrons administered their patronage; he also believed that the people should have some say in the appointment of their pastor – not least because sympathy between minister and congregation was essential if the ministry were to be a successful one. Lever, therefore, projected not the removal of patronage rights from the traditional holders but the institution of a congregational veto which might be exercised when the patron's nominee had served a probationary period in the parish. Lever never suggested that the power of the diocesan and his archdeacons as examiners be removed, seeing this new power in the congregation as an additional safeguard of pastoral standards.

Some years later, in the same diocese, Bishop William Overton produced a scheme which shared some of the characteristics of this earlier one as well as drawing upon the ideas of the chancellor, John Beacon.[33] Overton's scheme laid far greater emphasis upon the powers of episcopally appointed examiners to veto unsuitable candidates for both ordination and institution. Here, too, the candidate for institution was to undergo a practical probation of one month and then submit himself to the congregation for their approval or disapproval and referral back to the episcopal examiners prior to their final decision. It is unknown whether Lever's scheme was designed for national or diocesan use and no information survives concerning its implementation or its reception. It is known that Overton's scheme met with great opposition from patrons, particularly the crown, and that Overton was roundly rebuked by Whitgift for his efforts. Schemes which rode roughshod over the property rights of patrons and which smacked dangerously of 'democracy' stood no chance of success.

It is easy to establish that the crown and the hierarchy, both 'government' and 'reformed' wings, did have a set of principles which guided their approach to the question of initial recruitment into the Church and eventual employment of ordinands. But the actions of the Church's leaders were of necessity pragmatic. They were well aware that improvement in the quality of beneficed clergy rested upon educational expansion, especially as concerted attacks upon the prevailing patronage system were clearly doomed to failure. The inability of the bishops to reject unsuitable recruits has been over-emphasized by historians, but it is true to say that bishops were relatively helpless (except in extreme circumstances) before the conservative habits of patrons and their tendency to present known and often local men to benefices over and above well-qualified men.[34] The answer to this predicament was that the choice of clients before patrons must be limited initially to educated ordinands; clearly this could only be accomplished when sufficient graduates to meet the Church's pastoral needs presented themselves for ordination.

This dream became reality in the early seventeenth century. Between the beginning of 1600 and the end of 1606, 109 deacons were admitted in London diocese and, of this number, 82 were graduate and 12 were students. Recruitment via London in the 1620s was wholly graduate.[35] Educational standards had always been somewhat higher in London, however, and more significant is the improvement in remote, previously backward dioceses. There were 151 candidates ordained at Gloucester between June 1609 and May 1621; of the 87 deacons, 52 had degrees. Of the 60 ordained priest, 43 were graduates.[36] The four men who received both orders on the same day were also university men. Many of the non-graduates were students. This situation is to be compared with that of 1570 when none of the 36 ordinands had degrees. Even at Chester ordinands were better qualified. Of 314 candidates at Lichfield between 1614 and 1632, only 62 had no obvious university connection; recruitment was, therefore, at least four-fifths graduate and student.[37] All this is to leave out of account the staggering impression of university recruitment which can be obtained from an inspection of ordination lists at Oxford and Peterborough; huge numbers of students and graduates either leaving or remaining at university took orders here and, from an early date, recruitment was almost solely from the universities.[38] Neither is there any reason to suppose that the story of graduate recruitment in Ely and Lincoln changed in the early seventeenth century.

It is a simple matter to establish firstly that the crown and ecclesiastical leaders had a real interest in remodelling the ministry and particularly in making it a graduate group, and secondly that new recruits into the clergy were now almost all drawn from the universities. It is less easy to establish a causal connection. Was this spectacular improvement in the educational qualifications of clerical personnel attributable to the efforts of crown and hierarchy? Did it occur rather because patrons were showing strong preference for university men and therefore influencing the young to preface their clerical career with a university education? Was it simply the result of tremendously increased opportunity for secondary and higher education? Was it because career prospects in the Church had so improved that it now attracted graduates who would earlier have entered the law or government service?

A monocausal explanation seems both impossible and undesirable. Even hierarchical interest in raising the educational standards of the clergy was in accord with the general climate of the times. On the other hand, while provision of Protestant seminaries, the endowment of scholarships and fellowships, and bequests to schools provided the formal institutional framework necessary for expansion, they did not of themselves provide the incentive. The reasons for graduate recruitment into the Church were complicated. They deserve the attention of historians if only because the effects of this transformation upon the established Church and upon clergy–lay relations, especially during the Civil War and interregnum, will never be fully understood nor their magnitude appreciated without examination of the reasons behind and the nature of this change. Just a few of the issues must concern us here. Did the arrival of a graduate clergy significantly modify the way in which patronage was exercised? Did the clergy become more geographically mobile as a result, with increased pressure on the better livings? Is this to be attributed to a widening of the channels of communications through the university experience of both patrons and clients? Did the existing non-graduate clergy find it impossible to gain preferment because of new graduate competition? Were the 'new clergy' conscious of their position as an educated group? If so, what effect did this have upon professional development and clergy–lay relations?

To answer these questions it is first necessary to come to some understanding of the manner in which patronage was distributed in the Middle Ages and the early modern period. The prevailing picture was one of predominantly local recruitment into livings; local connection was of paramount importance when seeking a benefice.[39] This pattern may have been modified in certain instances, for example in the case of crown livings, but even here local influence was important in perhaps a majority of cases. This state of affairs can be explained in commonsense terms. The rules of the Church designed to prevent over-supply and under-employment of clergy by insisting that ordinands possess a title to a benefice, thus ensuring physical maintenance, naturally militated against large-scale migration because the inexperienced tended to obtain livings where they were best known. Thus the very structure of society supported preferment of local men. The patronage system provided opportunities for men to present both relatives and friends – this trend being heightened by the exercise of subsidiary patronage.[40] Of course, a man did not have to be a native of an area to obtain local connection. He might have managed to obtain temporary employment as teacher, curate or servant and eventually have acquired the necessary connections in this way.[41] Moreover, patronage was often extended through a chain of connections.

Broadly speaking it seems that locally distributed patronage had to remain the norm unless one of two situations arose. Either the horizons of patrons would have to be broadened considerably in a geographical sense, so that men from outside their immediate locality were more readily brought to their attention, or patrons, actively preferring graduate to non-graduate clerics, would have to be forced to look outside their own localities for just these men.

Superficially the huge expansion in secondary and higher education would seem to have created a climate congenial to the development of either or both of these situations: a large pool of graduate clergy willing to seek preferment anywhere, and a large number of gentry and yeoman patrons who had made new connections at university or at an inn of court and who were willing to extend their patronage either to these men or to their friends and relatives. When tested against the available evidence, however, this model seems to fall far short of the truth. Basically it assumes the existence of two separate groups of clergy: firstly, the uneducated men who entered the ministry before university expansion and, secondly, the graduates who flooded to ordination centres in the seventeenth century and especially in the 1620s and 1630s. It envisages competition between old and new men – educated versus uneducated. This would have been the case if the Church were now recruiting men from another group – if, for example, men who might in the 1590s have entered the law were now in the 1620s seeking ordination. This is a tempting proposition, but there is no evidence that more than a few men changed direction because of improved clerical career prospects or hierarchical persuasion. What little evidence there is of the social background of the clergy suggests no significant change other than that of the new social status conferred by education. To see the existence of two distinct groups among recruits warring for preferment is difficult if not impossible. It is surely significant that during the seventeenth century candidates for ordination were almost entirely university products. The lack of evidence of a competitive situation at the diocesan level supports this view. There are three possible explanations: that men who might have entered the Church decided not to because they foresaw insurmountable graduate competition; that the 'new' men were but the 'old' newly reformed; or a combination of these two.

Several interesting lines of approach suggest themselves. For some reason men seeking a clerical career were attending grammar school and university before placement. This movement was so widespread and dramatic that there was little room for competition for livings between non-graduate and graduate clergy, except where older men were looking for further preferment, and evidence presented elsewhere suggests that the clergy were never very mobile. It also appears that the large-scale, national improvement in educational qualifications implied little or no modification in the operation of patronage. The horizons of most patrons who attended university or inn of court remained as narrow as ever, for both colleges and inns had a marked regional complexion which cemented an existing network of connections rather than creating fresh ones.[42]

Accepting this interpretation, there is still no single explanation for the turning of the clergy to the universities before seeking orders. A plausible explanation is as follows. Initially the education of clerics at university derived from two broad developments: the declared desire of the Church's leaders and some, but proportionately very few, patrons to see a better educated clergy; and the increased interest in education arising from no direct professional motivation. Traditionally it has been thought that men put their money into education where they had previously donated it to religious foundations such as the chantries. In fact, however, it increasingly has been (not always explicitly) accepted that contemporaries both saw and sought to meet the social need for educational expansion and that some saw it as a vehicle for social engineering. Thus one notes the foundation of Protestant colleges for the training of ministers; grammar schools providing a classical education for those destined for the professions or local government; and English schools teaching basic literacy, arithmetic and accounting to apprentices. Education to a higher level was ceasing to be a luxury. To an appreciation of the value of literacy for the conduct of everyday affairs was added a conviction that the laity should be able to read the scriptures. The religious impetus behind the movement for mass literacy was strong. It may help the historian to realize why youths readily accepted the need for an educated ministry.

Both these developments had a profound effect upon potential recruits and their parents. At a time when few clergy were graduates or even students and when those who did have degrees were destined for early preferment, young men began to feel that the best chances of rapid promotion lay in the possession of such qualifications. Perhaps more significantly, parents and particularly clerical parents saw the situation in these terms. They encouraged their sons, nephews and godsons, with both words and financial aid, to pursue a university course prior to entering the ministry.[43] Of course, one must not be cynical in attributing a purely mercenary motive to these parents and sons – many shared the conviction of the Church's leaders that the standards of the pastoral ministry must be improved through education.

It is true that this change of attitude as well as changes in the character of recruitment took place at varying rates throughout England. For some time well-educated ordinands were able to move away from the remote provincial dioceses to find niches outside their native areas; there was always mobility from such areas into those of increased opportunity, which is probably why highly-educated clergy without benefices were much thicker on the ground in, for example, London than Coventry and Lichfield in the period preceding the Civil War. Poorer areas therefore had to over-supply rather than under-provide for their needs. The change in attitude was largely dependent upon the speed at which local educational facilities caught up with the Church's demands in that area. In fact in almost all cases educational provision increased rapidly and natural orientation of schools towards professional careers, combined with hierarchical interest in directing bright boys towards the Church via the universities, benefited the profession. A slow rate of turnover through death and resignation in the parishes meant that a relatively low annual recruitment of graduates was more than acceptable.

The development of secondary education in the diocese of Lichfield illustrates this point well. During the sixteenth century rather few native scholars were being sent to Oxford and Cambridge. An examination of Clark's *Tabular View of the Counties at Matriculation, 1567–1621* demonstrates that the four counties of the diocese – Derbyshire, Shropshire, Staffordshire and Warwickshire – sent very few students to Oxford when compared with other counties such as Devon, Gloucestershire and York-shire.[44] Whereas Derbyshire was in many respects a northern, rather than a midland, county which had definite connections with Cambridge, the other counties might have been expected to show a regional preference for Oxford. This remains true even when school connections, such as that of Shrewsbury school with St John's, Cambridge, are taken into account. Such a situation, when we recall the limited mobility into the area and the probable level of mobility out of it into richer and more populous localities, meant that the replacement of uneducated incumbents by graduate ones was liable to be slow. Real improvement in the diocese had to wait upon the desires of patrons and even more upon the improved internal supply of graduates.

Although there were schools in the diocese, some of them important, prior to 1558 it is certainly true that the reign of Elizabeth, and particularly the latter years of her reign, witnessed the first real expansion in the number of schools. Even the King Edward VI School, Shrewsbury, the largest school in the four counties and possibly in England, was in reality revived in the early years of Elizabeth's reign. Despite the fact that the documentation is incomplete, it can be shown that at least 200 parishes out of 388 in the diocese were at some time during the period 1584 to 1642 served by a schoolmaster, and that 93 of these parishes had a continuing tradition of education and probably a proper establishment.[45] The endowed grammar and the unendowed grammar schools (sometimes also providing more elementary instruction) grew up in the market towns and more populous areas of the diocese. Where the parish did not have its own school, the children were normally within walking distance of a school or might board during the week in a market town in the vicinity.

As shown elsewhere, ecclesiastical supervision of the schools was spasmodic; however, it is significant that in the case of the larger establishments, especially Shrewsbury, hierarchical interest and control was continuous.[46] There is every reason to believe that the pupils of such a school, or rather those who did not belong to the gentry or nobility, were directed towards the professions via the university and particularly encouraged to enter the ministry. This natural orientation of grammar school education towards the Church was further reinforced by two linked factors: in the first place, many of the non-gentle pupils were the sons of clerics; in the second place, the ministry had long had a strong dynastic element within it. Moreover, because many of the 'temporary' schools scattered throughout the diocese were run by vicars or curates, a good deal of the education outside the grammar schools proper was clerically directed.

It is easy to see that from this point onwards the re-routing of ordinands into the Church via the universities was self-generating. The chances of good preferment appeared to both insider and outsider to be slender indeed without a degree, or at least student status. Richard Baxter was almost deterred from entering the ministry because he believed that 'the want of academical honours and degrees was like to make me contemptible with the most, and consequently hinder the success of my endeavours'.[47] In fact, what little evidence survives suggests that local connection might still mean more to a patron than a good education – this is particularly evident in cases of older incumbents seeking preferment. Even so, it is evident that the hierarchical emphasis upon graduate recruitment and also the general climate of opinion in favour of education as the social ladder led contemporaries to a different assessment of the situation.

By the late 1620s and 1630s, however, men must have realized that a degree in itself could not prove a *positive* advantage to the man seeking placement, simply because every one seeking placement had a degree or was well on the way to obtaining one. Nevertheless, lack of such qualification could and did prove a serious disadvantage for some. Patrons might be unswayed by such considerations but the more conscientious bishops examined even graduates rigorously before ordination and, faced with a more than adequate supply of well-educated candidates, felt no scruple in rejecting unsuitable applicants.[48] It is true that the men the bishop of Oxford rejected in the 1630s found other bishops to ordain them, but they were graduate and, moreover, can scarcely have welcomed the inconvenience.

This examination of the situation has served to illustrate several important points. Firstly, one would be seriously in error if one judged the actions of prospective clerics in terms of the actualities of the situation; what they believed to be true was as important as, if not more important than, the truth in terms of professional development. Secondly, historians have tended to assume that changes in the nature of recruitment were gradual or that educational expansion was taken at a slow pace. In fact, such developments could make themselves felt almost overnight – as is demonstrated by the ordination lists. What is true is that the effects of changed recruitment might be slow in showing themselves in the parishes because of low rates of turnover and mobility among the clergy already ensconced. Thirdly, the move towards a graduate profession was, after a certain point – almost impossible for the historian to isolate – self-generating. There was a point when to have a degree was felt to be desirable, both for idealistic and professional reasons; soon the question of desirability was no longer at issue: a degree was essential for a career in the Church but it held out no promise of preferential treatment and no guarantee of the vocational training or aptitude of its owner.

This is not the place to discuss the value of a university degree to a minister nor to assess the academic worth of a university degree at this time although, obviously, these are important questions for anyone attempting to gauge the success of the re-forming policy of the hierarchy. It is true to say that whereas in the earlier part of the period many of the bishops laid equal weight upon attempts to produce graduate clergy and upon experiments to improve the vocational performance of ministers, by the 1620s and 1630s there was an increasing tendency among the bishops to hide behind the success of the first policy and shirk responsibility for further improvement. There are obvious exceptions; men like Thomas Morton and the bishop of Oxford were concerned that many graduates were unsuitable for the ministry and they acted upon their convictions. Nevertheless, the lack of evidence of attempts to reform the *type* of education offered the clergy points to the general truth of this conclusion.

It was largely because of this excessive reliance upon degree status and diminished emphasis upon pastoral performance and vocation that an unwelcome situation arose. This can be sum-marized very briefly. The clergy themselves were very conscious of their position as a highly-educated elite. They reinforced this position both consciously and unconsciously, sending their sons into the ministry via the university, and making their friends and confidantes largely among their own kind. As a result the clergy became markedly more caste-like. The Reformation itself had exposed a basic antagonism between the laity and the ministry – the laity could now only be reconciled to a ministry which provided adequate instruction and sympathetic service. Many pastors fulfilled this role. Many of the clergy, however, naturally set apart from the people by their life-style and their disciplinary, administrative duties, made themselves odious to their congregation by basing their claims to respect and to sole administration of the word and sacraments upon an education which to many laymen seemed irrelevant to the cleric's pastoral function. The picture was not, of course, so sharp, but it remains clear that clerical arrogance based on their separateness through education was at the root of much anti-clerical feeling in the mid-seventeenth century. The re-formation of the clergy seems a surface reformation only – the clerical profession, because of its self-awareness and occasional articulate arrogance, seemed more parasitic even than its Catholic predecessor and certainly provoked as much lay irritation and jealousy. Whether or not a deeper transformation more directed towards the fulfilment of the Protestant pastoral ideal would have brought harmony to relations between laity and clergy is debatable. What did happen certainly exacerbated the situation, the peasant among peasants was no longer and the pastor more often than not stood as the impersonal representative of an equally impersonal ecclesiastical discipline.[49]

One may conclude that the hierarchy did have a twofold policy for reformation of the ministry: increase in formal higher education; heightened vocational emphasis. For a combination of reasons the first of these goals was achieved with amazing ease. The second was more difficult to ensure: the patronage system proved an effective barrier to rejection of the unsuitable; it was far less easy to examine men for pastoral suitability than for possession of a paper qualification. In the event decreasing emphasis was placed upon this aspect by members of the episcopal bench. The effects of this situation were far-reaching and occurred where they might least have been expected.

# 3

## The role of the registrar in diocesan administration

## Rosemary O'Day

The role of the registrar in the administration of the Church in England has been somewhat neglected in the past by historians. This may be attributed to a feeling that the registrar's job was rather mundane – he recorded the activities of the bishop, the courts, or the archdeacon. Traditionally the registrar of a diocese has been classed among the lesser officials along with scribes, notaries, receivers, apparitors and messengers. Generally, as Dr Haines has said, 'the office of registrar does not emerge from obscurity until the second half of the fifteenth century'.[1] Whereas in Lincoln during the 1280s and 1290s John de Scalby acted as Bishop Sutton's registrar, the formal term *registrarius* was still rarely used in Worcester diocese in the fourteenth century. Men described as *scribae*, however, performed identical functions. In the registers there are no commissions of appointment to the office, which probably means that appointment was verbal and tenure only during the bishop's pleasure. Although the registers were in the custody of this scribe who travelled with the episcopal household, it appears that there was no formal *scriptorium* until the sixteenth century in Worcester. At that date a royal charter of confirmation was said to be 'in custodia episcopi Wigorn' in scrinio in domo registrarii in palacio episcopi sub sigillo'.[2] The first reference to a formal appointment to the post of bishop's registrar in Lichfield occurs in the mid-fifteenth century.[3]

If the office of registrar can scarcely be said to have existed in the Middle Ages, the work of the registrar or scribe was defined. He was responsible for keeping the bishop's registers. These were current compilations recording the formal activities of the bishop. Although they contained much of common form, they were not first and foremost precedent books. The content of the registers was to some extent fixed; ordination lists, institutions, licences, letters dimissory and royal writs all had to be recorded for reference purposes. Yet the selection of much of the registers' contents was determined very much by the scribe's opinion of what it was both relevant and important to record. Moreover, he would also receive directives from the bishop and other major officials calling for the inclusion of specific entries. Even at this point the historian can discern the possible influence of such a scribe.

Was the registrar no more than an exalted variety of scribe? An argument to this effect might well be constructed from the paucity of any documentation other than the episcopal registers, court act books, and instruments issuing from the register office, supported by the description of the medieval registrar. The historian today, however, influenced by the thought of Max Weber and deeply conscious of the considerable influence of the bureaucrat upon policy in contemporary society, will rightly be suspicious of such a view. The development of the Church's bureaucracy in the sixteenth century, parallel with an increase in the litigation before the church courts, should also make the historian look afresh at the registrar's role and avoid accepting the medievalist's definition as applicable in this new age.

During the sixteenth century the registrarship underwent a metamorphosis which is evident and yet difficult to document. On the one hand one senses that the registrar ceased to be primarily a member of the bishop's household; he is transformed into the diocesan registrar or principal registrar of the diocese and acquires an office. The principal registrar still has control over the registers but he is now also responsible for recording the proceedings of the consistory court (instance, correction and probate) of the diocese concerned. In the late Middle Ages the bishop's register was normally a complex compilation. Historians have noted the increasingly formal and bare character of the post-Reformation equivalent. The decline of the register, however, was not synonymous with a decline in the registrar's importance. Entirely separate records were now being kept of matters which had previously been recorded in the register. Thus in the sixteenth and seventeenth centuries there come into being subscription books which provide detailed information of a biographical nature for both ordinands and presentees to benefices; there are licensing books, records of resignations from benefices and so forth. The registrar's responsibilities showed an increase commensurate with the expansion of the work of the church courts during the period. At Lichfield, for example, records were kept of the proceedings of the three aspects of consistory. The registrar also kept records of episcopal visitations and the terriers sent in by churchwardens. Increasing involvement with legal work led to the production of detailed precedent books. The first of these extant at Lichfield dates from 1523.[4]

Of overwhelming importance for the development of the registrar's office was the fact that at some uncertain date it became usual for the holder of the office to be a notary public.[5] This meant that he had authority to issue legal documents. This development had a wider implication – it meant that the registrar's role became more complex as he no longer merely recorded the bishop's actions, letters and instructions but himself issued the instruments which gave these force of law. It was he who issued citations, certificates, demands for payment and so forth.

An office which was held responsible for all this documentation and more – for example, the large number of documents connected with the presentation and institution of clerics to benefices – was clearly too large to be run by one man. The registrar acquired deputies and clerks to perform the routine functions. There are several indications that ecclesiastical registries of the period employed quite substantial staffs. In some cases it is probable that the registrar himself was not a notary public, in which case his deputies almost certainly were. The deputies often attended court days in the registrar's stead. Some division of responsibilities was essential because most of the administrative work of the diocese thus devolved upon the registrar. It would be dangerous, therefore, to apply Dr Kitching's criteria for the importance of an official here.[6] The registrar, like the diocesan chancellor, was often replaced by his deputy in the courts, and no one could doubt the real importance of the chancellor in diocesan administration. As will become apparent, the registrar wielded much of his not inconsiderable influence outside the courts themselves.

An officer who possesses a deputy and a number of underlings automatically acquires prestige. A reflection of this new status is to be found in the fact that the registrar was now an officer appointed by formal letters patent and that he commonly held the office for life. The office was also lucrative and for this reason coveted. The table of fees adhered to at Lichfield under Bishop Overton demonstrates neatly that the registrar was in a position second only to the judge.[7] For instance, for each initial citation to appear before the court the judge of the consistory received 3*d*., whereas the registrar commanded a fee of 4*d*. A citation *quorum nomina* brought the registrar 1*s*. 1*d*. and the judge 1*s*. 6*d*. For a sentence the judge received 6*s*. 8*d*. and the registrar 3*s*. 4*d*. Letters of institution brought the registrar 4*s*. 4*d*. and the judge 10*s*. 0*d*. Even when it is accepted that the registrar normally had to pay the clerks within his office from his own fees, it is clear that the rapidly expanding business of the courts and the steady routine work of the diocese enabled the registrar to keep pace with inflation. This appears true even if we accept that the registrar engaged in no form of corruption.

Dr Kitching has expressed the view that the registrar's estimate of his own importance must be to an extent suspect; he cites in support of this argument the fact that the registrar's presence in court was not essential and that most of his routine functions could be performed by a deputy. He adds that it is, however, impossible for the historian to estimate how many hours' 'home-work' the registrar did.[8] This article contends that one cannot measure the registrar's importance according to his participation in the formal court procedure or in the routine work of his *scriptorium*.

In this sense Dr Kitching's point about the self-importance and self-glorification of the registrars is a significant one. The registrar's influence in the diocese progressed in harness with his self-esteem. The office became coveted (and expensive in all probability); others noted this fact and, believing that the registrar was influential in decision-making, corresponded with him on a wide variety of subjects, asking for advice and patronage. The registrar's position in control of the licensing of schoolmasters, preachers, curates, doctors and midwives, of the institution of clerics, and of the business coming before the church courts, assured him of the opportunity to influence decisions quietly. The insidious power of an efficient and expert bureaucracy was beginning to show itself. Moreover, the registrar still commanded the bishop's ear.

In the archives of Lincoln exists abundant evidence of the wide-reaching influence of the principal registrar of a diocese should he wish to exercise it. The correspondence of the diocesan and archidiaconal registrars falls into several classes. By far the largest surviving category is correspondence concerning court business. Some of this was of the simplest kind. For instance, on 23 November 1601, Edmund Riddull asked the registrar of Lincoln, William Stirrop, for a citation against Mr and Mrs Richardson of Saxby in connection with the detaining of a legacy: it is probable that Riddull was an apparitor.[9] Similarly William Corbell in 1602 wrote to Stirrop for a whole string of citations.[10] The influence of the registrar is apparent even in such mundane matters: should he choose, he might deny a citation after scrutinizing the case concerned and thus save the parties involved inconvenience and expense. Some of the letters, however, concerned more delicate matters. In June 1602 Robert Rustat protested to the registrar that certain inhabitants of Mountsorrell, Thorpe and St Ives had been summoned for offences of which they had actually been discharged several years before.[11] Hugh Reever, vicar of Ampthill, Bedfordshire, reported to Stirrop the J.P.'s failure to act upon a writ *de excommunicato capiendo*; the registrar was to see that something was done.[12] Other letters show more definitely the registrar using his own influence. In May 1603 George Eland inquired about the progress of a suit concerning Great Catford and asked Stirrop what the bishop's opinion in the matter was.[13] Later in the summer, Charles Dymoke appealed to the registrar for a release of fees for John Newton, a poor man standing excommunicate at Godmanchester court.[14] More significantly still, in November 1603 Gabriel Bewit, vicar of Harrington, asked Stirrop to deal leniently with one who was cited for defamation.[15] On several occasions people wrote asking Stirrop to forestall a citation before the consistory. John Bingnet, for instance, protested that he had been slandered about non-residence. Because his house had been robbed, he had let the parsonage out, boarded with a parishioner and sent his wife to live with his mother in Peterborough. Apparently Stirrop let the citation stand; in the following January 1605, Bingnet wrote that he had sent a certificate of residence to Stirrop.[16] It appears that because it was the registrar who effectively decided whether an offender should be prosecuted in the courts (unless his case was so important that the bishop or chancellor intervened) it became important to win the registrar over to one's point of view. There is certainly little suggestion that the registrar was passing on business such as this to his deputies or clerks.

The principal registrar was expected to have considerable legal expertise on a practical level. Of course, he was able to consult the many notaries public and advocates for advice on complicated matters. The chancellor of a diocese seems also to have been consulted regularly on day to day affairs. The absentee chancellor of Lichfield during the years 1683–9, Richard Raines, displayed a lively interest in and amazing knowledge of the work of his consistory court in his correspondence with the deputy registrars and registrar of Lichfield.[17] Yet the efficient and just administration of the courts was dependent upon the registrar's abilities and willingness to exercise his powers responsibly. However much the chancellor might urge the registrar to be more rigorous in correction cases, to guard against corrupt practices by court officers such as the proctors, to speed up processes, to scrutinize citations, and even to heed his legal advice, in the last resort the registrar made the decisions. It was difficult to control this official if he chose to pursue a given line stubbornly because so much of what he did was done quietly, even secretly. The exposure of some scandal, of course, meant some tightening up at the bureaucratic level but it was hard to ensure that reforms were really implemented.[18]

The clergy seem to have asked the registrar's assistance on legal matters. The precedent books doubtless proved of use at such junctures. The registrar was expected to advise on the legality of transference of cases from one court to another and on the respective jurisdictions of the courts within the diocese. Some of the most delicate matters requiring the registrar's tactful but expert attention concerned contested jurisdiction. In 1607 John Chippingdale reported that Dr Belley, the troublesome chancellor of Lincoln diocese, was in the habit of withdrawing cases which belonged properly in the commissary's court at Leicester; despite a declared intention to desist in future, Belley had continued to offend. Chippingdale washed his hands of the matter and left it to Stirrop to resolve.[19] This particular case is significant not merely because it shows the registrar in the 'hot seat' but also because it shows that it was he who on occasion lent definition to diocesan practice – if he allowed Belley to proceed formally uncontested, he was condoning, indeed underlining, the supremacy of the chancellor's court. Yet while the registrar was making independent decisions of some importance one also finds him seeking expert advice regarding the circumstances in which union of benefices was permissible, or the justification for granting a divorce or separation, and requesting mundane information – for example, a list of churches and chapels in the diocese.

The registrar was also expected to transmit these skills and his knowledge of the work of registrar to his deputies and clerks. For example, in 1626 John Prigeon, registrar of Lincoln, wrote to Walter Walker, deputy registrar in control of Leicester archdeaconry, a long letter full of instructions as to how and when the latter was to hold his courts. Prigeon continued to supervise Walker's activities as archidiaconal registrar throughout 1627. In February he reported that he had received complaints about Walker's exercise of the office.[20] He had a degree of control over the way in which Walker performed his duties. Thus, while we can say that the deputy registrars also had influence, it is true that their actions were circumscribed when the principal registrar chose to express an interest in the business involved.

In his work concerning the courts the registrar was, of course, responsible to the bishop and to his chancellor. He had to be willing to explain his actions and those of his deputies if requested to do so. At Lincoln sufficient correspondence survives to indicate that laymen and clergy often appealed directly to the bishop for help, occasionally against the registrar's decision. On 20 September 1603 Owen Hodges wrote to Registrar Stirrop on behalf of Bishop Chadderton. Some inhabitants of Rippingdale had complained to the bishop that they had been summoned to Godmanchester without reason. The bishop sought information from the registrar (whose responsibility it was to issue citations) and requested Stirrop to come to Holywell in person to discuss this and the matter of a commission being granted to the bishop of Peterborough.[21] In a different vein, the bishop was sometimes asked by someone cited before the consistory to excuse him of attendance and notify the court officers of this fact. To what extent the personal intervention of the bishop acted as a safeguard for the clergy and public against the registrars' abuse of their power is a moot point. Certainly when Thomas Bentham of Lichfield discovered in 1561 that the registrar, James Weston, was approving corrupt candidates for institution to livings, he immediately clamped down upon the registrar's freedom of action in examining presentees to benefices, taking steps to ensure that in future either the bishop or the dean had to be personally present at the examination.[22] At Lincoln in 1603 we seem to have a further example of the concern of the hierarchy to see that court cases were only brought when the evidence had been carefully scrutinized by the registrar's office. It was, however, difficult to ensure that this scrutiny was unbiased.

Much of the registrar's routine concern was, however, not with the work of the courts but with the clergy and, more specifically, with the exercise of ecclesiastical patronage. Although the registrar certainly had no official role to play in the administration of patronage, his intervention should cause no surprise in view of his involvement with all the formal milestones of a clergyman's career. He was present at ordination, asking a fee of 1s. for letters; at subscription, commanding a fee of 3s. 4d.; at institution, charging 4s. 4d. for letters of institution and 1s. 8d. for mandate of induction. He was instrumental in the issue and viewing of all manner of licences. Either he or his deputy sat in the probate side of consistory. He recorded clerical resignations from benefices, occasionally recorded exchanges, registered the *caveats* issued by patrons when livings in their gift fell vacant, and registered agreements of grants of next presentation. E. F.

Jacob postulated for the Middle Ages that there were perhaps 'unofficial information offices, run like an appointments bureau to which the prospective incumbents could resort' and where eager clerics were put in touch with possible patrons.[23] Undoubtedly in London the 'exchange' at St Paul's performed some such function, but within the provinces there was no need for any such bureau as the registrar and his clerks had at their finger tips all the knowledge required to arrange contacts between patrons and prospective clients.[24] The case of the Lord Keeper's patronage is of course an extreme one – there it was the registrar of benefices who, with the aid of examiners' reports and commendations, decided who should receive what benefice, with apparently minimal interference from his superior.[25] Yet clues from the records of Lichfield, Worcester and Lincoln suggest that the registrar's influence in the placement of personnel was accepted as normal.

One of the ways in which the registrar's office became aware of the occurrence of a vacancy was by the entry of a *caveat* against presentation to that living by anyone other than he who registered the *caveat* until inquiry had been made about the precise whereabouts of patronage. The entry of a *caveat* was not compulsory; it was probably only normal when disputed patronage appeared probable. *Caveats* were entered for a mere 41 vacancies at Lichfield between 1560 and 1579, a period which probably saw an estimated 380 vacancies.[26] *Caveats* at Lincoln seem to have been commonly requested by non-local persons who felt that their patronage might be trespassed upon in their absence. Where a *caveat* was felt to be necessary, the registrar was given extremely detailed instructions.[27]

A more accurate index of the number of void livings was provided by the registrar's record of resignations, and of the formal documents by which offending clerics were deprived. The registrar was bound by ecclesiastical and common law to inform the patron of a living when it became void by resignation or retirement. Failure on the registrar's part to do this could involve the bishop in tiresome, costly and unrewarding legal proceedings. There was, however, no formal procedure for recording the deaths of parochial clergy and the consequent voidance of their livings. The registrar through his probate work must have had a considerable working knowledge of the position, but he was not obliged to contact patrons to inform them of this opportunity to exercise patronage. This sometimes led to lengthy vacancies and to the patrons losing their *hac vice* right to present through lapse to the bishop or crown.[28]

Prospective patrons and intending incumbents often sought the bishop's assistance in their suits. Some, however, thought it worth their while to approach the registrar. Mr Wood addressed Registrar Stirrop in 1603 on behalf of his brother, a B.D., who had recently been nominated as rector of Somerby: 'In this case Sir I am to desire you in my owne that you would further him and acquaint my Lord with his cause that he may have present expedition, in which act you shall do a thing gratefull to Sir William, who after a manner accounts himself his patron . . . Sir William hath written to my Lord.'[29] The registrar was seen to have the bishop's ear; men were asking him to exert informal pressure on the bishop by bringing a particular suit to his attention. This pressure might merely succeed in expediting some piece of business in the court (which would save the suitor money) or a presentation to a benefice which was not really being contested, or it might be used in a more positive sense to influence the bishop's decision. Stirrop was called upon in 1601 by Edmund Riddull to influence the bishop's choice in the presentation to a benefice of '30l a yeare which is in the gift of my Lord bishop', adding that the bearer 'is very sufficient man for the place & I pray good cousin show him what favour you can'.[30] Two years later John Cooke appealed to Stirrop to help him to another living: his 'hearty desire is you would be a means to help me to some better place than that troublesome place with 2 churches that now I have: if it were but a place with some reasonable stipend until some living fall I would accept of it with thanks, for truly this toil of 2 churches is enough to weary any man be he never so willing a man'. Leaving nothing to chance, Cooke also wrote to Mrs Stirrop asking her to use her influence with the registrar to arrange a transfer.[31] Less specifically, in 1602 John Foster, vicar of Wigtoft, wrote a letter of commendation for a Cambridge graduate to Stirrop, requesting Stirrop's favour in his preferment.[32] Also in 1602, Stirrop was attempting to secure preferment for a client by using his diocesan knowledge. In February 1602 a cleric wrote to him explaining that he had done what he could to arrange for Stirrop's client to succeed him, but that his patron had probably already appointed to the benefice.[33]

The registrar's influence was not restricted to the preferment of clergymen to benefices. In 1606 John Dighton addressed Stirrop on the question of appointing a schoolmaster to Ketton parish: 'If Mr Little (pre[sently] vicar of Ketton) doe come to my Lord of Lincoln to get Licence to teache as a schoolemaster within the limits of Ketton parish, I pray you most heartily. Let me be sure that you will not but do all that may be don by you & your means to prevaile that such licence be not granted.' Moreover, Dighton was willing to go to some lengths to ensure that Little did not procure the licence in spite of this warning: 'Whatsoever he is to cite for the fee of such licence if he sped, I will give as much to have it withholden from him & I will (also) recompence them who shall be the means to obtain to be done.' If all else failed, Stirrop was enjoined at least to persuade the bishop to stay the licensing until Dighton had had a chance to present his case against Little in further detail. Stirrop, Dighton hoped, would also see Archdeacon Eland and attempt to see that he was not won over to Little's cause.[34] Evidence that bribes or incentives were offered to the registrar does not, of course, prove that such were accepted. Certainly, however, a diocesan registrar had ample opportunity for such under-the-table transactions.

In a much more generalized way the registrar of Lincoln was deeply involved with the problems of clerical personnel. It was his office which kept a careful check upon which clergymen had paid or failed to pay their subsidies, pensions, synodals, procurations and other fees. In July 1603 John Prigeon forwarded to Stirrop a list of those clergy who were behind with their subsidy payments and of those who had already paid; Thomas Rands sent the registrar £3 issuing out of the union of the benefices of Holton-le-Clay and Waythe; Francis Bullingham asked for particulars of the arrears of tenths and of subsidies collected to facilitate his accounting; and William Burneby, vicar of Helpringham, asked for respite for a payment as he was being harassed by an adversary.[35] It was the registrar who had to deal with the specific problems of collection arising out of sequestration of a benefice. Process of sequestration was carried out against John Parrott, vicar of Shillington, who wrote to Stirrop reproachfully. He claimed that the sequestration was unfair as he was perfectly willing to pay the subsidy levied but had never been informed of the place or date of payment.[36] Administrative inefficiency was also implied by William Folkingham who wrote that Mr Morrice, parson of Leasingham, had twice been asked for a sum of money for a sequestration which had already been paid. Henry Wilkinson made a similar claim in June 1602.[37] Before further action was taken, Stirrop (or rather his clerks) had to scrutinize the accounts.

In the context of the financial plight of the clergy, several letters were addressed to the registrar asking him to be lenient towards clerics in particularly difficult circumstances. Henry Vescy, vicar of Thorp St Peter, requested Stirrop directly to favour his cause as entry to his new benefice had cost him £80 in charges to king, bishop and court.[38] Elizabeth Goodryck requested Stirrop to be lenient over the charges on the estimable Mr Gust who had come to the small living of Ravesden on the urging of her husband.[39] Thomas Foster, hearing of the sequestration of his living of Great Stukeley, Huntingdonshire, asked Stirrop's aid.[40] Christian Savile asked the registrar for information regarding mortuary fees to the incumbent.[41] In 1605 Thomas Rainbow, vicar of Bliton, wrote to Thomas Rands, archidiaconal registrar, to forward to Stirrop his certificate of wearing the surplice.[42] Thomas Stirrop notified his relative, the registrar, that Mr Lathwett, although in possession of a dispensation to hold Little Carlton in plurality with Anderby, was being harassed by an adversary: the registrar was to see that no injustice befell Lathwett.[43] Samuel Watts, vicar of Great Dalby, sought the registrar's aid in 1603 to arrange the lease of his vicarage.[44]

The evidence available seems to demonstrate that whether the registrar had real influence with the bishop and in the courts or not, he managed to convince both clergy and lay suitors and litigants that he possessed considerable powers of persuasion. He was intimately concerned with the lives of the clergy in several respects. He could be expected to plead a prospective incumbent's case with the bishop in the case of an episcopal living; he might be willing to put a client in touch with a probable patron or vice versa; he might ask a retiring incumbent to influence his patron's next appointment; he might sway the bishop's decision in granting licences. On another level it was the registrar who supervised sequestrations, payment of taxes and fees by the clergy, and it was he who had to iron out the problems allegedly arising from administrative inefficiency and injustice. In his position as registrar of the consistory he had the opportunity to see also that the clergy were not the victims of similar inefficiency and to see that the foundation for a case against a clergyman was always scrutinized before charges were brought. He could also be expected to use his discretion in treating leniently those clergy who failed to pay fines, provide certificates, or do penance in response to the court's order. This official was not a judge or one who pleaded a case formally in the courts but, at the hub of the bureaucratic machinery and as the origin of all formal documentation, his activities could and did make an impression upon the lives and careers of the clergy.

Whereas the term lesser official may well have been applicable to the medieval functionary, it certainly does not seem to fit the registrar, at least in the diocesan context, during the early modern period. However, it may be the case that the post of bishop's secretary, just emerging into the limelight in the early seventeenth century, was to some extent eroding the registrar's position as confidante and adviser to the bishop. The examples of John Cosin, secretary to Bishop Overall at Lichfield and Norwich; of Richard Baddiley, secretary to Bishop Morton at Lichfield and Durham; and of William Easdall, secretary to Bishop Richard Neile at Lichfield, spring to mind.[45] Such men were part of the bishop's personal entourage, his protégés, who appear to have travelled with the bishop from see to see; unlike the registrar, their responsibility was not specifically to the diocese, in the form of the commissary general, but to the bishop in person, and they were much more likely to have a consistently good personal relationship with the diocesan than was the registrar.

It seems ironical that the one development which successive registrars so cherished – the confirmed hereditary nature of the office via reversionary grants – set the seal on this process. The practice whereby local men secured letters patent of appointment to the registrarship for life and obtained the grant in reversion for a son or other relative meant that whereas the initial recipient probably stood in favour with the bishop who appointed him, he stood in no special personal relationship with successive bishops and neither did his own descendants. The office of registrar acquired prestige when it became semi-hereditary but it may have lost some power during this process. One should consider alongside this surmise the fact that the registrarship tended to rest with a local family or with a family which had through long residence become local. The Westons at Lichfield, for example, who held the registrarship from 1561 until the third decade of the seventeenth century, were part of a prominent local family, and strengthened their connections with the local gentry throughout the period. Unlike the bishop's secretary they were therefore possessed of great local knowledge; they had at their finger tips the records of their office; and they had influence at least within the county of Stafford. All this helped them to maintain their position against the attempted encroachments of the bishop's household chaplains and secretary. But we must still accept a change in his position. The secretary dealt with the bishop's correspondence, both personal and official, and soon, because of his influence with the bishop, began to be a power in his own right. If the fifteenth century had seen the removal of the registrar from the household government of the bishops and had seen the creation of a formal registrar's office acting independently, though in close liaison with the bishop, the late sixteenth and seventeenth centuries saw the growth of a new informal position within the household which threatened to usurp the registrar's influence over episcopal patronage and decisions concerning administration and to cause him to be confined to his work in the consistory courts.

Despite this threat, the office of registrar certainly became much coveted during the period. In 1635 the corporation of Lichfield complained that while Registrar Archbold paid a low ship money assessment of £3, he had paid £2,000+ for the office.[46] The post must have been sufficiently lucrative to warrant such an outlay. Yet in examining the wealth of individual registrars and their position in society one must be wary of ascribing all of their prosperity to the fruits of office. Many came from gentry families and had come into property by inheritance. The will of James Weston, registrar of Lichfield, 1561–89, may be used to illustrate the economic category to which such a man belonged.[47] James had two sons, Simon and James. He provided for James with a yearly rent charge of £20 until he reached age 24, when it would be raised to £30 per annum. Simon, the eldest son, was to pay this rent charge out of property he inherited at King's Bromley, Armitage and Handsacre. James made further bequests of silver and small leases to his friends, kin and overseers of the will. The bulk of his property and moveable goods, however, were to be sold to provide for his three daughters and to prosecute a case of *quare impedit* for the prebend of Sallow which he had inherited from his brother, Chancellor Weston of Lichfield. Simon inherited a considerable amount of property (basically that which his father had himself inherited), while there was less concern for James's future, and a determination to use acquired property to provide for the three daughters – one of whom was married to Humphrey Wells, gent. James Weston's position as brother to the chancellor of the diocese had undoubtedly helped him financially; for example, from 1573 onwards he administered several leases of parsonages and prebends on behalf of Robert Weston's young daughters. Presumably being the diocesan registrar put a man like Weston in a position to acquire favourable leases of property, but the will is so undetailed that it is not possible to do more than say this.

Registrars certainly appear to have played their part in the money market of the day. The correspondence of Francis Bullingham, registrar of Lincoln in the late 1580s, shows that he made a practice of granting loans. In March 1585 he loaned £100 to Thomas Rands upon which he charged interest. At the same time a debt of £37 10s. 0d. was due to him from one Sutton and a little later, in 1586, a bond for a sum of £40 is mentioned.[48] Unfortunately we do not know how much interest was charged or the duration of the loans; apparently they were granted to people involved in the diocesan administration and their relatives. Bullingham certainly possessed considerable property and employed a steward. He held at least one parsonage which he leased out for 40 marks per annum. It is probable, of course, that the registrars loaned money which was temporarily in their hands by reason of their office, although there is naturally no evidence proving that this was the case. The registrar might also extend other financial favours to suitors; in December 1604 Francis Smith requested that Stirrop pay his court expenses which Smith would then repay according to a bond.[49] It would be interesting to know just how often the registrars came to the rescue in this practical manner.

Miss Jean Potter in her unpublished University of London M.A. thesis, 'The Ecclesiastical Courts in the Diocese of Canterbury, 1603–65' (1973), has attempted an estimate of the income accruing to the diocesan and archidiaconal registrars. She concludes that in 1603 the diocesan registrar was drawing a minimum of £27 from instance business in the consistory; by 1633 the amount had risen to £48 per annum. At the same dates the registrar of the archdeacon's court was drawing £31 and £44 respectively. Miss Potter concludes that the archdeaconry post was more lucrative than that of the consistory. Yet several questions are left unanswered. The estimate for the diocesan registrar excluded probable income from the probate and correction sides of consistory – presumably a sizeable sum; on the other hand one would assume that the archdeacon's court dealt mainly with correction business and probate. Moreover the registrar of the diocese was drawing a considerable revenue from fees which did not pertain directly to court business – licensing, letters of orders, resignations, institutions, inductions and so forth. Miss Potter's estimate, therefore, while helpful, yields only a minimum figure for the registrar's income at the diocesan level.

All the evidence which has thus far come to light suggests that the registrars were in a position to exercise considerable influence over the administration of the diocese at a practical level. Their conscientious industry was required to make the courts function efficiently and honestly. The bishop and the chancellor needed their fund of expertise and their connections in order to administer knowledgeably. Thus in 1603 Thomas Bullingham, son of Francis, wrote urgently to Registrar Stirrop urging his return to the diocese from London. The bishop was annoyed at his absence, especially as his personal secretary was sick. Many matters had arisen with which neither the bishop nor his servants could deal because they were too specialized.[50]

Although the historian will never know the whole truth about the registrars' influence within diocesan administration, because the workings of influence and patronage were generally quiet and undocumented, sufficient evidence exists to suggest that Weber's thesis might well be applied to his role. Because the registrar had to be an expert professional, with a fund of connections as well as knowledge, in order to run the administration efficiently at a bureaucratic level, there was a danger that he would turn naturally from the implementation of policy towards decision-making. His knowledge was technical, consisting of organizational know-how acquired through day-to-day experience with the minutiae of administration. 'The official's technical and organizational knowledge is a sign of his indispensability and hence of his power, unless he is controlled by people who possess not only the authority to supervise him but the knowledge to do so effectively.[51] The official's weapon against such expert supervision is to keep his business confidential. By intervening secretly at mundane levels of administration, he is able to wield considerable influence without publicizing the fact.

It is apparent, then, that during the early modern period the registrar of a diocese was indeed second in importance only to the chancellor. He may not have been in a position to initiate policy but with him lay the power to decide whether that policy was effectively implemented or not. Historians tend to forget that the courts Christian were not only instruments of law enforcement but of administration. To this extent they differed from the common law courts. It was incumbent upon the bishop and chancellor to supervise and control the registrar and his office. The canons of 1604 were a deliberate attempt to curb abuses. There were, therefore, checks on the registrars' exercise of influence but, because many of the channels of their power and patronage were on a very secret or a relatively unimportant level, such control could not be entirely effective. Indeed it was realized that such perquisites of patronage were as important as the fees themselves in making the official perform his administrative duties efficiently. While the post of bishop's secretary posed a potential threat to the registrar's extra-consistory influence, the registrar in the early seventeenth century still occupied an important and coveted position in diocesan administration and society, which has too long been overlooked.

# Finance

# 4

## Clerical tax collection under the Tudors: the influence of the Reformation

## Felicity Heal

I

The financial demands[1] which the Tudors made upon their subjects were irregular and uneven in incidence, the reflection of a society still essentially medieval in resources and organization. Nevertheless, fiscal control could be both comprehensive and relatively sophisticated when circumstances permitted, as they did most obviously in the English Church after the Henrician Reformation. Even before the Reformation the Church was a valuable source of revenue for the crown – the best estimate suggests that about £12,000 per annum may have gone to line the royal coffers, exclusive of those benevolences, loans and amicable grants that were expected as of right in time of war.[1] This is particularly significant when contrasted with the papal attempts at money-raising: no general tax could be sent to Rome without royal permission, which was hardly ever given, and from traditional dues such as Peter's Pence, and the fees paid on promotion to benefices, the papacy probably received under £5,000 a year.[2] Yet the clergy still retained a certain economic independence, and an attitude to taxation similar to that of the laity. The king had the right to demand of them certain custom- ary dues, and all necessary revenue in times of crisis, but their obligations were still limited and feudal, and in no sense were their goods and revenues wholly at the disposal of the crown. After the Reformation the government was able to exercise a completely different degree of control over church wealth, and this was reflected as much in the increased incidence of taxation as in the more dramatic appropriation of the property of the monasteries.

The major taxation change for the clergy was, of course, the introduction of first fruits and tenths. Although the first fruits were based upon the old common services and annates, payable at the papal curia upon provision to benefices, they were now extended to the whole body of the clergy, and with them came the totally new grant of a tenth of annual income. This dual exaction was added to the pre-Reformation subsidy or tenth, which was once again from the 1540s required of the clergy whenever a lay parliamentary subsidy was granted. The establishment of first fruits and tenths as the main form of clerical taxation considerably improved the crown's regular income, and at the same time emphasized the distinction between the laity and the clergy in this field. The latter were shown to be subordinated to the Supreme Head of the Church. Between 1535 and 1547 the average annual yield of first fruits, tenths and subsidies was £47,000, and even after the disappearance of the monasteries, chantries and religious guilds, the Tudor government could reasonably expect to raise £30,000 from these taxes.[3] Only in Mary's reign, when the crown renounced its claims to first fruits and tenths, and depended wholly upon subsidies, did the yield fall to its pre-Reformation levels. Not only new taxes, but a new standard of assessment helped to improve Henry VIII's profits. Whereas money had previously been collected according to the survey prepared for the taxation of Pope Nicholas IV in 1291, this was now supplanted by the great *Valor Ecclesiasticus* prepared in 1535 by royal commissioners to give a true estimate of the value of church property.[4]

So sharp was the transition to a new form and level of clerical taxation at the Henrician Reformation that discontinuity might be thought to be the obvious feature of this aspect of ecclesiastical affairs. Yet here as elsewhere, the crown and Church built upon a system that was already in existence, rather than beginning wholly anew. Some of the taxes might be novel – the sums that they were required to pay came as a grievous shock to the parish clergy of the 1530s – but the methods of payment were largely familiar, the product of the experience of several hundred years which the Church had already had as tax collectors to the crown. Both before and after the Reformation it was the bishops who had the principal responsibility for the collection of royal dues, and a selection of the bishops' own deputies who appeared in the parishes to demand payment. The system of tax collecting among the clergy has never been discussed in any detail, but it is a subject both interesting and valuable in its own right, and germane to the general theme of continuity and change in the sixteenth-century Church. It provides an admirable example of an administrative process fundamentally unchanged by the great upheavals of these years, yet subtly amended by the will of the crown, and by the pressures generated after the Reformation. The bishops, who stood at the centre of the tax-collecting network, are a particularly fascinating subject for study. They themselves were liable to some of the largest of royal demands, and they were cast in the ambiguous role of chief tax collectors and leading protectors of the clergy. This dual role led to many tensions and difficulties, which raised larger problems about the status of the bishops, and threatened their position as spiritual leaders of the Church.

2

The pre-Reformation system of royal taxation involved the bishops both in the process of agreement and the task of collection. It was commonly royal policy to ask Convocation for the grant of a subsidy or tenth at the same time as Parliament was asked for a lay grant. The clergy were even less likely than the laity to refuse such a request, though in theory they retained the right to deny the king. The money might be a lump sum, such as the £25,000 granted in 1489, or the £40,000 voted by the southern Convocation in 1496.[5] The £118,000 voted by the clergy in 1531 in gratitude for their escape from the threat of *praemunire* is the last example of a fixed payment of this kind.[6] More commonly a tenth or subsidy was granted; individual liability was then based in theory upon the 1291 taxation lists, which the Exchequer took as their guides in deciding the general amounts owed by the Church. The Exchequer had no right to intervene in the detailed business of tax collection; this was left to the bishops, who performed the same role as the sheriff in lay collections. If the tax was a lump sum the clergy in convocation divided it up into the amounts that each diocese could be expected to pay, and then the bishop was left to handle local apportionment. When a tenth or subsidy was given, Convocation granted activating power to the crown, and the diocesan was then normally commissioned as collector, and ordered to make returns into the Exchequer, or the revived Chamber, by a specified date.[7]

The scattered surviving evidence suggests that the bishops organized tax collection in a similar manner, whatever the nature of the original grant. The financial demand was passed to sub-collectors, who in this period were almost always heads of monastic houses. At Durham, for example, the prior of the cathedral was regularly the episcopal deputy in matters of taxation; at Ely it was again the prior of the cathedral, sometimes aided by the abbot of Banwell, and at Hereford in the 1520s the abbot of Flaxley had this responsibility.[8] Little is known about the manner in which these men set about their task; it must be presumed that they in turn deputed other men to tour the dioceses and collect the actual money. Receipts for tenths paid over by William Latimer, master of the college of St Laurence Poultney, London, show a different collector on each occasion, suggesting that the sub-collectors employed deputies on a casual, short-term basis.[9] Some of these deputies would also have had the onerous task of conveying the money to London, and obtaining Exchequer acquittance on the bishop's behalf, for it was always the bishop who was accountable to the crown when he had been commissioned as collector. From time to time the bishop was also commissioned to levy arrears of tenths and subsidy by the traditional ecclesiastical method of sequestration.[10] The existence of these commissions for the early Tudor period suggests that a system was already in existence for exonerating the collectors from illeviable debts. This probably followed on the same development in lay taxation: before the Tudors reformed the system the sheriff had been accountable for all debts, however bad they might prove.[11]

There were few major difficulties with this system of revenue collection, beyond the familiar problem that not all taxes could be raised in full. The two potential problems lay with the apportionment of liability and the accounting to the Exchequer. Liability or accountability formally rested with the bishop, but it was rarely he who oversaw the raising of revenue, and his deputies must have been left very much to their own devices. This difficulty of controlling deputies who actually handled the money was to be a recurrent theme in later episcopal correspondence on taxation. In the early sixteenth century, however, only one example has been found of a real problem: in 1512 part of a tenth due from the diocese of Hereford was not paid because of the death of the bishop. As a result the sub-collector, the abbot of Flaxley, became liable for the payment, but he in his turn died and his unfortunate successor was left to struggle with the outstanding debt.[12] Accounting in the Exchequer was always a tedious and time-consuming process, but one which lay collectors had to suffer just as much as the clergy. As early as the reign of Henry VI the crown on occasions by-passed the lumbering Exchequer machinery; in 1464 a papal subsidy designed to finance a campaign against the Turk was supervised and collected by the crown, ignoring the Exchequer, because of the 'dread' that the clergy had of being accountable to that worthy institution.[13] Under Henry VII most of the numerous clerical grants were handled by the Chamber.

Henry VII taxed the clergy more consistently than any of his predecessors. Between 1487 and 1496, for example, there were four separate grants of tenths, and in addition the richer clergy were asked for benevolences and loans.[14] This occasioned no significant protests, even though the higher clergy were also subjected to a game of ecclesiastical musical chairs, in which the bishops were moved from see to see partly to increase the royal revenues from vacancies and fines at restitution of temporalities. The only crisis of the pre-Reformation period that did arouse vigorous protest was Wolsey's attempt to raise war finance in the 1520s. In 1523 the clergy granted the very unusual subsidy of half the value of all benefices, payable over five years.[15] To this were added substantial demands for loans and benevolences, and then a further request for a subsidy of a third of the value of all livings. It was the last demand that provoked Archbishop Warham to write in protest to Wolsey that, even if the king was willing to reduce this from one-third to one-sixth, he believed there was 'more untowardness than towardness' among the clergy in paying the tax. Many of the clergy, especially the religious, alleged that they had had to mortgage lands and sell jewels to raise the money, and the situation was made more difficult because there had been no repayments on the earlier loans. Warham himself was owed 2,500 marks, and most of the bishops were owed between £500 and £1,000. The archbishop also suggested that the heavy taxation of the laity was having an indirect effect on the clergy's ability to produce the money: his own farmers were reluctant to pay their normal rents because of the demands of the government.[16] It was the hostility of the laity that forced Wolsey to withdraw his demands in 1525, and the higher clergy seem on the whole to have co-operated loyally in the task of extracting money from the Church, but comments such as those of the archbishop suggest that they too could question the wisdom of royal policy.

Their doubts were probably made more compelling by the difficulties which they had in raising personal taxes and loans to satisfy the king. Bishop Sherburne of Chichester had to sell almost £700 worth of plate in order to loan the king £1,000 in 1522, and Bishop West, when he had found the £500 required of him, complained that he had not been 'barer' of money since his second year in the see of Ely.[17] At one of the subsidy payments demanded in these years, on the other hand, Richard Foxe of Winchester actually paid £50 more than the necessary sum, in order to please the crown.[18] Good relations with the crown were of prime importance to the bishops, and, until the Reformation decades, economic self-interest rarely conflicted seriously with this political need. Nor was it often necessary for the bishops to speak in defence of the weak lower clergy on the matter of taxation. Few of them were subject to loans and benevolences, and even the subsidy did not touch the poorest sections of the Church.[19] Payments upon promotion to benefices were normally reserved to those who had an income of more than 100 florins a year, though these could again be a source of grievance. Most bishops and others who had to pay annates and common services were forced to borrow heavily for the first few years of their tenure of new promotions. Cuthbert Tunstall went so far in 1525 as to refuse a provisional offer of the see of Ely because he feared that the debts incurred would be a burden to his relatives in the event of his early death.[20] Despite these difficulties, and the occasional crisis of the 1520s, matters of taxation rarely seem to have been a major anxiety to the bishops or, so far as can be judged from the lack of surviving evidence, to their lowlier colleagues in the parishes.

3

For a brief period during 1534 it appeared that the Reformation might actually relieve the clergy of part of their tax burden. After the restraint of annates and other payments due to Rome, and before the introduction of the first fruits and tenths legislation, the only money being paid by the clergy was the £118,000 granted by the two convocations in gratitude for their escape from *praemunire*. The interval of calm was shortlived; by 1535 the vital first fruits and tenths legislation had destroyed any illusions the clergy might have had about the generosity of Henry VIII.[21] The Court of First Fruits and Tenths not only taxed the Church anew, but redefined in detail the duties of the higher clergy as financial agents of the crown. The bishops were assigned responsibility for the collection of the annual tenths, their duties falling to dean and chapter, rather than to the sub-collector, *sede vacante*. First fruits, on the other hand, were to be paid directly to the Exchequer, or some other central court, each cleric compounding to pay the money within a specified time. Even then, the bishops had to furnish the Exchequer with annual lists of vacancies and new appointments in their dioceses, and act as the support of the government to ensure that no benefices went untaxed. The tenths, for which the bishops were directly accountable, were to be collected by 1 April each year, though this date was later amended to allow time for the inclusion of the Easter offerings. All normal means of levying money, including sequestration, were at their disposal, and the crown now added to these the right to make distraint on moveables or land in the case of obdurate refusal of payment. If part of the money could not be levied by any means, the Exchequer must be certified within 24 days, and the bishop was then exonerated from those sums. With minor amendments, these remained the basic rules for the collection of tenths until the end of the century.[22] In general pattern they differed little from the arrangements already in force before the Reformation, but the tone and precision of the orders leaves no doubt that initiative lies wholly with the crown. The regularity of first fruits and tenths removed from the clergy in Convocation even the rights of consenting to taxation, and of sometimes deciding upon the precise methods of apportionment and collection.

At the time when this tightening of royal control placed the bishops in a more vulnerable position than before, the introduction of new taxes, based upon a new assessment, for the first time aroused widespread protests among the ordinary parish priests. The *Valor Ecclesiasticus* assigned a taxable value to even the most impoverished benefice, and the first fruits legislation swept into its net whole sections of the Church that had not been taxed before. Many of the affluent clergy found themselves paying at a more realistic, but unpalatable, rate for the first time for several centuries. The bishops themselves suffered: for example Chichester, which had temporalities worth £591 according to the *Valor*, had been paying on a previous assessment of £463; Worcester was raised from £485 to £980, and Hereford from £449 to £748.[23] Where the bishops led the rest of the Church followed and the combination of higher assessments and new demands became potentially explosive in the 1530s. The support which the Yorkshire and Lincolnshire clergy gave to the revolts of 1536 was conditioned partly by resentment at the impositions of the government, and opposition to the new levies was a recurring theme in both uprisings.[24] So explosive was the issue of the tenths in Yorkshire that, at the beginning of 1537, Archbishop Lee was still reluctant to embark on collecting them. Since he was already under a cloud for his part in the Pilgrimage of Grace, he drew a very tart rejoinder from the king when he dared to propose a postponement of the levy. Henry indicated that it was a calumny upon his northern subjects to suggest that they would deny him money after clemency had been extended to them, and that the bishop had an easy role to play, since he could refer any obdurate clergy to the Exchequer.[25] The tenth was eventually collected, but with elaborate precautions, for some of the laity also feared the passions that it would arouse. Even when no bloody uprising was feared, the bishops had plenty of problems with the collection of revenue, ranging from treasonable statements by their clergy, to the sheer difficulty of using a new tax list. As Tristam Teshe reported from Yorkshire before the outbreak of revolt, the king would inevitably lose much money before the minor errors in the *Valor* had been corrected.[26] The case of Archbishop Lee also suggests that the bishops were forced to devote more personal time and attention to the delicate business of tax collection in the 1530s than they had in earlier decades.

The tensions of this first decade of the new system tended to disguise another unresolved problem of tax-collection. This was the question of accountability; of who had the responsibility to the Exchequer for revenues raised. The basic pattern remained as it had been before the Reformation: the bishop had the duty of accounting for all monies that should be paid over, of certifying the debts that were illeviable, and of gaining an Exchequer acquittance. In practice, his hands never touched the money, and it was invariably a deputy who took it from the parishes, deposited it in the Exchequer and obtained the *quietus est*. The dissolution of the monasteries meant that the most reliable source of sub-collectors was lost to the bishops. The duties perforce had to devolve, either upon an existing member of the episcopal administration, or upon a completely new official. The strains were often too great for the existing administrators; for example, Richard Spaceford, receiver of Hereford, was left in 1536 with the unenviable task of collecting the new tenth and remitting it to London entirely alone, since his bishop was on embassy in Germany.[27] Throughout the century examples can be found of episcopal officials with other promotions also acting as deputy collectors, but there was a tendency to regard this as a separate office, to be filled by the bishop's letters patent, and usually to be filled by local laymen. Whoever the deputy, he was in these early years answerable only to the bishop, and had usually entered no bond to save the bishop harmless if he failed to collect taxes through negligence or fraud. Even if the bishop died, it was now the dean and chapter, rather than the deputy collector who became accountable in the Exchequer. This problem of responsibility was not new, but the increased demands of the 1530s gradually brought it into prominence, and it remained most stubbornly resistant to solution for the rest of the Tudor period.

Although some of the episcopate were already having difficulty in managing their deputies, and keeping their tax arrears low in the 1530s, the first real test of the fiscal arrangements came in the early 1540s, when the French war greatly increased the government's need for money. There are obvious similarities between the demands made in these years and those of Wolsey two decades earlier. The whole Church was asked for an unusually large amount of tax, and the higher clergy were asked for the inevitable loans. In the 1540s the increases in taxation came from the reimposition of subsidies, which had not been demanded in the 1530s because of first fruits and tenths, and then the raising of the subsidy rate from 2s. in the £ per annum, to 3s. in the £.[28] The true situation of the Church was, however, different from that of the 1520s. Royal authority was now unchallenged, any section of the Church that resisted the royal will might suffer the same fate as the monasteries, and even the laity offered no support and comfort, since they acceded willingly to all the king's demands for war supply. The clergy contributed £53,000 to the royal budget in 1541, and perhaps £48,000 in 1544, while in theory the increased rate of subsidy for 1546 should have brought in a further £12,000, to produce a grand total of £60,000.[29] Even these large sums did little to satisfy the king's need for money; by 1544, therefore, the bishops were being pressed to anticipate the payment of taxes by several months, in order to provide the government with ready cash. On 26 December 1544 the council urged Cranmer to hasten the day of payment for both tenths and subsidies, and see that the money was paid over to First Fruits and Tenths by the end of January, although it was not all due until the following midsummer.[30] In June 1545 a circular letter was sent to all the bishops telling them to arrange for the immediate payment of tenths and subsidies due the next Christmas, on the very dubious assurance that the clergy would then be acquitted of the next payment.[31] The council also intervened directly in the business of tax-collection; one of the bishops was castigated in 1545 for failing to raise enough money for the crown, and in 1546 Cranmer was charged with being too lenient in the allowance he made during the collection of subsidy in his own diocese.[32]

This last charge suggests both that the clergy were finding difficulty in meeting the crown demands, and that some of the bishops were sympathetically disposed to those who pleaded poverty. On the other hand, the new impositions generated none of the heat and passion among the clergy that had been sparked off by the introduction of first fruits and tenths. Times had changed, the clergy were more cowed, and less disposed to challenge the rights of the crown. Moreover, the demands of the 1540s were not in fact new; they merely revived old taxes, and did not draw new groups into the net of taxation as first fruits and tenths had done. Even the bishops were not willing to complain of the burden of taxation; most paid about a quarter of their gross revenues in taxes and loans in these years, and some, who had to find first fruits, paid considerably more.[33] Some of the episcopate apparently had a struggle to raise the necessary capital; these years saw a marked increase in some dioceses of the use of such revenue-raising devices as leases in reversion and the grant of the rights of presentation to a benefice for one turn. Nevertheless, the most active surviving complaints of the bishops concern the length of time they were allowed for the payment of first fruits, rather than the general plight of the lower clergy or their own large tax burden.

The lower clergy certainly found it difficult to pay all that was asked of them, and the lists of arrears in episcopal accounts increase noticeably in the early 1540s. The way in which these arrears grew can be demonstrated by a particularly full set of accounts for the diocese of Rochester.[34] In 1539 the bishops owed the crown a large sum, but this was merely because some of the money was delivered late to First Fruits and Tenths. Thereafter, until 1543, the account was almost clear. In 1543 £44 was missing from the tenths and by the next year this had grown to £61, while £91 was owed on the subsidy. Although attempts were evidently made to prevent further arrears accumulating, by 1546 the two sets of arrears stood at £74 for the tenths and £181 for the subsidy. This was in a small diocese, where the total sums due annually for the tenth were of the order of £250. Rochester's difficulties could be explained partly by a lack of administrative continuity in these years: between 1540 and 1548 there were two changes of bishops. Evidence from other dioceses shows the same pattern of accumulating arrears, and difficulties in the collection of revenue.[35] The main explanation is surely therefore the high level of taxation, though to this should be joined the demoralization and inertia of some of the bishops. Some of the episcopate, notably Voysey of Exeter and Reppes of Norwich, virtually abdicated their positions in the decade after the Reformation, pressed into doing so by the financial demands of the crown and laity, by their own weakness as administrators, and by distaste for religious change. It was in dioceses presided over by these men that some of the heaviest arrears were allowed to accumulate, and this must reflect their failure to supervise their deputies as well as the financial difficulties of the clergy.

Not until the early years of Edward's reign did the fiscal pressures upon the clergy really produce very large arrears. Demands for subsidy continued, although after 1548 the young king's advisers reverted to a request for 6s. in the £ payable over three years.[36] Changes in government religious policy, and the continuing appropriation of the goods and property of the Church, did nothing to strengthen clerical morale and created an atmosphere that was not conducive to the efficient collection of taxes. The graft and incompetence of central government under Protector Somerset also meant that the inefficiency of the clerical administrators was not kept in check. Arrears in the payments of tenths and subsidies therefore continued to mount in various dioceses. In 1549 Bath and Wells owed £1,176, while in 1551 even the poor diocese of Llandaff owed £502. The worst example was that of Exeter, which by 1553 had a total debt to the crown of £2,353.[37] These sees, of course, were peculiarly incompetently run, and often had corrupt officials, but the problem of arrears troubled many bishops who were careful to supervise their deputies, and to return their correct certificates of non-paying clergy. By 1553 only Durham, Ely, Lincoln, Salisbury, Winchester and York were entirely free of debt – it is interesting that these are on the whole the larger and richer bishoprics, which had the finance and administrative expertise to create a fairly efficient tax-collecting system.[38]

Those sees which were heavily in debt by the end of Edward's reign often had absentee and indifferent bishops. Voysey of Exeter lived in Sutton Coldfield, and ceased even to check if money was being collected in his diocese. When the full tally of the debts was uncovered, the bishop sought to blame the whole affair on his deputy, Strowbridge, who probably was the immediately guilty party, but was only following the example of the bishop in neglecting his duties.[39] The Voysey case was so scandalous that in 1552 the government took the unusual step of persuading him to resign in return for the large pension and personal exoneration from his debts. Other bishops who defaulted on royal payments were liable to have their goods seized as debtors to the crown until the money was forthcoming. If the bishop thought that the fault lay with his sub-collector, he could of course try to extract the money from him. There is no evidence under Somerset's régime that the bishops were pressed particularly hard to make up their arrears, or that their goods were distrained to pay for their debts. Under Northumberland, on the other hand, there was a distinct tightening of financial administration, and it is from this period that we have a few cases in which the bishops tried to extract money from their deputies. The most interesting and full example concerned Robert Aldrich, bishop of Carlisle, and his sub-collector, Edward Michell, clerk.[40] Tax collection at Carlisle had evidently been rather casually organized; Aldrich had delegated the work to his official principal and registrar, who in turn had recruited Michell to collect the subsidy due in 4 Edward VI. No bonds or formal patents had been written at any stage of this process. Michell was supposed to pay the money to Christopher Oakland, one of the bishop's servants, who was responsible for conveying it to London. Either Michell or Oakland appropriated £163 of the money, and forged an acquittance from Thomas Leigh, auditor of the Court of First Fruits and Tenths. Inevitably Michell accused Oakland and vice-versa, and since neither of them was liable in law for the payment, it seems likely that Aldrich was forced to pay the arrears.

Incidents such as this, and the widespread evidence that the bishops could not always control the men who actually collected the royal revenues, led the crown to rethink the question of accountability. An obvious way to improve the situation was to tighten the central control of the Exchequer or Court of First Fruits, and make the sub-collectors more directly responsive to the will of the government. From at least the middle of the Edwardian period, when the first surviving recognizance volume of First Fruits and Tenths begins, sub-collectors were called to account for their own arrears, and bonds were taken from them for payment of debts.[41] Thus for example, John Payne, the collector for Bath and Wells, was required in 1551 to pay £600 of the £1,800 that he owed, on a bond of £1,000. Such action was only possible for the crown if the bishop already had a sufficient bond from his deputy to be discharged harmless from any debts. Some bishops were already taking these bonds in the Henrician period, but the Carlisle case shows that they were not universal, and that some members of the episcopate neglected to make any adequate arrangements for the collection of money. Northumberland's government recognized this, and intervened with legislation in 1552.[42] All under-collectors appointed by episcopal patent were to be bound by recognizances in First Fruits and Tenths to answer for such sums as were due from their jurisdictions. The collectors were also to agree to save the bishops harmless from these dues. The Act was intended, in the words of its preamble, to help the king, who 'hath been greatly defrauded of the said duties and many of the bishops [who have been] sore troubled to their great hindrance and utter undoing'.

Legislation was supported by the actions of the council. In 1552 the bishops were told that sub-collectors would only be accepted by the Court of First Fruits and Tenths if they had authorization under the episcopal seal, and that certificates of defaulters prepared for the court must have full circumstantial detail attached to them.[43] Later in the same year the council ordered that the bishop of Lincoln should be discharged from a portion of subsidy due under his predecessor, and a variety of other minor and local aspects of clerical tax collecting were subject to its scrutiny and comment.[44] This would suggest that the Tudor government was moving slowly and perhaps unintentionally towards assuming responsibility for the control of all clerical collections, since the bishops themselves had been shown to be incapable of the task. Such a development, in which the bishops would have retained at most a nominal involvement and the pleasure of paying the deputy collectors, was a logical outcome of the movement begun at the Reformation, away from the exercise of clerical initiative and discretion in the matter of taxation. Most of the episcopate would probably have welcomed such a move, since their lack of control over the amount and style of taxation made them merely intermediaries between crown and Church in this very contentious area. However, before the government could take further initiative, the whole of the structure of Church–State relations was thrown into disarray by the accession of Mary.

The Marian solution to the difficulties generated by heavy taxation was to return first fruits and tenths to the Church. This measure was not introduced until the middle of the reign, and its full implementation took even longer, but meanwhile the queen sought ways to help the most heavily indebted of the bishops. A group of new bishops – of Gloucester, Chester and St David's – were forgiven the debts of their predecessors, probably because in these cases the previous bishops had been guilty of appropriating royal funds to pay their own debts.[45] When the fault lay with the under-collector the crown was not so lenient; John Payne, of Bath and Wells, was still being pursued in the Marian period, and ended in debtors' prison at least once, because of his failure to keep to the term of his bond.[46] It was characteristic of the Marian government that it did the minimum necessary to help the poorest sees, but remained cautious about giving money indiscriminately to the Church.

The new generation of Mary's bishops were required to pay their first fruits, but already Mary was responding to the urgings of her cousin, Cardinal Pole, and to the promptings of her own conscience, and planning a more general restitution to the Church. This finally emerged as legislation in 1555, when first fruits were abolished, and the tenths were ordered to be paid to the bishops, who were to use them for the good of the Church and the augmentation of poor benefices.[47] The disadvantage of this arrangement for the Church was that the bishops had to assume responsibility for the payment of all ex-monastic pensions and corrodies previously handled by the Court of Augmentations. These pensions represented a diminishing commitment, as the old inhabitants of the monasteries were dying fast, but when the first survey after the legislation was prepared, they amounted to £36,000, whereas the tenths yielded between £15,000 and £16,000. The difference was apparently made up by a continuation of first fruits, even though these had been formally abolished in 1555. The abolition of the crown's claims to first fruits and tenths also created further administrative problems for the bishops. They once again assumed a comprehensive control over tax collecting, without the coercive machinery of the state to support them. Administration of the tenths proved more complicated than before, since money had to be passed from diocese to diocese in order that those with many ex-monks should be able to pay the necessary pensions.[48] There were problems of organization and control; for example, Bishop Tunstall of Durham complained in 1558 that he could scarcely pay the pensions in his diocese, because the tax money came in so slowly.[49] By this date, other comments suggest that the advantages of the new system to the Church were beginning to outweigh the disadvantages. The bishops were recovering their initiative in financial matters, and the process of augmenting benefices could soon begin. Then, once again, the structure was swept away by the death of the sovereign, and a complete change of religious policy.

Before turning to Elizabeth, it is necessary to glance at the other side of Mary's economic policy towards the Church. After the loss of first fruits and tenths, Mary and her advisors felt themselves legitimately entitled to continue demanding subsidy, which, since it was a pre-Reformation tax, was not tainted by the schism. These subsidies proved little easier to collect under Mary than under Edward, for the tax burden upon the clergy had only been eased very slightly, and the Church was still in some confusion and disarray. In February 1557 the bishops had managed to collect only £2,739 of approximately £15,000 due in the previous month, and in August of the same year the Privy Council had to order the bishops of Norwich, Winchester, Coventry and Lichfield, Llandaff and Rochester to make further payments of subsidy immediately.[50] The collector of Rochester was required to appear in person before the Privy Council to exhibit his Exchequer acquittance and the collectors of Norwich actually had to be apprehended by the sheriff and made to give a bond to appear before the council within 15 days.[51] Substantial parts of this last Marian subsidy were never collected, and the debts remained to trouble the bishops under Elizabeth. Mary's government clearly found exactly the same problem that Northumberland's had done: that only a section of the episcopate had the energy and/or luck to be able to collect their taxes efficiently. They needed the coercive support and pressure of government, and they also needed conditions more settled than those of the last years of Mary's reign, when the ranks of the episcopate itself were decimated, and many clergy died in the influenza epidemics.

4

One of the first legislative actions of Elizabeth's government was to return first fruits and tenths to the crown. The queen followed the example of her father and brother in levying subsidy from the clergy as well, though there was only one occasion on which her demands reached the levels attained in the mid-1540s. Subsidy was granted by the clergy on 11 occasions during the reign, the most common grant being 6s. in the £, payable over three years.[52] Only at the end of the reign did the financial problems of the Spanish war force the rate up, and in 1598–1600 the very unusual rate of 4s. in the £ per annum was required. There were eight years during the reign when no subsidy was demanded, but in general the parish clergy must have become accustomed to paying tenths and a regular annual subsidy. As William Harrison remarked in his *Description of England*, the payments of the clergy, unlike those of the laity, 'are certain, continual and seldom abated'.[53] The regularity of this taxation, and the more settled conditions of the Elizabethan Church, should in theory have made the task of the bishops somewhat easier. They should also have been helped by some of the details of the 1559 and later legislation. The precedent of Mary's reign was followed in grading the rates of subsidy tax, so that benefices worth under £5 paid nothing at all, and those under £8 only 6s. 8d.[54] Some further help was given in handling those who refused payment; from the subsidy Act of 5 Elizabeth onwards the bishop or collector was allowed to sell the goods distrained from these men, and to remit the money to the Exchequer.

Procedures within the Exchequer itself were tightened as a precaution against fraud, and new rules were laid down for speedy auditing and the granting of acquittance.

None of these minor attempts to improve the system had much effect upon the role of the bishops, to whom the crown very emphatically returned full responsibility for the collection of taxes. Under Elizabeth the Privy Council rarely intervened in this field, and the bishops were left to operate the system with little direct support from the government, but under the very real threat of penalties if they failed to perform their duties. The bishops' awareness of their vulnerability led them to be more careful in appointing deputies, and getting adequate bonds from them. When Archbishop Parker appointed Henry Seath and William Woodward to collect the tenths and subsidies of Canterbury diocese in 1561, he asked them for a bond to discharge him from any responsibility for faults in their accounts.[55] In this case the tenths were to be paid to the archbishop himself, who had been granted them as compensation for manors he had lost in an exchange with the crown in 1560. For the collection of these the two men were to receive a fee of £20, while for the subsidy to be paid to the crown, they were allowed the traditional $2\frac{1}{2}$ per cent of all monies collected. Since two men were involved in this commission their individual remuneration for a difficult and thankless task was not very great, and the temptation to embezzle funds must have been correspondingly large.

The classic case of embezzlement and inefficiency under Elizabeth was that which involved Bishop Parkhurst of Norwich. The story is well known, and need only be recalled briefly here.[56] Parkhurst's collector, George Thimbelthorpe, was already well entrenched in office when the bishop entered the see, having first been appointed by Bishop Reppes in 1544. Parkhurst reappointed him, and at that time apparently took from him a bond to be saved harmless from all debts. Thimbelthorpe's own deputies fell into arrears with their payments, and he himself probably appropriated funds, so that by 1571 he was heavily indebted to the crown. About this time one of the sureties' seals was removed from the bond which Thimbelthorpe had given Parkhurst, thereby making the bishop's legal position far less secure.[57] The result was that Parkhurst found himself liable to pay the crown

£1,126, which he was compelled to repay at the rate of £400 *per annum* from a total income of about £750. Of course, recent research has suggested that the total money income taxed under the *Valor* was probably not representative of the gross money income collected by the bishops by the end of the century. Nevertheless, it was a considerable achievement that the bishop died four years later free of debts, but in order to repay the taxes he had been forced to live in retired poverty on his manor of Ludham, a situation that did nothing to enhance his already shaky spiritual authority in the rest of the diocese.

One result of the Thimbelthorpe affair was yet another attempt to legislate the sub-collectors into a sense of responsibility. Parkhurst himself promoted legislation in the Parliament of 1572 by which the lands and moveables of under-collectors were made liable to seizure for arrears in tenths and subsidies.[58] Bishops, or deans and chapters *sede vacante*, were exonerated from as much of the debts as could be met from the possessions of their deputies. The problem, of course, was that the assets of these men often did not meet the debts they had incurred, either because of skilful concealment, or because through genuine incompetence they had failed to enrich themselves or collect the taxes. The legislation failed to limit the number of cases in which the bishops became debtors to the Exchequer – indeed, these seem to have increased during the 1570s. One further suggestion for legislative action was made in 1580/81. This was a draft bill by which the crown was to be given powers either to continue the existing system for the collection of clerical tenths, or to take the task directly under the control of the Exchequer, appointing collectors who would have the same powers as the bishops.[59] The bill urged the need for this second alternative because many bishops failed to pay all their taxes, and died indebted leaving 'her highness long unanswered of her due, and their successors grievously charged and encumbered therewith'. This seems a document more likely to have come from the Church than the crown, and it did not reach Parliament. Whatever the disadvantages of leaving revenue-raising to the bishops, it was consistent with the policy of Elizabeth's government to avoid the responsibility and expense of new tasks which could still be fulfilled by its subjects.

The author of this second piece of legislation may have had specifically in mind the case of William Bradbridge of Exeter, who had died in 1578.[60] Exeter was a poor see after the Reformation, and so remote from London that it had become almost as undesirable a promotion as the Welsh bishoprics. As a result, its Elizabethan bishops were not noted for outstanding piety, energy or learning, and debt and poverty were their common lot. Bradbridge's predecessor, Bishop Alley, had been indebted to the crown, and Bradbridge himself was therefore careful about the precise bond that he took from his newly-appointed collector of tenths, Henry Borough. However, Bradbridge, like Parkhurst, then left the powerful interest groups already entrenched in the diocese to go their own way, and further debts began to accumulate. By 1577 even Bradbridge suspected that he was in debt, but close questioning of Borough reassured him, at which the bishop 'rejoicing drank to the gentlemen, and said that he would not be indebted to the queen for anything'. His illusions were short-lived and before his death he had begun to make systematic enquiries into his deputy's conduct.

Borough was so busy deceiving the bishop that he even intercepted a servant that the latter had sent to the Exchequer to find out his true situation. He also managed to extract acquittances from the bishop for all the monies he had supposedly paid to the crown, though on the last encounter Bradbridge refused to sign until he had seen the Exchequer acquittance. This last sum of £237 went unacquitted, but it seems that Borough then merely forged the bishop's signature to complete his tale of dishonesty. After his death Bradbridge was found to owe £1,235 to the crown, and his goods were seized because of his exonerations of Borough. An Exchequer enquiry into the bishop's goods gradually revealed the collector's duplicity, and he ended in a debtors' prison when it was established that much of the arrears were his direct responsibility.

Parkhurst and Bradbridge provide particularly vivid examples of the hazards of tax-collecting and dependence upon deputies. Other bishops who came to grief can easily be cited: for example, Richard Cheney of Gloucester in the 1570s, Edmund Freke of Worcester in the 1580s and Thomas Godwin of Bath and Wells and John Aylmer of London in the 1590s.[61] The difficulties of some of these men sprang entirely from the dishonesty of their deputies, and their own failure to supervise the accounts prepared for the Exchequer. Others, notably Richard Cheney, and Marmaduke Middleton of St David's, were themselves guilty of embezzling funds in order to keep their very shaky episcopal finances afloat.[62] Some of the Edwardian bishops had adopted the same expedient – indeed Anthony Kitchin of Llandaff probably adopted it under Edward, Mary and Elizabeth – but the Elizabethan government did not allow its servants to escape through laxness or generosity.[63] All bishops who were in debt, however plausible their excuses, and unfortunate their situations, were required to settle their accounts, either in person or through their executors after death. Debts, and the seizure of episcopal goods to pay for them, became a drearily routine part of the Exchequer's handling of clerical taxation. Thus, to take an apparently typical year, in 1581 the dean and chapter of Gloucester owed £162, the bishop of Coventry and Lichfield £296, the bishop of St Asaph £179, the bishop of Chichester £84, and the collector of Bristol, where there was no bishop, £970. All these were debts that could not easily be cleared, and in each case an order had been made for seizure of goods to cover the money owed.[64]

Even efficient diocesans, who had competent deputies, found their duties as tax collectors irksome in the Elizabethan period. The determination of the government to receive all monies owing to it gave them little respite, and cast them in the role of oppressors of the poor clergy. At the very beginning of the reign this was clear to Edmund Grindal, who was faced with royal demands that he collect from the diocese of London the remains of the Marian subsidy, as well as all the money owed to the new régime. In 1564 he wrote a determined letter to the Marquis of Winchester, pointing out that the current subsidy had been collected 'with much difficulty, and many complain of want of money'. It was therefore impossible to raise the Marian remnant without some reasonable allowance of time, although a distraint had already been issued on his goods and on those of the dean and chapter. It would be just, he concluded, if the council did not expect them to pay their predecessors' debts, but only their own.[65] This was not, unfortunately, the Exchequer view of justice, and some of the bishops continued to be troubled for years to come on the minor matter of these old subsidies. In 1573, Richard Cox of Ely tried to solve the problem by paying from his own pocket the £15 alleged to be outstanding, only to find that the see still owed £40 or £50, and in 1580 John Parker, the son of the archbishop, was summoned before the Barons of the Exchequer to explain why his father had not collected the remnant of the subsidy for Canterbury diocese.[66]

Other minor examples of friction between the bishops and the financial officers of the government could be multiplied. In 1573 Pilkington of Durham was complaining of the dangers and expense of transmitting money to London, a difficulty which all northern collectors faced, but about which they rarely grumbled.[67] In the mid-1570s Horne of Winchester wrote in highly critical tones to the Exchequer when he was made accountable for monies which he believed he did not owe, though in this case the government may have been in the right, for he died owing over £900.[68] The sharpest encounter of all came in the mid-1580s, when Bishop Overton of Coventry and Lichfield accused Thomas Fanshawe of being too rigid in his interpretation of the rules governing the issuing of process against debtors.[69] This last clash is of more general interest, since it was occasioned by an apparent change of policy by Burghley in the 1580s. The usual arrangement had been to issue process against any bishop who had failed to pay less than half his subsidy by the term after the due date. So many bishops were failing to attain this target that there was presumably some danger of the whole episcopate being brought into disrepute by recurrent demands from the government. Burghley therefore exercised his discretionary powers on a number of occasions, and stayed the issue of process until some terms for payment could be agreed with the bishop.

It might be expected that the tensions between bishops and central government would be reflected in the bishops' relations with the clergy they had to tax. If central government insisted on the full payment of all dues then the intermediaries had to do the same to those actually paying the money. Evidence on this point is unfortunately much less full, though general complaints about taxation from the lower clergy are common enough. The bishops often informed the government that it was very difficult to collect extra levies above the tenths and subsidies; to take just one example, Bishop Overton was expected to raise over £400 in lance money from the richer clergy of his diocese in 1581, but could only get £200, because most of them were very 'untoward'.[70] This reluctance to produce taxes only increased to overt hostility when the bishops themselves tried to supplement their own income by levies and imposts. Both Overton and John Wolton of Exeter were accused of attempting this in the early 1580s, when they were heavily indebted.[71] Even the legitimate claims of some bishops to the tenths of their dioceses under the exchange arrangements made with the crown in 1559 could cause tension. Bishop Cox of Ely, an efficient but financially ruthless diocesan, used the weapon of sequestration against clergy who defaulted on their payments so often that this was made a major complaint when he was charged with various offences by Lord North in 1575.[72] On the whole, however, complaints from the clergy themselves about the behaviour of the bishops as tax collectors are conspicuous by their absence. Indeed, the bishops did on occasions make serious attempts to act as protectors of the Church against the excessive demands of the monarch. The most famous example was Archbishop Whitgift's determined opposition to a proposal made in 1584 to replace the *Valor Ecclesiasticus* by a new assessment. He argued strongly that many sections of the Church were in fact poorer than when the original estimates had been prepared: only parsonages not on long leases were likely to have improved significantly in value.[73] Cox also wrote in defence of the clergy at an earlier date when a similar rumour was in circulation; he pointed out that the clergy were already despised and oppressed by the laity, despite their contribution to the establishment of true religion, and that further taxes could only weaken their authority.[74] By such spirited opposition to the crown, the leading bishops may have done something to protect the Church from new exactions.

Despite the tensions and difficulties that beset the bishops as tax collectors, a remarkable amount of money was actually paid to the government by the Church. To take the example of the 1590s, for which the surviving evidence is particularly good, most of the regular taxes were paid almost in full. The figures for the tenth between 1594 and 1598 are given below.

Tenths of the clergy: 1594–8[75]

Anticipated annual yield approx.   £12,970

Actual yield 1594            £10,028
         1595            £12,925
         1596            £11,980
         1597            £11,800
         1598            £12,891

(The years 1594–7 saw exceedingly bad harvests, amounting
sometimes to famine, which probably formed the worst series of
the century. That the crown still succeeded in obtaining payment
of taxes from the clergy suggests that the assessment was based on
an under-estimate of clerical income.) Subsidy at 2s. in the £
was worth about £13,000 per annum, but actual receipts
fluctuated more widely than the tenth. In 1594 there was a very
low intake of £9,039, but later in the decade it was never less
than £12,000, and after the increase of the rate there were several
yields of £16,000 or £17,000. Arrears, of course, continued to
exist, and with the increased demands at the end of the century
they began to rise again, but there is no evidence that they
reached the very large sums recorded under Edward VI.

The continuous pressure which the Exchequer applied to the
bishops is one obvious reason for this achievement. The case of
Parkhurst became a *cause celèbre* in the Church, and the bishops
were anxious to do all they could to avoid his fate. Bishop
Godwin of Bath and Wells, who did fall into the same difficulty,
expressed this feeling very well when he was faced with process
from the Exchequer: '[this] is so terrible to me and so disgraceful
to my place, the credit whereof I would fain maintain, for the
bettering of my service'.[76] It was the bishop of Bangor's proudest
boast that after 16 years in his very poor see he did not owe a
penny to the crown.[77] This fear of being brought into social and
political disrepute for failing to collect all the royal taxes preyed
upon the minds of the bishops, and meant that they were ready
to make the most unlikely sacrifices of their own income when
they found themselves in debt and the crown required them to
compound for repayment. No doubt Burghley and the other
royal advisers were well aware of the advantages of being able to

use the fear of the bishops in order to increase the queen's income, though they were also careful to avoid bringing the hierarchy too far into disrepute by imprisoning any of the bishops for debt, or by depriving them of their sees.

Yet fear alone would not have been sufficient to make the clergy pay and the bishops collect their money fairly efficiently. Throughout the period the concepts of the duty and obedience owing to governments, and the commitment of the subject to aid the prince, provided a positive justification for all taxation. Under Elizabeth this emphasis upon duty and gratitude to the prince was probably the most effective weapon in the hands of the clerical tax collectors. The queen had delivered the Church from the bondage of popery, and later in the reign protected the realm from the tyranny of Spain. In these circumstances no good cleric could refuse to pay, as far as he was able, the taxes asked of him, or as Bishop Sandys put it, 'we must readily and willingly pay unto them [princes] tribute and custom, for God hath so appointed and they have so deserved'.[78] Such a conception of duty, both of the taxed clergy and the collecting bishops, was difficult to fulfil in the economic conditions of the late sixteenth century. The bishops, in particular, suffered more in this period because of their administrative inefficiency and failure to control their deputies, than they had done earlier. Nevertheless, the concept of obedience and duty governed their approach to taxation, as it did the approach of most of the lower clergy. A most vivid illustration of this attitude, drawn from the ranks of the lower clergy, is the tale of a Cornish clergyman who became involved in the Bradbridge–Borough case at Exeter.[79] He was the man chosen to pay subsidies from a group of parishes to Borough, and was given a meeting place in Cornwall to hand over the money. Borough did not appear, and so the cleric undertook the long journey to Exeter to seek him out. When he finally found him Borough refused to take the money, which he alleged should have been paid to his deputy, but he took over £1 from him for his pains. The deputy, John Roberts, then insisted that he should pay the full amount, and the unfortunate cleric dutifully borrowed the £1, so that his account should be clear. Such persistence in the face of blatant dishonesty suggests either weakness, or a genuine conviction that the queen's money must be paid, and the story itself is enough to indicate that the clergyman concerned was unlikely to be a complete weakling. A similar tenacity on the part of many of the bishops no doubt helped them to cope with the mounting problems of clerical taxation, and to fulfil a role which had grown from a pre-Reformation situation of relative simplicity, to an Elizabethan situation of economic and political danger on which the fortunes of a number of the episcopate foundered.

# The New Foundations

# 5

## The Durham dean and chapter:
## old abbey writ large?

David Marcombe

Today, more than four centuries after the dissolution of the monasteries, the boys of Durham School still refer to the cathedral as the 'abbey'. Similarly, the thousands of visitors who flock to Durham every year are coming primarily to see one of the finest monastic churches remaining in England: they visit the monks' dormitory rather than the later cathedral library. The historian working amongst the Chapter Archives does so in the pleasant surroundings of the Prior's, not the Dean's, Kitchen. Indeed the casual modern visitor might be forgiven for going away with the picture of the present day dean and chapter as some great ecclesiastical cuckoo haunting the magnificent nest which it has neither built nor inspired. The Calvinist deans of the sixteenth century proved themselves to be well aware of the dangers implicit in this sense of continuity with the past by the way in which they systematically destroyed many of the ancient relics of medieval Durham.[1] But although Mrs Whittingham could destroy the magical banner of St Cuthbert in the flames of her kitchen fire and Dean Horne could stamp angrily on the bricks and mortar of the Corpus Christi Shrine, their activities were in a sense a measure of the frustration they felt in the face of a persistent ghost which refused to lie down. In the 1590s Catholics were still gathering information about the life lived by monks of the convent and in the High Church atmosphere of Charles I's reign the cult of St Cuthbert enjoyed something of a revival.[2] The sense of emotional continuity, then, was strong but in what real sense was the new dean and chapter the successor of the prior and convent?[3] To what degree did it represent innovation or draw on traditions from elsewhere?

In England the cathedrals of the Middle Ages fell into two categories, secular and monastic chapters. Apart from taking care of their own ample interests and generally acting as corporations in their own right, the cathedrals shared the function of acting as watchdogs over the power and privileges of the see and, in practice, the power which the bishop exercised over his chapter was usually small.[4] The great monastic cathedrals, such as Canterbury and Durham, invariably owed their first loyalty to their rule and, although the bishop was admitted as an honorary, if powerless, abbot, the chapters were generally reluctant to take on too many non-monastic obligations.[5] The great secular cathedrals, on the other hand (for instance, Salisbury and York), displayed a flexibility which their cloistered brethren lacked; they differed from the monastic chapters by their greater integration with the world outside their walls.[6] By the fifteenth century, for example, a good deal of the routine work of the secular cathedral was being undertaken by the vicars choral, thus freeing the prebendaries for valuable work in the universities or the secular or ecclesiastical administrations.[7] This traditional pattern was shattered by Henry VIII's reformation. The old secular cathedrals were considered valuable enough in terms of patronage to be allowed to survive with only minor changes, but the surrender of the larger religious houses and the resultant anomaly of the 'chapterless' bishop raised the necessity of some fundamental reassessment of the situation of these churches.

The king's solution was characteristically conservative. The idea of converting redundant monastic houses into secular cathedrals had first been broached by Wolsey in the 1520s and received widespread backing, the king believing that the social services offered by the new churches might prove to be 'a universal remedy for all the ills which beset the realm'.[8] In all, Henry VIII revived 16 monasteries, comprising the eight medieval monastic cathedrals, six of the more important monasteries which became the centres of the proposed new sees, and the short-lived collegiate churches of Burton and Thornton; collectively these churches, re-endowed as secular chapters, became known as the cathedrals of the 'new foundation'.[9] According to Professor Knowles the refoundation was haphazard, and certainly there was little consistency in the timing, extent, or constitutions of the new houses.[10] For the purposes of propaganda the king was eager to emphasize the breach with the 'corrupt' monastic past and this was generally done by ostentatiously changing the dedication of the house, but in fact there was a substantial degree of continuity, with the new cathedrals retaining the same property and personnel which they had had in the 1530s.[11] Thus by the time of Henry's death England's full complement of cathedrals, either of the old or new foundation, had been made up.

At Durham the convent was guided through these troubled times by the influential Bishop Tunstall and the conciliatory Prior Whitehead and, partly by judicious use of bribery, the monastery ensured its continuation largely unscathed.[12] Cromwell, Wriothesley and, later, Somerset all received pensions from the chapter, and the prompt surrender of the cells and finally of the mother house in December 1539 convinced the government of the convent's good faith.[13] A submissive policy was certainly in the best interests of all parties concerned. In 1536, for example, the house received a favourable report from the visitors, the revered body of St Cuthbert was saved, and the somewhat rash grants of lands and advowsons made by the chapter during the last two years of the priory's existence were not examined too closely by the government officials.[14] But the most important advantage lay in the smooth changeover from monastic to secular cathedral. When the refoundation eventually came in 1541, apparently with the pious intention of restoring religion 'to its primitive and genuinely unalloyed pattern', zealous Protestants could be forgiven their surprise at finding the entire corporation from dean to minor canons staffed by those same monks who in the words of the king had 'woefully transgressed their bounds'.[15] In all, about half of the Durham monks, the most articulate and intelligent members of the monastic community, were provided for in the new foundation, reflecting the deep-seated conservatism of the Henrician reform which was based as much on the king's own religious views as on a desire to save money by keeping the number of pensionable monks to a minimum.[16] The pensions often proved to be a temporary outlay as the new corporation soon showed its determination to use its patronage in favour of ex-members whenever possible. George Cliffe, for example, was presented to a prebend by Bishop Tunstall as late as 1558, and when he died at the advanced age of 86 in 1595 he finally ended the personal link between priory and cathedral which had existed since the foundation.[17]

If an examination of the deed of foundation tends to indicate a high degree of continuity, then so does a brief glance at the deed of endowment, which scarcely bears out Professor Scarisbrick's description of Henry VIII's 'cheese-paring' attitude in endowing the new foundations.[18] Overall figures might justify this remark, but it would be difficult to include Durham in his rather gloomy picture. The endowment was very generous because the catheral received the bulk of the monastic estates in Durham, *infra aquas* as it was termed,[19] along with property in Yorkshire and Northumberland.[20] Generally speaking only the property of the outlying cells was retained by the crown. This may well have been a blessing in disguise because these lands obviously created problems of administration and the possession of some of them, such as Lytham, had been hotly disputed in the fifteenth century[21] Significantly enough, in this context, it was peripheral property in Northumberland and Yorkshire which gave rise to the long and costly disputes in which the Elizabethan chapter was engaged.[22] In addition to its landed estates, the new chapter retained intact most of its ecclesiastical patronage as well as the peculiars over which it enjoyed archidiaconal jurisdiction. In fact, the new corporation was granted 'all spiritual rights and ecclesiastical privileges which the priory had held or enjoyed . . . or should have held or enjoyed', a clause which gave the dean and chapter the right to recover the monks' usurped ecclesiastical jurisdiction.[23]

Continuity with the past was clearly demonstrated by the determination of the new dean and chapter to exercise this last principle to the full. Traditionally the medieval priors had stood as the champions of the palatinate against outside forces which had threatened to usurp the liberties of St Cuthbert, a mantle which the legalistic deans of the sixteenth century accepted with some enthusiasm. The most serious of these conflicts was the running battle which had gone on with the archbishop of York since the thirteenth century over rights of spiritual jurisdiction *sede vacante*, visitation, and the priory's peculiars in Yorkshire.[24] In 1286 the archbishop agreed not to visit the dioceses *sede plena* but was accorded such rights during vacancy.[25] In 1507/8 Prior Castell revived the conflict by refusing to accept commissions *sede vacante* from either the archbishop or dean and chapter of York; the precedent was followed by Dean Horne during the vacancy following Tunstall's deprivation in 1553.[26] The most bitter disputes concerning this issue took place under Dean Whittingham in 1576/7 and Dean Matthew in 1587/8, yet despite a favourable judgment by King's Bench in the 1590s the issue remained a vexed question until the twentieth century.[27] In sueing the archbishop of York and the bishop of Durham before the Court of Delegates the Elizabethan Calvinist deans proved themselves to be working very closely in the context of the monks who had gone before them.

Indeed, apart from a brief interlude under Edward VI when Dean Horne shocked Durham by bringing his wife into the cathedral precinct and engaging in the first blatant acts of iconoclasm, the tranquil life of the Durham close saw little apparent change until the accession of Elizabeth.[28] The prebendaries were still acutely aware of their Benedictine past, describing themselves in 1545 as 'late monks of the late dissolved monastery of Durham'.[29] By then they had already provided for the reinterrment of St Cuthbert in a decent though less sumptuous fashion, and were still using the great paschal candlestick and the image of Christ in the Easter services.[30] It is hardly surprising that the reconciliation with Rome in 1554 was celebrated with feasting in the dean's house, bonfires and the music of minstrels.[31] During the summer months the Halmote Court still made its leisurely tour of the chapter's Durham manors and the official still dispensed spiritual jurisdiction from his seat in St Oswald's church. Knowles' conclusion seems to be completely confirmed: 'the change over at the cathedrals ... was affected with a minimum of dislocation ... the monks who remained ... found themselves living a life that differed little from that in the monastery'.[32] Professor Hamilton Thompson went even further, asserting that the new foundations still continued to shut out the outer world: 'there was no breach of continuity at the reformation: the new foundations were considered entirely from the traditional point of view . . . and without a thought of their possible application to general diocesan purposes'.[33]

Up to a point these conclusions can be accepted, but they provide nothing like the complete answer. As Knowles realized, the decisive question was one of chronology.[34] The ex-monks in the chapter were keen to perpetuate the old ideas and some attitudes, such as the dispute with York, lingered on almost to the present day, but fundamental changes were gradually taking place. The Marian statutes of 1555, for example, reveal that even a Catholic sovereign was conscious that the new corporation should be fulfilling a substantially different role from that of the monastery or, indeed, of the older foundations. Residence was more strictly enforced than in the older secular cathedrals; the Durham prebendaries were encouraged to hold diocesan cures and to undertake regular preaching activities therein.[35] This outward-looking attitude, the presence of which Hamilton Thompson denied, is neatly illustrated by the newly constituted cathedral grammar school which began to take in the sons of increasing numbers of local merchants and gentry rather than concentrating on potential recruits for the monastery.[36]

Gradually, as the number of ex-monks in the chapter declined, so did the monastic attitude of the corporation as a whole. Death took its steady toll from the 1540s onwards and the 1559 visitation and the Puritan purges of the following 20 years sent a number of monks into premature if not inactive retirement.[37] William Todd was deprived by the High Commission in 1567 for wandering about muttering popish prayers to the annoyance of his Puritan colleagues; in 1572 Stephen Marley lost his stall for refusing to subscribe to the articles of the previous year.[38] These old prebendaries were being replaced, moreover, by a very different kind of man.

What were the major areas of distinction between the new cathedral and the priory; how did the cathedral differ from the old secular foundations; to what extent was Durham typical of other English cathedrals?

Constitutionally the new cathedral did not closely resemble either the priory or the old secular foundations. The medieval secular pattern was to share power between the dean and the three great cathedral dignitaries: the precentor, chancellor and treasurer. In chapter the dean was very much *primus inter pares* and the basic constitution of these bodies has been described as republican, a fact best illustrated by the long and sometimes violent dispute between John Macworth, dean of Lincoln, and his prebendaries in the fifteenth century.[39] The traditional monastic pattern, on the other hand, gave almost absolute power to the abbot, although in practice the strict letter of St Benedict's rule was not always viable in the larger houses.[40] At Durham the prior was forced to look to his senior monks for advice and support and the actual administration of the monastery was conducted by the prior in conjunction with eleven obedientiaries. As Dr Dobson says, 'it would be dangerous to assume that the will of the prior was always the source and origin of all policy. At Durham it was notoriously difficult to distinguish the actions taken by the superior on his own initiative from those arising out of consultation with the senior monks of chapter.'[41] Nevertheless, the prior still retained ultimate control over most departments. Especially useful was his undisputed authority to choose the heads of most of the Durham cells and to move monks between them at will; John Burnby, prior in 1546, averted a crisis by immuring his ambitious rival, Richard Bell, for the next eight years as prior of Finchale.[42]

On this vital question of authority the Marian statutes of the cathedral were vague and contradictory, attempting to steer a middle course between the power structures of the secular and monastic chapters. The dean certainly appeared powerful and his authority over some aspects of chapter activity was wide: the receiver and treasurer, the main administrative officers, were his deputies rather than his equals; so far as the discipline of the minor members of the corporation was concerned, the dean had absolute jurisdiction.[43] What was in doubt, however, was the old matter of the precise relationship between dean and chapter and the relative powers allocated to each. In some matters the dean was unable to act without the consent of the chapter, while in others he was only obliged to seek its advice.[44] Some of the

Elizabethan deans of Durham tried to exploit the implied power of their position to the full but were invariably faced with the sort of belligerent claim put forward by Robert Swift in 1570 that 'neither jurisdiction, nor any other thing, is . . . given to Mr Dean alone without the Chapter, nor by any law can be, they both together being one body politic and by civil imagination one self person'.[45] In practice the dean could usually rule peacefully with the backing of at least half the chapter but, if determined opposition grew up, the situation became very difficult.[46] On two occasions before 1640 serious dissension broke out, instigated by the Puritans Ralph Lever and Peter Smart, and in neither case was the dean able to deal effectively with the situation.[47] Thus, although in some ways the position of the dean was comparable to that of the prior, the practical limitations on his authority reflected the medieval secular tradition.

In the hope of resolving internal differences, increased visitorial power was granted to the bishop, although very few bishops courted unnecessary bad feeling by using these powers to the full. 'We have two governments in this country', pointed out some of the prebendaries in 1580, 'the one pertaining to the dean and chapter, the other to my lord of Durham: these both have their limits how far and in what sort to deal'.[48] Thus the chapter was keen to perpetuate its independence even though a good deal of this had been lost at the refoundation. The struggles of the twelfth and thirteenth centuries had resulted in the acceptance of the bishop as a titular abbot who enjoyed no actual power in the monastery; as diocesan, however, he retained his right of visitation although his powers of correction within the priory were vague and ill defined.[49] The Marian statutes attempted both to clarify and rationalize this position. Although the bishop still lacked regular jurisdiction over the chapter it was made clear that the cathedral was basically the *sedes episcopalis* by according him place of honour in the choir, superseding even the dean, and allowing him to minister and preach in the cathedral whenever he thought fit. He was to hold triennial visitations (or when called upon by the dean and two prebends) and in these investigations was given full power to correct offenders. Moreover, if the statutes or the election of officers stood in doubt then the chapter was obliged to turn to the bishop as arbiter.[50] Bishop Barnes, for one, used these powers to the full and, while he engendered a good deal of resentment by so doing, he also proved the degree of episcopal control which could be exercised by a determined bishop: 'we have almost no chapter . . . but first direction must be had from Auckland . . .', complained the bishop's enemies.[51]

The important question of patronage represents a similar break with the past because Bishop Barnes' influence in the cathedral was based as much on a group of *client* prebendaries within the chapter as it was upon his visitorial powers. Despite pressures exerted upon it by the laity the priory had always remained an independent corporation as far as recruitment was concerned. The election of the prior, who was chosen by the chapter, did not require the approval of either king or pope, and the monks seem to have secured their positions by personal recommendation, thus making the monastery a 'self perpetuating corporation'.[52] In 1541, however, several valuable benefices were created and the chief of these, the deanery, the 12 prebendal stalls, and the 8 secular almsrooms, were reserved for the crown. The only change to this pattern came in 1556 when Mary granted the patronage of the prebends to Bishop Tunstall, a move which brought Durham into line with the other secular cathedrals and which was perhaps designed to compensate for the patronage which the bishop had lost through the dissolution of the collegiate churches.[53] The move was an important one because it forged a much closer link between the bishop and his chapter. Occasionally the bishop was heavily influenced by a layman (Essex was behind the preferment of Henry Ewbank; Strafford was behind that of Thomas Carr) but normally bishops used the prebends to provide for their favourite preachers and administrators – it was common for the chancellor and the archdeacons to sit in the chapter, as in the old secular cathedrals.[54] The deanery remained a piece of royal patronage to be fought over by the various court factions, as, for instance, during Toby Matthew's long campaign for the post between 1581 and 1583.[55] There were two non-resident deans: Thomas Wilson, one of Elizabeth's secretaries of state, and Adam Newton, tutor to James I's children. On both occasions the lack of competent leadership had adverse effects upon the chapter by sharpening factional interests.[56]

The changes in patronage ownership had wide ramifications.

Now both crown and bishop had a much better claim on chapter time and energy and consequently an increasing burden of administrative obligations fell on the cathedral. Dean and prebendaries, ever conscious of the prospects of higher preferment, were normally prepared to render such services as were required. The priory, it is true, had not been completely divorced from the world of secular administration. The monastery had collected clerical subsidies for Durham and had provided hospitality for royal officials on business in the North, but apart from this the degree of extra-mural work undertaken was generally up to the will of the individual prior.[57] Attitudes varied. Wessington refused to treat with the Scots in 1444, allegedly because he feared reprisals against the priory's Northumberland possessions, but reluctantly agreed to undertake a 'quasi-judicial role' as arbiter in the disputes between the Herons and the Manners in the 1420s and the rival branches of the great house of Neville in the 1430s.[58] Bell, on the other hand, whose ambition eventually took him on to the bishopric of Carlisle, was only too pleased to act as border commissioner under Edward IV.[59] Similarly, the obligations of sixteenth-century deans varied, but their dependence upon the crown for preferment brought them into further contact with the secular world of politics and administration. All of the deans were J.P.s in Durham, Northumberland and Yorkshire and members of the Council of the North.[60] Dean Skinner was basically a lawyer who owed his appointment to the fact that he promised to be a loyal and competent administrator in an area which was generally considered to be unsympathetic to the Elizabethan government. Archbishop Parker thought him 'learned, wise and expert' and the officials of the bishopric were ordered to consult him in complicated cases in his capacity as temporal chancellor of Durham.[61] Toby Matthew undertook extensive administrative duties including the collection of information for Robert Cecil about Scottish court factions in the 1590s.[62] It was partly because of their proven ability as administrators that Watson went on to the bishopric of Lincoln, Horne to Winchester, James to Durham, and Matthew eventually to the archbishopric of York.[63] In a mere 50 years the Tudor deans had secured more prestigious ecclesiastical preferment than had the priors in the entire history of their house.

The exercise of patronage by bishops and differing court factions led to the presence of diverse and conflicting interests within the chapter and of conflicts which were often difficult to resolve. Early in Elizabeth's reign there was obvious tension between the old Catholic prebendaries backed by the Nevilles and the incoming Protestant clergy backed by court families like the Russells and Dudleys.[64] Twice these patronage conflicts led to serious crises. During the 1560s and 1570s Bishop Pilkington and the Dudleys had built up a powerful faction in the cathedral and diocese which caused alarm at court because of its religious radicalism and general antipathy to secular interests. As part of the general attack on puritanism dating from Archbishop Grindal's suspension in 1576, the new bishop, Barnes, backed by more moderate forces at Court, attempted to supplant Pilkington's group and a head-on collision between the old interests and the new ensued.[65] Later Bishop Neile managed to recruit a formidable following in the chapter because of a series of timely deaths or resignations; his supporters included John Cosin, a protégé of the proto-Arminian Bishop Overall, and Augustine Lindsell, thought by the Puritans 'to sit at the stern of Popish Arminianism in England'.[66] Neile's group inevitably clashed with the older prebendaries nominated by Calvinist bishops such as Hutton, Matthew and James.[67] In 1621 Robert Hutton preached against the new trends in the cathedral and, although prosecuted by the High Commission, he continued to register his protest by absenting himself from communion.[68] Then, in 1628, came Peter Smart's famous and vitriolic attack on Neile's 'spiritual fornicators' and their 'superstitious vanities, ceremonial fooleries, apish toys and popish trinkets'.[69] On the very afternoon of his sermon Smart was called before a special court of High Commission and this incident inaugurated a period of bitter dispute and recrimination which was only to end when the Long Parliament released Smart from 11 years in the King's Bench prison.[70] An examination of patronage and its effects clearly places the cathedral in the medieval secular tradition, because in the priory problems of this sort rarely arose and, if they did, there was machinery available to deal with them quickly and effectively.

But perhaps the most outstanding contrast lay with the personnel. The typical Durham monk was a man of middling social status (generally from the yeoman/artisan class) who had been born in the locality. Most had studied at the almonry school and in the fifteenth century about half had spent some time at Durham College, Oxford, though a smaller proportion had actually received degrees.[71] The priory, of course, had produced some outstanding scholars such as Uthred of Boldon and Prior Wessington, but little is known of the general intellectual climate of the house except that the reading tastes of the monks, reflected in their library, were conservative.[72] The opinions of sixteenth-century Protestants of the quality of monastic learning at Durham were unfavourable: Robert Dalton and Nicholas Marley were thought to be unlearned and Thomas Sparke 'neither a preacher, learned man, nor honest', despite the fact that all three were bachelors of divinity.[73] At least one of the sources was capable of reporting favourably on the academic attainments of other Catholic clergy. Morally the monks lapsed occasionally: as late as 1567 William Todd was said to have 'used himself so excessively in drinking that he had been miskempt and drunk'.[74] Despite this the priory received a reasonable report from the king's visitors in 1536 and Dr Dobson concludes that the monks were 'generally successful in conveying an impression of moral respectability'.[75]

If the monastic community formed a large group chiefly remarkable for its mediocrity, then the personnel of the Elizabethan and Jacobean chapters represented an important break with the past. Although many were still northerners, the later prebendaries were recruited from a much wider area and included Scotsmen like John Weemes and Anthony Maxton and southerners such as John Calfhill and Henry Ewbank.[76] The majority came from substantial landowning families: the Pilkingtons, for instance, were squires of the Lancashire village of Rivington and had built the church there, while the Blakistons were amongst the most ancient and respected gentry of the palatinate.[77] Distinguished university careers were common and the chapter as a whole encompassed a huge range of experience and talent; theologians and lawyers were always in the majority, but the Elizabethan chapter could also boast experts on such diverse subjects as siege warfare, medicine, chess, drama, mathematics, logic and cartography.[78] Some of the prebendaries such as Thomas Sampson,

Thomas Lever and John Foxe were men with international reputations, well known to Calvin and the leading reformers of Europe, while others like Francis Bunny and Hugh Broughton were justly famous for their wide learning and extensive writings.[79] In short, this second generation of prebendaries comprised a very remarkable group of men amongst whom, except in the matter of financial corruption, serious moral turpitude was either virtually unknown or exceedingly well disguised.[80] They enjoyed higher social status than their monastic counterparts; had a broader experience of life; and possessed more varied talents. Moreover the certainty of election of Calvinists such as Lever gave a certain resilience and toughness which pulled them through the most difficult situations and allowed them to admit no man as their better.

These characteristics of the prebendaries, and the fact that they were usually married, had important repercussions for many spheres of chapter activity. The monks were generally insular in outlook; lacking experience in the secular world, they approached that world with caution and trepidation. Prior Castell summed up this feeling when he expressed his fears of undertaking high office in 1494 'being young in years, not having the use of great practices of temporal business'.[81] The result was that the priory relied heavily upon lay 'professionals' for advice, protection and estate administration. Chief amongst these lay protectors were the Nevilles, who enjoyed close and profitable relations with the priory from the fourteenth century onwards; their lavish benevolence was repaid by the monks with offices and privileges. Ralph, Lord Neville, was the first layman to be buried within the monastic church of St Cuthbert.[82] The estates of the convent were usually supervised by the Nevilles or Neville clients and as late as 1549 the Earl of Westmorland received an annuity of £10.[83] The connection lasted until the end: in 1571 George Cliffe was presented to Brancepeth by Lady Adeline Neville after showing support for the rebels in 1569.[84] Despite the fact that the Nevilles were capable of issuing sharp and sometimes insulting rebukes to refractory priors, Wessington sincerely believed that the secret of success lay in 'cherishing and keeping in of the love of my lords Westmorland and Neville'.[85]

The Nevilles were not the only group which the priory had to

heed and Knowles certainly exaggerates the status of the prior
in putting him on a par with the great magnates of the North,
arguing that his 'standards were those of the peerage rather than
those of the country squire'.[86] The convent was under continual
pressure from a variety of noblemen to provide patronage for
their clients and it was partly to satisfy this demand that the
collegiate churches of Howden and Hemingbrough were founded
in the early fifteenth century.[87] Under Edward IV Bell was
buying the support of Warwick and Gloucester by using the
priory's patronage in their favour: blank letters of presentation
were handed out by the prior and in 1464 he advanced £24 to
Warwick out of a clerical subsidy.[88] The convent did not give
unqualified support to this policy, but it had a sound enough
grasp of the realities of the situation to appreciate that resistance
would have been difficult. In 1446 the monks acknowledged
their need to respect 'the demands and requests of the lords and
magnates whom we cannot offend'. Thirty years later Bell complained that 'I and my brethren are so oft times called upon . . .
by divers lords of right high estate that we may not have our
liberty to dispose such small benefices as are in our gift to our
friends like as our will and intent were for to do, as God knoweth
and me repenteth'.[89] The monks were not equipped by status or
temperament to resist the encroachments of the laity and in the
context of the lawless society of the fifteenth century the problem
was especially marked. In a controversy with the Hiltons over
rights in Monkwearmouth a number of monks were threatened
and attacked; during the dispute Baron Hilton's son accosted
William Lyham, Master of Monkwearmouth, pulled down his
hood 'and asked him in stoor manner "who was thy sire?"'.[90]
Significantly enough, we cannot answer Hilton's question, and
this is doubtless one important reason why Dr Dobson was led to
his conclusion that 'patronage . . . was utilised in the interests of
secular lords rather than the monastery'.[91]

The later prebendaries were in a very different position. True,
they were working in an age which generally showed more
respect for the law, but their advantages of experience and social
status gave them the freedom of action which the monks usually
lacked. As members of the landed classes themselves, possessing
the charisma of the 'gentleman born', the prebendaries could

deal with the gentry as equals and speak to the lower orders with authority. Moreover, their social and often actual kinship with the local civil and ecclesiastical judiciaries meant that they approached potential legal crises with a high degree of confidence. It was alleged in 1576 that the enemies of the chapter could not receive justice in Durham because of the close alliance between the chapter and Bishop Pilkington who had *jura regalia*.[92] Advantages such as these, coupled with the fact that prebendaries preferred to hand down their lands to their own kin rather than to amenable gentry, enabled the Elizabethan chapter to run its own estates for its own undisguised profit.[93] Under Whittingham and his successors the chapter tenants were forced, very reluctantly, to accept new 21-year leases of their lands and the gentry were gradually forced off the 'corpes lands' in order to restore them to the prebendal stalls.[94] Typical of the new approach was Dean Hunt's sequestration of the lease of the Rectory of Bywell St Peter, enjoyed by Sir John Fenwick, in order to help pay for Cosin's repairs to the cathedral and his 'strange Babylonish Ornaments'.[95]

The magnates still shared much the same attitude to the corporation as they had in the days of the priory and, indeed, the movement towards secularization had been strongly reinforced by the Henrician and Edwardian reformations. Yet substantial changes were occurring. After 1547, if not earlier, the position of the Nevilles was gradually deteriorating as new 'Court' groups, notably the Dudleys and Russells, began to establish themselves in the government of the North. Eventually the power of the Nevilles, though not their influence, was effectively destroyed by their abortive coup in 1569.[96] Predictably, the new prebendaries courted the new families but, although they shared radical Protestant religious opinions with them, they did not always see eye to eye with them on the question of the endowment of the Church.[97] Generally speaking, the chapter was reluctant to support its patrons in schemes of further secularization. Dean Horne, for example, was certainly involved to some degree in Northumberland's scheme to take over the diocese of Durham and he was marked out at an early date to succeed to the new, reduced bishopric. As the full implications of the plan gradually unfolded, Horne made it clear that he was reluctant to give the duke his full support and it was Ridley who was finally nominated to the new bishopric.[98] Similarly, Dean Whittingham was quite capable of resisting secular interference when he felt that the general welfare of vested interests of the chapter were threatened: at Sacriston Hugh he resisted the encroachments of Leonard Temperley, who was supported by Baron Hunsdon; and at Brantingham he fought a long and successful suit against Walter Jobson, a client of the earl of Leicester. Warwick, Whittingham's patron, was heard to complain 'once or twice' of the dean's 'ingratitude'.[99] The contrast between old monk and new prebendary is a real one but it should not be overplayed. In 1538, soon before the surrender of the house, Prior Whitehead refused Henry VIII's request for a lease of Rilly for Stephen Brackenbury, yet in 1580 the chapter responded at once to a letter from the queen and granted the tithe corn of Aycliffe to Lord Eure.[100] The priory did not endure complete subjection any more than the new cathedral enjoyed complete freedom, but the general tenor of the argument holds good. Despite pressures exerted upon it the later chapter, whether Puritan or Arminian in tone, was usually capable of taking a much stronger stand than the monastery and of using its patronage as it thought best.

Thus, to link the cathedral and the priory too closely together would be dangerously superficial. This is not to argue that the cathedral was in any sense a 'better' institution than the priory, simply different. Although by the fifteenth century the priory had moved away from the ideals of the monastic fathers, it had shown a remarkable stability in a society of intense social and economic change; there was probably less dissension and corruption in the administration of the priory, and the priory was never as unpopular with the laity as was the cathedral.[101]

How typical was the case of Durham? Generally speaking, the new foundations appear to share the broad pattern described – an endowment deeply rooted in the past with the temporary perpetuation of the old ideas in a first secular chapter invariably made up of ex-monks of the house. Carlisle is a case in point. Here the new cathedral was endowed with most of the property of the old Augustinian house and a highly conservative régime consisting of ex-canons ruled the roost until the 1560s when the first reformers, such as Gregory Scott and John Macbray, were injected into the chapter by the Puritan Bishop Best; only then did the substantial alterations conceived in the statutes of 1545 begin to take effect.[102] After a point, however, broad comparisons become exceedingly difficult and tenuous. The whole life and tone of a cathedral was governed by its statutes and, much to the frustration of the historian seeking comforting generalizations, no two sets are alike. The constitutions of the old foundations especially varied enormously, partly because of the ease with which individual chapters could add to or subtract from their statutes.[103] Residence qualifications were quite different, for example, at Salisbury and Lincoln; the value of a Lichfield prebend was much less than a York one; and Exeter's constitution included certain archaic regulations quite foreign to other cathedrals.[104] Even within a cathedral there was great diversity, the value of the Lincoln prebends ranging from nothing to £70 per annum.[105] However, the fact that the various medieval 'uses' were being merged into the generally-accepted 'use of Salisbury' indicates a degree of interaction; some common features were emerging by the fifteenth century.[106] The new foundations – the products of a master plan rather than of indigenous growth – are predictably more similar, but even here there is significant variety. Norwich was governed by a highly idiosyncratic code largely devised by the chapter itself; Durham's statutes had heavy Catholic overtones including masses for the souls of Philip and Mary; and distinct examples of individuality existed at Canterbury, Worcester, and Carlisle.[107] The common practice of quietly ignoring the statutes, either for religious reasons or because they clashed with some general vested interest, simply added to the general confusion. Under Elizabeth, for instance, there were heated arguments at Durham and elsewhere about the obedience due to 'popish' statutes and at Carlisle the chapter had unlawfully reverted to the old secular practice of electing its officials for life.[108]

Thus any generalization about post-Reformation cathedrals must be approached with extreme caution. Nevertheless, it seems fair to attempt some sort of summing up and to determine where the *raison d'être* of the new foundations lay, if not in their monastic past. The new cathedrals owed their greatest debt to the medieval secular cathedrals, the broad pattern of which they followed. Yet they were far from being mere carbon copies, because the clerics who framed the statutes for the new foundations were well aware of the problems faced by the old cathedrals and consequently were able to sidestep the worst pitfalls. Ironically, it was often by falling back on the example of the more centralized monastic chapters and mingling this with the prevalent secular tradition that the new foundations evolved their unique constitutions.[109] Thus, when we compare the new cathedrals with the old, we are faced with a picture of continuity only a little more pronounced than that offered by comparison with the priories. Basically the new foundations perpetuated the medieval secular ideal by creating chapters which were supposed to integrate with the world as well as care for the *opus dei*. The bishops' patronage of the prebendal stalls and the consequent involvement of the prebendaries in the ecclesiastical administration was common to both old and new foundations, as was the notion that members of the chapter should be maintained by an apportionment of land annexed to their stalls, although at Durham this practice arguably had monastic antecedents.[110] In practice the old and new cathedrals were staffed by remarkably similar men whose wide-ranging abilities were not always given full scope in the introspective and petty-minded faction fighting which was common. Dr Edwards' conclusion that the 'modern reader might form the impression that the medieval cathedral clergy spent most of their time in "bickering"' is thoroughly confirmed by a study of their counterparts in the new foundations.[111]

Yet there were significant innovations in the constitutions of the new cathedrals. The role of the bishop was more clearly defined and his powers of visitation and correction were greater than those enjoyed over the old foundations; all cathedrals were jealous of their independence, but significantly Barnes found it easier to exert pressure on the Durham chapter than Curteys did at Chichester.[112] The dean was nominated by the crown instead of being elected by the chapter and, although the power of the deans of the new foundations has often been exaggerated, their authority undoubtedly owed something to the legacy of the priors. The great endowed dignitaries of the old foundations, who often vied for power with the dean, were replaced by officials subject to annual election, more reminiscent of the monastic obedientiaries.[113] The chapter itself became smaller and more select. The medieval secular pattern had been that of a 'small resident executive' dominating the cathedral while the majority of prebendaries resided elsewhere and engaged in other pursuits. Even when many of the old chapters were substantially pruned at the Reformation, non-residence remained a major problem in churches such as Lincoln and York.[114] The new pattern was to create smaller chapters in which a high proportion of members were expected to reside in the diocese if not actually in the cathedral close. The ideal, of course, was not always adhered to, although at Durham the level of complete non-residence was small and certainly no match for the absenteeism of the old foundations.[115] Moreover, the power of the minor corporations was established and maintained at a low level in the new foundations; certainly the minor canons of Durham could not match the vicars choral of York in either privilege or prestige.[116] The general picture which emerges is of a much more tightly knit corporation in a cathedral of the new foundation, lacking the diversification, divided responsibility, and flexibility of the older chapters. Such a corporation, watched over by a diligent bishop and guided by a Court-appointed dean, was quite in tune with the ideals regarding Church and state held by the Tudor sovereigns.

The new foundations, then, were hybrids, drawing on a number of sources both secular and monastic, but with the secular in the ascendancy. This is not to be uncomplimentary – the new cathedrals, born out of compromise, were quick to establish an identity of their own even in face of persistent local traditions such as those already noted at Durham. The authors of the Rites would surely not have bothered to pen their memoirs unless they had a nagging fear that the Calvinist deans were having a measure of success in obliterating past traditions. By the end of the sixteenth century there were clear signs of changes in attitude, and Peter Smart was hitting out at the monkish as well as the Arminian view of the *opus dei* when he criticized Marmaduke Blackiston's belief that he was doing 'enough to God and the Church' by sitting through the services in choir like 'an idle drone'.[117] Much more was expected of a prebendary than this. Hamilton Thompson had little time for the nineteenth-century notion of the cathedral as 'a centre of diocesan activity' when applied to the sixteenth century. Although in some ways he was correct, he failed to take into account the fact that the sixteenth-century changes in general, and the creation of the new foundations in particular, at least began the trend towards the smaller and more active chapters which was to culminate in the nineteenth century.[118] At Durham, for example, the administration of the diocese became gradually rooted in the chapter after 1541 and the prebendaries undertook important work in the area as highly articulate parish clergy or masters of hospitals. Bishop Barnes summed up the changing attitude when he declared that it was the duty of the cathedral clergy to assist 'him in his great cure and parish'.[119] This was a far cry from the monastic ideal and, if the cathedral occasionally clashed with the same bishop it was supposed to be assisting, it only serves to prove that in the sixteenth century, even more than in the fifteenth, 'the importance of the Cathedral . . . often transcends that of the diocese of which it forms the *matrix ecclesia*'.[120]

# 6

## Finance and administration in a new diocese: Chester, 1541–1641

### Christopher Haigh

In 1568 Bishop Downham of Chester complained that he had 'the least revenue that any man of my calling have in this realm', and in 1603 Bishop Vaughan claimed that it was well known 'how little able the small revenues of this see is to defray the charge thereof'.[1] Within the limits of pardonable exaggeration the two men were right, for with one of the lowest of episcopal incomes the bishop of Chester was expected to rule one of the largest and most difficult of English dioceses. The new see was endowed in 1541 partly from the revenues of the archdeaconries of Chester and Richmond, which provided £283 a year for the bishop. Any further property would have to be sacrificed by the king from among the lands and tithes of the suppressed monasteries. It is thus not surprising that Chester and the other new sees were endowed at a level far below that of the older bishoprics. The crown provided monastic property for Chester worth only another £190 4s. 8d., to give an estimated gross annual revenue of £473 4s. 8d., while essential fees and pensions reduced the net endowed income to £369 4s. 7d., though by various measures the first bishop was in fact able to raise about £495 in the early years of his rule and the see was assessed for tax purposes as having an income of £420 1s. 8d. These sums may be compared with an average net pre-tax income of £1,568 7s. 6d. a year for the 17 English sees existing in 1535, when only Rochester at £411 1s. 9d. had a taxable income lower than that of Chester.

By 1575 the average taxable income of 20 bishoprics, the 17 old
sees and 3 of the new ones, was £1,084 14s. 4d., when the Chester
figure was still £420 1s. 8d. and the bishop's actual net income
was £669 16s. 6d. At that time only the old see of Rochester
and the new sees of Gloucester and Peterborough had taxable
incomes lower than that of Chester, and the bishop of Chester
was clearly one of the poorest on the bench.[2]

The revenues of Chester were untypical in their source as well
as their size. The incomes of the older sees came predominantly
from land, and 'spiritual' revenue from appropriations accounted
for perhaps 10 per cent of the total in 1535, but in 1541 two-
thirds of the revenues of Chester were 'spiritual' and from 1547
the bishop had no income at all from land. The nature of Chester's
endowment had two important results. First, between 1541 and
1546 the bishop held only one manor, and throughout the period
1541–1641 there was only one episcopal residence in the diocese,
the palace at Chester; the bishop could not emulate his peripatetic colleagues, supervising his diocese closely as he moved
from manor to manor, but had to rule from his inconveniently-
situated cathedral city. Second, the bishop's opportunities for
the exploitation of his property were limited, as there were no
demesne lands to provide food and cushion the episcopal household against rising agricultural prices, there were no assets such
as woods which could be sold, and there were no perquisites
arising from manorial rights. If the bishop of Chester was poor
in 1541 he would, unless there was outside help, be poor in 1641,
and his revenues would never reach the level needed to support
a traditional diocesan administration.

The financial advantage to the crown of combining low
revenues with the largest possible administrative area, and the
desirability of using existing jurisdictional boundaries, created a
diocese of massive proportions. Chester was 120 miles long at its
longest point and 90 miles wide at its widest; it covered 5,200
square miles and was the third largest diocese in England. But
the two larger dioceses, York and Lincoln, had revenues about
four times the level of Chester's, so that heavy administrative
costs were less serious a burden for their bishops. When the
Reformation changes presented ecclesiastical government with
problems of enforcement and discipline far beyond the tasks

which had hitherto faced diocesan bureaucracies, the administrative resources of even well-established and relatively well-financed dioceses were strained.[3] But the poorly-endowed new sees of 1541 were ill-equipped to answer the demands placed upon them, and this was particularly true in the unwieldy diocese of Chester.

Bishop John Bird faced major administrative, political and financial problems when he was translated to the new see of Chester in 1541. The creation of a new diocese by letters patent was a simple exercise, but it was a much more difficult proposition to turn an official fiat into an administrative reality. Bird, in 1541, had to create a new jurisdictional structure for the Church in the North West of England, recruit a corps of officials to staff his new institutions, and impose his authority on the far-flung parishes of his diocese – and all this had to be accomplished within the constraints imposed by the meagre endowment of the see. The immediate problems which faced the bishop forced him to take decisions which determined the organization and effectiveness of diocesan administration until the Civil War.

The new diocese was formed by the amalgamation of the archdeaconries of Chester and Richmond, and as the old archdeacons had enjoyed considerable independence from the authority of their respective bishops it was necessary to extinguish their jurisdiction and vest it in the bishop of Chester, for otherwise the new episcopal power would have been negligible. The bishop was empowered to devolve as much or as little jurisdiction as he wished to two new archdeacons, to whom he was to pay annual stipends of £50 each.[4] Such salaries would, however, have reduced the bishop's new income by more than a fifth, to a level at which it would hardly have been possible to maintain a proper episcopal presence, so at least as a temporary measure Bird elected not to appoint archdeacons. Instead of paying stipends to archdeacons, Bird devolved some of his powers to rural deans, who paid him rent for the profits of their jurisdiction.

In the archdeaconry of Chester the authority of rural deans had been vested in the archdeacon, and Archdeacon Knight had retained the deaneries in his own hands, bestowing part of his jurisdiction upon deputies to whom he leased the revenues of their administration. Thus when in 1541 the powers of the archdeacon were vested in Bishop Bird, the authority of the rural deans was likewise extinguished and the bishop was able to create a new structure. In the absence of archdeacons it was essential that there should be an alternative link between the cathedral city and the parishes, and Bird built upon Knight's example. The bishop nominated powerful rural deans, who were to proceed in all disciplinary cases except simony and heresy; grant probate of wills, except for those of knights and clergy, where the estate of the deceased was worth less than £40; and collect synodals and procurations for the bishop. In return for the profits of this jurisdiction, the deans paid to Bird an annual rent, which brought in £24 10s. 8d. from the 12 deaneries in the archdeaconry of Chester. As the rural deaneries in the archdeaconry of Richmond fell vacant, Bird imposed the same system upon them, beginning in 1550 with a grant of disciplinary and probate jurisdiction in the deaneries of Kendal, Lonsdale and Catterick, and when all the Richmond deaneries had been leased out they produced an income for the bishop of £11 15s. 4d. These arrangements, designed to increase Bird's net income by £136 6s. 0d., remained characteristic features of the administration of the diocese; Chester was never to have archdeacons with real authority, and until a little before the Civil War the deans leased their considerable powers for life.[5]

The calibre of the rural deans was to create, as we shall see, serious problems for bishops of Chester, but the character of the officers who were to staff the two consistories was even more significant. Richard Smith, rector of Bury, had been an official of the archdeacon of Chester's court, but he was certainly unpopular and apparently inefficient and corrupt and Bird, after employing him as a temporary commissary, soon dispensed with his services. The archdeacon of Richmond's court had been presided over by John Dakyn, the vicar-general, but when Archdeacon Knight became bishop of Bath and Wells Dakyn followed his patron south to a new career.[6] Bird therefore had to build a new administrative cadre, and it is indicative of the weakness and delicacy of the position of the first bishop of a new diocese that he felt it necessary to recruit his staff from prominent local families. As his chancellor Bird nominated a member of the powerful Savage family of Cheshire, perhaps through the intercession of the bishop's colleague Edmund Bonner, half-brother of the new chancellor. George Wilmesley was already an ecclesiastical administrator of some standing, having been registrar and a proctor of the chancellor's court at Oxford, vicar-general to Bishop Hilsey of Rochester, and dean of Archbishop Cranmer's peculiar of Shoreham. If Wilmesley was to be attracted from the beginnings of a successful career under the eye of an archbishop to the fastnesses of his native Cheshire, then a tempting bait was needed. Bishop Bird united the three main diocesan offices of official principal, vicar-general and commissary-general, and gave them to Wilmesley as chancellor; three years later he allowed Wilmesley to purchase the office of registrar from the first holder. Bird paid salaries to Wilmesley as commissary and as registrar, in addition to the fees he received, and three rural deaneries, with their attendant probate fees, were bestowed upon him. Finally, the bishop gave his chancellor long leases of episcopal property and grants of patronage, providing further opportunities for profit.[7] Such terms could hardly be refused and George Wilmesley moved north, but the decisions Bird had taken were of lasting importance; thereafter the diocese was ruled by a succession of powerful chancellors, with life-grants of the offices of official principal and vicar-general and three rural deaneries, and Wilmesley's leases crippled the finances of the see.

As commissary of the consistory at Richmond the bishop appointed Robert Layburne, rector of Lamplugh, who had probably known Wilmesley while both were at Broadgates Hall in Oxford. The first commissary was presumably a relation of Sir James Layburne, a leading Cumbrian, and in 1544 the post passed to a member of another prominent local family. Miles Huddleston, LL.B., was the pluralist rector of Whittington in Lonsdale, where his family held the manor and the patronage of the rectory. The position of commissary was also made attractive by the addition of a salary to the income from fees, and again Bird was able to recruit men of standing and expertise to bolster his own authority.[8] The bishop tried in other ways to lessen the necessarily parvenu character of his new diocesan administration, by binding the interests of the gentry to himself and the see.

Annuities were granted to influential local men, including three grants totalling £14 a year to William Glaseor, a leading official and citizen of Chester. Others were favoured with generous long leases of episcopal property: Thomas Holcroft, a protégé of the Earl of Hertford and a considerable purchaser of monastic lands in Lancashire and Cheshire, had a 21-year lease from the king of the rectory of Weaverham, and when the appropriation passed to the bishop Bird confirmed the lease and added another to follow it, at the same rent, for 99 years. Robert Tatton and his son profited similarly, with a 40-year crown lease of the rectory of Bowden followed by a 99-year lease from Bishop Bird. These and other leases seriously depleted episcopal revenues later, and in 1587 an Exchequer decree on a group of Bishop Chadderton's rectories, including Bowden and Weaverham, complained of 'very extraordinary long leases made by the predecessors of the said reverend father, which are very beneficial unto the lessees for above double or treble the rent yearly answered to the said bishop.' In the 1620s Bishop Bridgeman scribbled furious marginalia on copies of Bird's leases, for example that 'This execrable lease hath also passed away this benefice from the Church and all churchmen for ever, a true sign of that bad bishop's sacrilegious and ungodly disposition'.[9]

But for all Bridgeman's strictures, Bird's purpose is easy to see and it was not an improper one for a bishop in his position. Before 1541 the North West had been on the periphery of the ecclesiastical structure, and the authority of the church courts had intruded only marginally. Bird therefore faced the major task of introducing real episcopal power into the area for the first time, and of making his rule acceptable to a gentry class which had only recently shown itself contemptuous of ecclesiastical authority.[10] The magnitude of the problem, and the early failures of episcopal discipline, may be illustrated by the royal commissions of 1543 and 1550, appointed to combat the sexual laxity of the gentry and their reluctance to contribute towards the repair of ruined churches, matters which properly fell within the competence of the church courts. Bishop Downham was later to follow Bird's example in attempting to ingratiate himself with the local gentry, granting out the patronage of prebends in the cathedral, giving long leases contrary to statute, and angering

others by his reluctance to proceed against gentry offenders.[11]
John Bird was thus forced to pursue two essential but incompatible policies: he saw that it was necessary to buy the services
of influential officers and the friendship of the gentry, but the
expenditure this entailed conflicted with his efforts to maximize
the net income of the see. He saved £100 by dispensing with
archdeacons and brought in £36 6s. 0d. by leasing the deaneries,
while when he leased out his property he was able to save the
£18 he had paid to estate officers. But the bishop's careful
economies were dissipated by his generosity to George Wilmesley
and by his improvident leases to the chancellor and others.

The profitability of the endowment of the see had already been
reduced when it came to Bird, for at least seven of the ten
rectories had recently been leased out by their former owners,
for terms of between 60 and 99 years. The nuns of Chester foresaw the demise of their house, and in 1538 they leased Llanbeblig
rectory for 99 years and Over for 81 years, the latter grant to
follow the expiry of an existing lease, while Archdeacon William
Knight was clearly very well-informed. Knight must have heard
of the discussions which preceded the introduction of a bill into
the Lords in May 1539 to give the king power to create new
dioceses, and he must have seen that his own archdeaconries
were ripe for reorganization. Thus in November 1538 and May
1539 he leased out four of the six rectories appropriated to
Chester and Richmond, for periods of 60 or 61 years. It may be
assumed that archdeacon and nuns raised heavy fines for their
leases, but in doing so they limited the ability of the bishop of
Chester, who soon took over their rectories, to do so. Bird was
able to take fines in 1546 by leasing the rectory of Bidston and
the site of the former Chester nunnery, but thereafter the next
opportunity a bishop would have to raise a fine on the original
endowment of the see was to be in 1596, when a lease of
Llangathen rectory was due to fall in.[12] Not only was the rental
of the bishopric fixed for many years in a period of inflation, but
the bishop could not supplement his income by fines for new
leases.

In 1545 the Act for suppression of chantries and colleges
presented Bishop Bird with what he thought was an opportunity
to alleviate both his administrative and his financial difficulties.

He petitioned the king that if Manchester College was to be confiscated he himself might be 'preferred to the house, lands and tithes thereof, proportionately for the exchange of other lands as much in value, to the king's grace's use'. The bishop hoped that the college would provide a convenient administrative centre, as he 'hath no house of residence within his large and ample diocese but alonely his house at Chester', and he anticipated some financial gain too. If the college property passed to him, Bird intended to make both a new foundation and a profit, and though he offered the king the manor of Weston in Derbyshire in exchange he hoped that lands and tithes in a rapidly-growing town would prove more profitable than a manor 'which lieth above forty miles out of the said bishop's diocese, so that he cannot use the commodities thereof so well as of lands near'. But the exchange into which Bird was instructed to enter was less advantageous to the see, for late in 1546 he had to surrender Weston and his other lands to the king, receiving in return five appropriated rectories and the advowsons of eight other rectories, together with licences to appropriate them as they became vacant. The bishop lost lands worth £153 18s. 0d. a year, and had to continue paying tenths on the properties as if he still owned them, and received instead five rectories guaranteed to yield at least £81 3s. 0½d. net and an annual pension from the king of £83 9s. 9d., so that in the short term he lost £169 5s. 9½d. and gained £164 12s. 9½d. The crown pension was in lieu of the other eight rectories, and as each one became vacant the bishop was to appropriate it, institute a vicarage and retain the profits, with a *pro rata* reduction in the pension until it was extinguished. The king guaranteed that the new rectories would eventually bring in at least £111 4s. 6d., so that in the long term Bird would lose £169 5s. 9½d. and gain £81 3s. 0½d. plus £111 4s. 6d., and so make an annual profit of £23 1s. 9d.[13]

The results of the exchange were, however, very much less beneficial to the bishopric than the plans of 1546–7 had anticipated. One of the rectories assigned to Bird had already been granted to someone else, and there was no compensation until 1558, while the bishop was forced into a short-sighted policy with the properties he received. The negotiations of 1545–7 were costly, and Bird's financial position was weakened by the rapid inflation of 1546, so that he had to raise money by granting long leases in return for fines. Bird had not, as far as we know, made any leases in 1541–5, but in 1546 he took fines for leases of the two parts of the original endowment which were as yet unburdened and in 1547–50 he was involved in the granting of ten leases of between 60 and 99 years on the rectories he received by the exchange. Four of the five new appropriated rectories had recently been leased, and for these Bird granted consecutive leases until Bowden was rented until 1655, Weaverham until 1660, Backford until 1665 and Castleton until 1704. As for the rectories which still had incumbents, two were leased out for 90 years each by Bird and the rector, two more were leased out by Bird for 80 years each from the next vacancy, and another was immediately appropriated and burdened by two leases for a total of 152 years. The average length of the leases of 1546–60 was 88 years, and their length was presumably dictated by a need to raise heavy fines; the leases probably produced nine fines which went wholly or partly to the bishop, giving him perhaps £500.[14]

In 1541 Bishop Bird had so organized the administration of the diocese as to maximize his net revenues, but his precautions appear to have been insufficient and in the late 1540s he had to exploit the endowment in the only way available. Most of his property was already burdened with leases which fixed rents, and the piecemeal increase of rents as leases fell in provided no answer to immediate difficulties; all Bird had to sell was the future, if necessary by consecutive leases, and long leases with high fines formed the only way in which his property could be exploited and his revenue raised. Bird's successors had little choice but to follow his example, but its disadvantages are clear. The average length of the 11 leases Bird granted on possessions which remained in the hands of bishops of Chester was 88 years, so that on average he fixed rents until 1635, but by that time the total rental of £273 8s. 10d. on these rectories was worth only £106 at 1547 prices.[15]

The pressures which forced Bird to make long leases were personal as well as financial. Three of the leases, each for 80 years, were to Edward Plankney, the former registrar of the diocese, perhaps in compensation for the office he had sold to

George Wilmesley in 1544. Four leases, for a total of 368 years, went to the chancellor himself, two of them 'in consideration of the good and diligent service, labours and pains that the before-named George Wilmesley hath taken in labouring the matters of exchange of lands'. Bishop Bridgeman, 80 years later, was not impressed by Bird's reason for the leases nor by Wilmesley's achievement in the exchange, for he scribbled in the margin of one lease: 'a wicked and illegal consideration, for he made away the temporalities of the bishopric and took only advowsons etc. of benefices then with cure and full of incumbents, which also he made away to this Wilmesley'. Bridgeman's anger is not sur-prising, for the actions of Bird and Wilmesley had severely limited his own income, especially in the case of Bradley rectory, which was valued at £17 6s. 7d. a year in 1535 but was later leased to the chancellor for 80 years at a rent of only £1. Wilmesley soon capitalized his asset, selling the lease to a Staffordshire man, and Bishop Bird not only confirmed the transfer but agreed that on the expiry of the lease the rectory would pass to the lessee's heirs in fee farm for ever. Bird's successors challenged the grant in the courts without success, and they even found it difficult to extract the nominal £1 rent.[16]

Though Bird must have raised large sums by fines, this did little to alleviate his desperate financial situation. It was dis-covered in August 1553 that £1,087 18s. 0½d. in tenths and sub-sidies granted to the crown in 1550 had been collected by the bishop and his agents but had not yet been paid into the Exchequer. The sheriff of Lancashire was instructed to sequestrate the episcopal revenues in the county, but it is probable that Bird had used the taxes to pay off his debts and the outstanding sum could not be recovered. In May 1554 it was found necessary to release the next bishop from the debt he had inherited, and these manoeuvres represented a gift to the see of over £1,000.[17] The infusion made possible a minor reorganization of diocesan government, and in the autumn of 1554 Bishop Coates was able to nominate two archdeacons at the stipends of £50 each stipulated by Henry VIII. Coates could not grant them archi-diaconal jurisdiction, since this had already been leased to the rural deans, but the two posts provided officers who could play an important role in diocesan government. Robert Percival, archdeacon of Chester, became commissary-general and official principal, while John Hampson, archdeacon of Richmond, was made a special commissary and usually presided over the consistory as Percival's deputy.[18] The appointments, however, reduced the bishop's net income by about a fifth, and, though Coates was allowed to hold at least three benefices 'in commendam' with his bishopric, his finances must have been stretched. His successor, Bishop Scott, was in an even worse position during the 'price explosion' of 1556–7 and he seems to have appealed to the crown for help, for in February 1558 Mary made a substantial grant to the see. In compensation for the rectory of Workington, which had never passed to the bishopric after the exchange of 1546–7, Mary gave the reserved rent of £143 16s. 2½d. which she received from the estate of St Bee's to the bishop, less a pension to the crown of £63 8s. 4½d., and the profit of roughly £80 was very much greater than the revenues of Workington. In addition, Scott was given help towards the stipends of his archdeacons, with a grant of the rectories of Cartmel and Childwall and a licence to annexe them to the archdeaconries. Scott and his successors preferred, however, to retain the rectories for the see, and they were soon bringing in £112 13s. 8d. in rents. As happened in the dioceses of Bath and Wells and York, the reign of Mary saw a considerable improvement in the finances of the see of Chester.[19]

Although the gross income of the bishop increased by almost 40 per cent between 1547 and 1558, it remained true, as William Downham complained in 1568, that 'I have of the bishopric nothing but bare rent, and much of it evil paid, and the least revenue that any man of my calling have in this realm'. We are accustomed to the strident claims of poverty made by Elizabethan bishops, and they were no doubt meant for the ears of rapacious courtiers, but Downham had no need to pretend and the real impecuniousness of the see protected it from spoliation and even attracted assistance. In view of the 'exility' of the bishopric, Matthew Parker was able to ensure that the Marian augmentations remained, and though in 1561 Elizabeth imposed a reserved rent of £11 15s. 5d. on the rectories of Cartmel and Childwall the see was not subjected to leases or exchanges under the Act of 1559.[20] As personal chaplain to the queen Downham was forgiven about one-seventh of his first fruits from the see, and in November 1561 he was given a promise of £26 12s. 3d. a year and arrears of £532 3s. 4d. when it was discovered that a pension which was to have been included in the original endowment had never been paid. Ten years later the bishop was forgiven arrears in the tenths on some of his rectories, and at some stage he was freed from the payment of subsidies on five rectories. But these were minor adjustments which did no more than make poverty a little less oppressive, and when Bishop Downham died in 1577 he was heavily in debt.[21]

William Chadderton succeeded to the see in the midst of a financial crisis. Somehow he managed to pay his £42 0s. 2d. as composition for first fruits, after pleading with Walsingham for help lest he should 'not be able to fulfil the least part of my duty'. But he then had to go cap-in-hand to his own clergy for a benevolence of 5 per cent of their income, 'to contribute unto divers extraordinary charges laid and happened upon the said reverend father'. Such assistance would not, however, be forthcoming again, for the diocesan clergy agreed to contribute only on condition that they should never be put to a similar charge, and it proved insufficient to deal with the bishop's problems. In 1592 Chadderton had still not paid the £378 1s. 6d. outstanding on his first fruits, and in that year he had to agree to pay the remainder within five years. In 1587, however, the bishop had been able to ease his position slightly, when he pleaded to the Exchequer that he could not possibly pay the £415 13s. 6d. accumulated arrears in tenths on some episcopal rectories, and he managed to have the debt forgiven and the burden for the future transferred to the farmers of the rectories. But the net revenues of the see remained far too low, and Chadderton complained that he had only £73 7s. 4d. as 'all his allowances towards the charges of his house, servants and other necessaries borne and sustained all this winter past to this 19 of June 1595', though it is true that the bishop had miscalculated and the sum was in fact £123 7s. 4d. In 1603 Bishop Vaughan told Robert Cecil that everyone knew 'how little able the small revenues of this see is to defray the charge thereof'.[22]

Vaughan's comment was in justification of his succession to the rectory of Bangor to supplement his 'poor bishopric', and it was usually necessary for a bishop of Chester to hold a rich benefice *in commendam*. William Downham held two benefices in addition to the see, including Bangor, and in 1568 the impending expiry of his licence for pluralism caused him some consternation. Chadderton held the wardenry of Manchester College as well as Bangor while he was bishop, and even before his formal nomination to Chester Hugh Bellot was pressing for *commendams* so that he could make ends meet. Bishop Lloyd held the rectories of Thornton and Waverton, Thomas Morton held Stockport, and John Bridgeman had the rich rectories of Wigan and Bangor as well as canonries at Exeter and Lichfield. Some bishops needed other expedients; Downham leased the rectory of Huntingdon from the dean and chapter and Lloyd's wife and sons had a lease of Shotwick from the same source, while Chadderton used some unknown means of raising money which aroused the disapproval of his successor.[23]

As appropriations and as *commendams*, several benefices supported the administration of the diocese and the household of the bishop rather than attracting well-qualified parish clergy. In 1595 Bishop Chadderton was paying the stipendiary vicars of his appropriations an average of just over £11 a year, less than half the income of all south Lancashire vicars and only 40 per cent of what was thought necessary to support an incumbent; even where the bishop had shifted the burden of stipends to the lessees the vicars fared little better, and the average stipend paid by the farmers was under £14. The bishop and his farmers were also less than diligent in their maintenance of the fabric of appropriated churches; Bolton church was in ruins by the fault of the appropriator in 1595, 1598 and 1604, and at Childwall there were similar complaints in 1563, 1592 and 1604. It was difficult to recruit clergy of high calibre to serve in such unpromising conditions, and in 1590 only one of the bishop's six appropriations in Lancashire had a vicar who could preach, while in 1610 Cartmel was 'meanly served only with a reading minister'.[24] Perhaps worst of all was the case of Ribchester, where the chancel and the old rectory house were said to be in decay in 1578 and, though the farmer claimed that repairs had been carried out, by 1583 the house was near collapse and a new one had to be built. Between 1574 and 1616 the vicar of Ribchester was Henry

Norcrosse, who held two benefices and served both himself, was unpopular among his parishioners and was accused, apparently with some cause, of simony, and who tried to increase his income by selling ale and victuals, to the neglect of his ministerial duties; Norcrosse was finally deprived for drunkenness and violence.[25]

Bishops of Chester reduced their costs at the expense of vicars and parishioners, but their net revenues were still insufficient to finance an orthodox diocesan administration. Bird had taken the unusual step of assigning salaries to the chancellor, the commissary of Richmond and the registrar, presumably because many of the fees which might have accrued to these officers would in fact go to the rural deans. But it had not been possible to set the stipends at a realistic level and it was necessary to supplement the officials' incomes from other sources. Chancellor Wilmesley secured four leases of rectories from Bird, and he purchased the registrarship from the holder, gained the reversion of the post for his sons and leased the profits to a deputy for a rent of ten marks. Other episcopal servants were also rewarded with leases, Edward Plankney having three from Bishop Bird and Edward Gibson receiving two from his master Bishop Downham. The office of chancellor was partly supported by leases of the profits of the deaneries of Chester, Malpas and Bangor, and from 1567 the commissaries of Richmond leased the profits of at least Kendal, Lonsdale and Catterick; the deaneries were probably sub-let to deputies.[26]

The peculiarity of Chester's deaneries resulted from arrangements made necessary by the poverty of the see and the size of the diocese, but the system was far from satisfactory. The leasing of deaneries for life and the granting of reversions made the office a source of profit rather than an administrative trust, and having paid their rents the deans were eager to maximize their profits. In 1571 six deans were found to have been commuting penances without the permission of the bishop and pocketing the proceeds, while two were said to have taken bribes to conceal offences. In 1578 and 1595 deans were reported for commuting the penances of sexual offenders, and commutation seems to have been a regular source of revenue. Even legitimate exploitation of the deaneries brought in considerable profits, and Bishop Bridgeman was able to increase the rents of some deaneries by four or five times while still leaving the leases as worthwhile investments. Some deans sub-let their offices to the highest bidder, so that the bishop had no control over the calibre of staff at deanery level; Downham tried to dismiss the sub-lessee of Manchester deanery for commuting penances, but the deputy dean continued to exercise his functions, and under Bridgeman a sub-lease of the deanery of Middlewich passed to a woman – the bishop only managed to invalidate the lease when the woman was found committing adultery.[27]

As life interests in the deaneries and even reversions had been granted, and as the bishops needed the rents which the leasing system produced, it was difficult to overturn the arrangement completely, but it was clear by the 1590s that the deans had to be brought under episcopal control. In 1594 Chadderton instructed the deans to submit annual reports on their proceedings, and those who failed to do so were suspended from office. Bishop Vaughan called the deans before him in 1599, examined their records, organized a new system of regular deanery courts, and tried to impose a common registrar of his own choice on the deans. This officer was regarded as an episcopal spy and the deans appealed to the archbishop of York against Vaughan's intrusion, but they submitted to his demands when he threatened them with suspension. Bishop Lloyd had further difficulties in 1606, when he had to proceed against the deans of the archdeaconry of Chester for contempt of his jurisdiction. In 1615 Lloyd abandoned his attempt to control the deans in the archdeaconry of Richmond, and granted seven rural deaneries to the joint commissaries, an arrangement which became the norm in Richmond. Bishop Bridgeman was also forced to retreat, and he gave up his claim to nominate a registrar for the deans, but his relations with the deans led to a more fundamental change which, though it improved the bishop's finances, may have decreased official authority in the diocese.[28]

As the deanery of Amounderness and the deaneries in the archdeaconry of Chester fell vacant, one by one Bridgeman increased the rents substantially and granted them to the archdeacons of Chester and Richmond. In May 1635 the bishop was able to grant the deaneries of Chester, Malpas, Bangor, Fordsham, Middlewich and Nantwich to Dr George Snell, archdeacon of Chester, who already held the deanery of Wirral. The rents of the deaneries were increased to a total of £50, which cancelled out the stipend which had hitherto been paid to the archdeacon, and thereafter Snell could live on the profits of his ruridecanal jurisdiction. At the same time the deaneries of Warrington, Leyland and Blackburn were granted on the same terms to Dr Thomas Dodd, archdeacon of Richmond, and Bridgeman planned to reserve the deaneries of Manchester and Amounderness for his chaplains. In fact, Manchester remained in the hands of Dove Bridgeman, the bishop's son, and Amounderness was given to the diocesan chancellor in compensation for the three Cheshire deaneries he had surrendered to Dr Snell. Two weeks later, the two archdeacons assigned the jurisdiction and profits of their deaneries to Chancellor Mainwaring, who was to pay each of them £50 a year as rent.[29]

It is difficult to assess the administrative impact of these changes, for the coming of the Civil War meant that they did not last for long. In a similar situation in the archdeaconry of Richmond, Commissary Craddock found it necessary to lease his powers as rural dean of seven deaneries to deputies, and unless the chancellor adopted a parallel expedient for the Chester deaneries the middle tier of diocesan government was effectively abolished. If, conversely, deputies were appointed in the Chester deaneries, then the pre-1635 situation with its inefficiency and corruption, was reproduced, except that the deputies leased their powers from the chancellor instead of the bishop. Bridgeman's motives were, however, financial rather than administrative, and his gains were considerable. He saved the archdeacons' stipends of £100 in all, and the old rents of Macclesfield, Manchester, Wirral and the eight Richmond deaneries continued to be paid; the rents of nine deaneries were lost, and the bishop was left with a profit of £82 4s. 0d. a year. His intention in the long term was to assign Macclesfield to the archdeacon of Chester and to increase the Richmond rents to £36 6s. 0d., which had been the total rent for all 26 deaneries, and if this had been done the total profit would have been £107.[30] Again, the administrative structure of the diocese was dictated by financial considerations.

Bridgeman's reorganization of the deaneries was merely a part of a wide-ranging attempt to increase his revenues and cut his costs.[31] When he became bishop in 1619, Bridgeman discovered that the see had, as he put it later, 'no charters, evidences, registers, rentals, counterparts, nor any other escripts or records to be found concerning his bishopric or the revenues thereof'. He therefore set his servants to work compiling a collection of records concerning the see, its appropriations, its taxes and its revenues. In 1627 the charter of erection of the see and other documents were copied from the original patent rolls, and a collection of leases was made in a volume on which Bridgeman noted that 'as many as by any means I could get I have caused to be registered in this book. The rest have been lost by my predecessors' neglect'. These investigations revealed a number of ways in which net income might be increased; the bishop discovered, for example, that he was not bound to pay subsidies on five rectories 'which are freed by an old order in the Exchequer, though I paid divers subsidies err I knew of that order'. Bridgeman drew up elaborate accounts for all the revenues he claimed and marked each one as paid or unpaid as the money became due, increasing each year the range of sources from which income actually came. He found that a pension due from the rectory of Preston had not been paid since 1607, and in 1624 he secured a Duchy decree for payment of the pension and arrears. The bishop also demanded pensions from 11 other benefices, but he was successful with only one of them. In 1624 he sued some of the tenants of St Bee's for non-payment of rent for two years, and when they claimed that they could not pay he had their revenues sequestrated. In 1626 he was able to force the warden of Manchester to pay £21 12s. 0d. in accumulated synodals and procurations, and he also gained arrears from Brigham and Aysgarth. By a new lease of the rectory of Bidston he obtained synodals and procurations long unpaid, and he reported the recovery of many lost fees in the archdeaconry of Richmond.[32]

Bishop Bridgeman was able to persuade his clergy to grant benevolences totalling £269 17s. 4d. in 1619 and 1620, but such expedients did not lessen his need for a much higher regular income. In only one case, however, is the bishop known to have increased the rent of an appropriation, when in 1622 he renewed Sir Rowland Egerton's lease of Budworth and doubled the rent to £1. Bridgeman exploited his rectories by taking higher fines rather than by increasing rents, for the gains he could make in the short term by the latter method were limited. The average fine charged for leases of tithes, recorded in the reports of the Commonwealth surveyors of ecclesiastical property or Bishop Gastrell's collections, for the years 1566 to 1618 was £50, but in the same sources the average fine during Bridgeman's episcopate was £114; in the period 1660–1708, the average was £115. In fact, a surviving account book shows that Bishop Bridgeman took an average fine of £192 11s. 11d. for tithe leases, and the known fines do not provide a fair sample of the fines taken. To achieve a 'weighted' return of fines, the ratios of fines to rents and to the annual value of rectories as estimated by the Commonwealth surveyors have been used to provide average fines for the epis-copal rectories as a whole. In the period 1566–1618, fines aver-aged half the value of a rectory and twice the bishop's rent, so that the average fine must have been about £80. During Bridge-man's rule, however, fines averaged one and one-sixth times the value and ten times the rent of the appropriations, and the average fine was £200, thus roughly confirming the accuracy of the method used, since we know that Bridgeman actually took almost £193. Thereafter, in the years 1660–1708, fines were four-sevenths of the value and four-and-a-half times the rent of rectories, giving a probable average of about £100. It seems that Bridgeman more than doubled the fines taken by his predecessors and far exceeded those of his successors. The fine for a lease of the tithes of Raskelf had been £50 in 1601, but in 1624 Bridgeman took £80 for exactly the same terms, and though the fine for a lease of the tithes of Kirkby chapel had been £10 in 1601 Bridge-man took £40 for the same terms in 1638. In 1637 Bridgeman's fine for a lease of the rectory of Kirkby Ravensworth was £180 or even £200, but the fine for the same terms in 1687 was only £112. In addition, Bridgeman raised £240 over 20 years for altering the terms of existing leases and in fines on leases of tenements and vicarage houses. Income from fines thus played an important role in the bishop's finances, and it was presumably his need to maximize fines which led him to disobey Charles I's order of 1634 restricting the length of leases.[33]

Although his policy of extracting high fines while maintaining low rents might be presented as selfish and shortsighted, Bridgeman's conduct in the case of the rectory of Ribchester showed a greater awareness of the long-term interests of the see. In 1603 Bishop Vaughan granted a new lease of Ribchester to the Sherburne family for three lives at the old rent of £39 16s. 8d.: the property was thought to be worth £350 a year by 1650. In 1621/2 only one life remained in the lease and the Sherburnes began to press for renewal. The bishop, however, found that the 1603 grant had been made while a 90-years' lease of 1548 was still in being. From 1624 he refused the Sherburnes renewal on the grounds that they were not in any case the true lessees. His legal advisers warned Bridgeman that as he had tacitly acknowledged the Sherburne claim by accepting their rent in the past he was unlikely to win any litigation and so the bishop again accepted the rent. He continued, however, to resist pressure for renewal even though the farmers offered a fine of £700 and he himself thought that he might succeed in securing a fine of £1,000. Bridgeman's intention was to allow the lease to fall in, augment the vicarage and reserve the rest of the profits to the rectory for the bishopric. This plan fitted well into Laud's scheme 'To annexe for ever some settled commendams, and those, if it may be, *sine cura*, to all the small bishoprics'. In 1632 Bridgeman and Laud secured from the king an order that Ribchester be annexed to the bishopric when the lease expired because Chester was one of the sees in which the revenues 'have been so diminished that they suffice not to maintain the bishops which are to live upon them according to their place and dignity'. Although Laud mentioned Chester as a see in which his plan had been fulfilled, in fact his only achievement was the dispatch of a royal letter; the project was interrupted by the Civil War – in 1661 Bishop Walton leased Ribchester to a servant in trust for his own wife and son. In 1639 Laud had suggested the appropriation of the £600-a-year rectory of Wigan to the see and set about raising money to purchase the advowson. Bridgeman evidently thought Wigan a more desirable prize than Ribchester, suggesting that half the money for the purchase of Wigan might be raised by a fine on a new lease of Ribchester. The scheme remained incomplete.[34]

Bridgeman used a range of methods to increase his income; he was also able to reduce his costs. He shifted the burden of the archdeacons' stipends from his own purse to that of his chancellor.

He seems to have discontinued the salaries of the chancellor and the commissary of Richmond, presumably regarding the profits of the deaneries as sufficient compensation. By agreements negotiated in 1624 and 1629, the bishop ensured that all or half of the individual stipends of vicars of six appropriations were paid by the farmers thereof although the existing leases placed this burden on the bishop. Less reputably, he failed to pay salaries to curates or to the vicars of Chipping, Kirkby Ravensworth, Patrick Brompton and Ribchester, although these had been stipulated by the king in the 1547 indenture of exchange, of which Bridgeman had a copy. In all, Bridgeman prevented a drain of £198 13s. 4d. a year from the episcopal exchequer.[35]

Bridgeman's policies as bishop were matched by his conduct as rector of Wigan, where his relations with his parishioners became so bad that he had to be warned by the government to take care. As rector and lord of the manor, Bridgeman tried to overthrow tithe prescriptions, recover lost rents and impose tolls and fees for the market, and even to make the people tenants at will by virtue of their attendance at his court. Such proceedings gained him a reputation for rapaciousness and legal subterfuge, and made him many enemies. In 1633 he was accused of retaining the profits of the work of the ecclesiastical commission, which should have gone to the crown, and of using the sums raised by the commutation of penances for his own purposes instead of giving them to charity. The charges seem to have resulted from a drive by Bridgeman against adultery and fornication, in which he used a new form of penance and imposed higher fees for commutation, and this led to stories that he was taking bribes from the gentry to tolerate their indiscretions. The accusations were made by two deprived clergy and a disbarred solicitor, and the main charges appear to have been untrue, but many witnesses came forward to protest against the bishop's exactions and there was enough circumstantial evidence to prompt the bishop to try to silence his accusers and the investigators sent by the king. There were dark hints of simony and nepotism, and it is true that Bridgeman's brother-in-law and two sons were wellbeneficed with episcopal promotions, and in 1633 he intended to make another son diocesan chancellor until prevented by the intervention of the king and Laud.[36] Bridgeman's efforts to improve his financial position seem, in fact, to have destroyed the good relations with the local gentry which his predecessors, and especially Bird and Downham, had fostered, and there are grounds for suggesting that in his pursuit of the Caroline stress on the dignity of the episcopate the bishop had to forgo an efficient diocesan administration and a fruitful relationship with the gentry.

The bishops of Chester, from Bird to Bridgeman, had to rule one of the largest dioceses in England on the basis of one of the smallest incomes, and they tackled the problem in the same way, by leasing out all they could, including jurisdiction, and raising ready cash by fines on new leases. But at least until the latter part of the reign of Elizabeth it is probable that leases fell in only infrequently, and the consequent dependence on a low rental income must have been one of the causes of the financial crises of 1553, 1557, 1579–80 and perhaps 1587. The poor finances of the see, however, prompted the crown to occasional acts of generosity, as in 1554, 1558, 1561 and 1587, and protected the bishopric from spoliation, while the bishops managed their finances intelligently within the constraints upon them. The money incomes of the archbishop of York and the bishop of Bath and Wells declined during the sixteenth century, but at Chester the episcopal income increased considerably and the improvement continued into the seventeenth century. The net income of the see at its erection in 1541 was to have been £290 14s. 2d., though by failing to appoint archdeacons and increasing some rents Bird increased this to £494 12s. 5d.; by 1587 the net revenue had risen to £849 9s. 6d., and by the time some of Bridgeman's reforms had taken effect in 1637 the net total was £1,122 8s. 10d. This means that by late in Elizabeth's reign the money income of the bishop, which in 1541 had stood at about a quarter of the income of the sees of Bath and Wells, Ely and York, and one-sixth of that of Canterbury, was about the same as that of the bishop of Bath and Wells, almost half that of their colleagues at Ely and York, and about one-third of the income of the archbishop of Canterbury.[37] This bishop of Chester had been a near-beggar among his colleagues in 1541, but a century later, especially with his *commendams*, he was among equals.

The rise of the bishop of Chester was, however, only a relative one, for in real terms he remained as poor as ever while his fellows declined to his level. When the revenues of Chester are plotted against the Phelps-Brown and Hopkins price index, it is apparent that the real income of the see declined despite the efforts of crown and bishops. Though the expenditure pattern of a bishop, no matter how poor, was rather different from that of the craftsman for whom the index was designed, the bishop of Chester had no demesne land to exploit and no woods to sell, so that he was almost totally dependent on his depreciating money income, and the following table demonstrates the changes in his position.[38]

| Year | Net income in £s | Index | Real income in £s at 1541 prices |
|------|------------------|-------|----------------------------------|
| 1541 | 495 | 100 | 495 |
| 1547 | 490 | 140 | 350 |
| 1558 | 621 | 140 | 444 |
| 1561 | 670 | 172 | 389 |
| 1587 | 849 | 300 | 283 |
| 1619 | 860 | 300 | 287 |
| 1637 | 1,122 | 376 | 300 |

There was a serious decline in the real income of the already poorly-endowed see until 1587, for though the net income increased this was not sufficient to withstand the pressures of inflation; thereafter, the bishop's real income remained steady, partly because the rate of inflation slowed down and partly as a result of the efforts of Bishop Bridgeman. In 1541 the endowment had been inadequate to support an orthodox diocesan administration, and Bird and his successors were forced to adopt unusual expedients in the establishment and maintenance of a new ecclesiastical jurisdiction. Over the following century the real revenues of the bishopric declined despite vigorous efforts, and the structures adopted in the 1540s could be amended only to a limited degree. Bishop Bird prevented disaster by the abolition of archdeacons; Bishop Bridgeman prevented disaster by the abolition of rural deans; the bishop remained solvent only by abdicating from the real government of the diocese.

# 7

## Some problems of government in a new diocese: the bishop and the Puritans in the diocese of Peterborough, 1560–1630

### William Sheils

Henry VIII's first queen, Katharine of Aragon, had been buried in the great abbey church of Peterborough in 1536; this fact may have had some influence on the troubled conscience of the king when it was decided to spare the church and establish it as the cathedral for the new see of Peterborough created in 1541. A more practical consideration bearing on this decision was the need to dismember the vast medieval diocese of Lincoln, within which Peterborough was located. Accordingly, two of the arch-deaconries in that diocese were elevated to the dignity of sees, but Peterborough, unlike Oxford which had already been a centre for archidiaconal business, had not been previously an administrative centre within the diocese. As the location of a wealthy landowning monastery Peterborough was no backwater in the early sixteenth century, but the archdeaconry courts and offices at that time were situated at Northampton, a more central and, in some respects, a more obvious place for government. The new diocese, therefore, comprised the old archdeaconry of Northampton and was co-terminous with the counties of Rutland and Northamptonshire. During the century after its foundation the diocese witnessed the growth of a vigorous and persistent Puritan tradition which the authorities were never able to contain. Stemming the tide of Puritanism was not the only task facing the ordinary but, in historical terms, it may have been the most significant one. It is in this particular context that the problems facing the bishops and their officials are to be considered.[1]

Peterborough abbey had owned extensive properties, most of them in Northamptonshire, which were assessed at an annual net profit of £1679 15s. 8⅝d. in 1535. It was from this source that the endowment of the new bishopric and cathedral chapter sprang, the portion of the bishop amounting to a net yearly income of £368 11s. 6⅞d. in 1541. This income formed the major part of the episcopal revenues, because the profits formerly accruing to the old archdeaconry of Northampton, including most of the revenue from probate jurisdiction, remained with that official.[2] The bishop of Peterborough was therefore even more poorly endowed than his colleague in the new diocese of Chester, but he did not have as large a diocese to govern as his northern counterpart. The diocese was said to contain 301 livings and 327 churches early in Elizabeth's reign and this figure stayed fairly constant throughout the period. In 1575 the episcopal income was assessed at £414 19s. 6d., less than that of any other English see except for Gloucester, another new foundation. The economic status of the new compared with the older bishoprics can be indicated by comparing the income of Bishop Scambler of Peterborough with that of his colleague at Chichester, who governed an ancient diocese of similar size and responsibility but had an income almost one and a half times as great. In one respect the bishop of Peterborough was better off than his colleagues in the other new dioceses like Chester because most of his income derived from lands rather than from spiritualities. The bishop had been granted much of the demesne land of the old abbey together with the manors of Burghbury and Eye in Peterborough, the manors of Werrington, Walton, Paston and Gunthorpe at Paston, the small manor of Sowthorpe at Barnack, and the manor of Thirlby in Lincolnshire.[3]

The manors were grouped closely together in the soke of Peterborough, but any advantage in having a compact group of estates was offset by the administrative and social difficulties arising from their location. The soke formed a promontory at the north-east corner of the diocese, having relatively little economic contact with the great sheep pastures of Northamptonshire. In addition to the abbot's house at Peterborough which served as his palace, Bishop Dove had a residence at near-by Castor, but for most of the period the bishops had no mansion elsewhere in the diocese which they could use as a residence. In common with his colleague at Chester the ordinary was dependent on the hospitality of others if he wished to travel round his diocese – a situation which could have been avoided if the see had been endowed with other monastic property in the area, such as the large manors of Oundle or Kettering which were very centrally placed. In addition to facilitating his movements around the diocese, ownership of such estates might have given the bishop a position among the Northamptonshire squirearchy, that thrusting group who were to prove so capable of thwarting episcopal policy. Throughout the period neither the bishops nor any members of their families were able to penetrate county society except within the soke where, with the exception of the Fitz-william family of Milton, none of the major landowners of the diocese were based.[4]

The economic problems of the bishops during the period were increased by the financial demands of the crown and, in Scambler's case, by those of William Cecil, his predatory patron, as well as by maladministration. Within a year of his appointment Bishop Scambler had granted a lengthy lease of the hundred of Nassaburgh to William Cecil who, in 1562, was also coveting the lead roof of All Saints' church, Irthlingborough, for Burghley House. All Saints' church was no longer needed because St Peter's, the former collegiate chapel, now served the town as parish church. Seeing the opportunity John Mountstevinge (a local gentleman who enriched himself by his exercise of several patents from diocesan officials and by his zeal on behalf of Sir William Cecil) approached both the bishop and the chapter, under whom he held several offices, on Cecil's behalf and was apparently successful in acquiring the lead. Cecil had secured several favourable leases of Church property in the diocese by 1576 when the most infamous transaction of all took place. Scambler was induced to make a scandalous alienation to the crown of the episcopal manors of Thirlby and Sowthorpe, the lordship of Nassaburgh, and Tanholte pasture at Eye. These properties were valued at £84 a year, approximately $\frac{1}{4}$ of the taxable income of the bishop in 1575, and were granted almost immediately to Cecil by the crown. In 1581 the queen received a 60-year lease from Scambler of property in Peterborough worth approximately £10 a year. His willingness to comply with requests from that quarter was said to encompass more than his temporal possessions. In August 1580 it was alleged that the bishop had taken the fruits of the rectories of Syresham, Cottesbrook, Brockhole, and Norton Davy into his own hands for the use of the queen. Scambler's impoverishment of the see was notorious, and it has been suggested that his translation to Norwich owed more to the crown's hopes of profit from that wealthy see than to any merit in the bishop himself.[5]

Even when long leases to the crown were unfavourable to the see, however, they could be profitable for the bishop himself or the members of his family. A 70-year lease to the crown by Bishop Dove in July 1601 was used as a means of transferring the property concerned, the Spittle in Peterborough, to the use of his son William, to whom the residue of the lease was assigned by William Hake, the grantee from the crown. Dove and his family also received favourable leases of capitular property from the dean and chapter, who were no more careful of the long-term economic effects of such a policy than were the bishops. In fact, in one particular instance the dean and chapter, who were troubled by litigation resulting from a series of forged leases granted by Edward Baker, their receiver-general, in 1587-8, connived at ignoring a forgery 'because the prebendaries favoured the bishop' and Thomas Dove was permitted to remain their tenant in 1630. Bishop Dove diverted much of the income of episcopal and chapter estates to the use of himself and his family but, even so, found the cost of maintaining the ancient palace at Peterborough exorbitant. In 1629 he was granted a licence from the archbishop to demolish part of the building, but died before executing the work; after his death his son claimed to have had to spend £500 on the palace to restore it.[6]

The demands of self-interest and the exactions of the crown impoverished an already poorly endowed bishopric to such an extent that Thomas Cecil wrote to his brother Robert in 1695 in the following terms: 'The place [Peterborough] is of small revenue, and but for the title of a bishop, I think few will affect it, but to step forward to a better.' Such a situation clearly influenced the quality of the bishops recruited. The first Elizabethan bishop, Edmund Scambler, did in fact proceed to a better see, but not through his administrative abilities; neither of the other bishops, Richard Howland and Thomas Dove, achieved promotion, although Howland aspired to the archbishopric of York in 1595. Howland's appointment in 1585 was by way of being only a fourth prize – he had already been unsuccessfully recommended for the sees of Worcester, Chichester, and Bath and Wells by his patron, Archbishop Whitgift. Clearly the see did not attract men of the first rank as its bishops and the effect of this on the diocesan administration will be considered later. Prior to that, one further area of possible influence must be considered, namely the use of the patronage at the disposal of the bishops.[7]

The bishop had very little patronage in this diocese beyond the collation of the six prebendal stalls in the cathedral granted by Queen Mary.[8] Owning only four advowsons, one of which was claimed successfully by Thomas Cecil at the end of the century, to livings in the soke of Peterborough, Bishop Scambler reduced the number still further in 1563 by alienating the patronage of Paston to John Mountstevinge. Such limited patronage gave the bishop no real control over the personnel of the parochial clergy of the diocese and in fact the bishop of Peterborough had less patronage in the area than his predecessor, the bishop of Lincoln, who owned several advowsons. Any episcopal influence on parochial appointments had to be exercised indirectly.[9]

All ordinaries had the right to present to livings *per lapsum temporis* when patrons proved negligent. A zealous bishop could also seek to influence the extensive patronage in the hands of the crown, much of which was administered through the Lord Keeper. The *per lapsum* patronage in this diocese was not significant statistically and, in fact, from 1580 it appears to have been encroached upon increasingly by the crown which, from the accession of James I, appeared to exercise this right on all but three occasions. This presumably brought financial advantage to the crown and can be seen as a further example of the way in which the fiscal demands of the monarchy emasculated the episcopate. On the three occasions when Bishop Dove was allowed to exercise his right there were peculiar circumstances and as a result the bishop was involved in confrontation with some of the leading gentry supporters of the Puritan ministers deprived in 1605. The livings of Fawsley and Byfield, in both of which the veteran Sir Richard Knightley of Marprelate fame was patron, and of Whiston, which became a notable Puritan centre under Percival Wiburn following the suppression of the order of Northampton, remained unfilled by the patrons who chose to ignore the sentence of deprivation and to support the former incumbents financially. It was in such circumstances, where the exercise of his right carried unpleasant social consequences for the bishop, that the crown graciously refrained from encroachment.[10]

Within the diocese the *de iure* patronage of the crown was extensive and its administration provided the bishop with the opportunity to extend his influence considerably. The crown appointed to almost one-third of livings that fell vacant during the period. Most of these appointments were made after petitions were presented by interested parties to the Lord Keeper and, in the early years of the period, Scambler worked hard to exploit this source of indirect patronage. During Nicholas Bacon's tenure of the Lord Keeper's office Scambler was noted as the petitioning party on 23 of the 98 occasions when such appointments were made. Despite Scambler's other shortcomings this figure, in addition to the concern he showed about non-residence in the diocese, does indicate that he had considerable interest in the standards of pastoral care. Unfortunately, figures for the later period are not easily established and comparison between Scambler's record in this respect and that of his successors is not possible. An examination of the appointments to crown livings at Peterborough suggests that both administrative control and episcopal influence diminished here as elsewhere, with the paradoxical result that, as the sympathies of the government and the Puritans drifted apart, so more and more Puritan clerics were able to find livings nominally under the patronage of the crown. The most trenchant illustration of this was the presentation of Francis Wigginton, the less celebrated brother of Giles, to the royal living of Laxton in 1599, despite his having already incurred episcopal censure for nonconformity.[11]

However limited their influence on the personnel of the parochial clergy, the bishops of Peterborough could determine the character of the administrative machinery of the diocese through their choice of officials. The problem at Peterborough, as in all new sees, was that of creating the instruments of episcopal government where none had existed previously. During the early years at Peterborough continuity with the early sixteenth century was provided at archidiaconal level both in institutions and personnel. Since 1506 the archdeacon of Northampton, sometimes referred to as the archdeacon of Peterborough in the early 1540s, had been Gilbert Smith, who remained in office until 1548. Much of the archdeaconry's business was carried out by his official John Sylvester, who occupied that position from at least 1533 until his death in 1543, conducting the archdeacon's court either in the chapel of St John's Hospital, Northampton, or at All Saints' church, with occasional visits to Oakham.[12] The official of the archdeaconry remained an independent appointment until 1587 when it was combined with that of vicar-general and official of the bishop in the person of Henry Hickman. For most of the remaining period the archidiaconal and episcopal posts were filled by the same individual.[13]

The archdeacon was an important figure in the diocese and his relationship with the bishop was a significant factor in diocesan government. The income of the archdeacon was assessed at £140 15s. 6d. in 1575, when Nicholas Sheppard held that post together with parochial livings outside the diocese. Following Sheppard's death in 1587 Bishop Howland secured the appointment for his son James, a precedent followed in 1612 by Bishop Dove, whose son Thomas was archdeacon for 17 years from that time. Nicholas Sheppard was the only archdeacon to show any sympathy for the Puritans; he may have been influential in the establishment of the Puritan order of Northampton in 1570 soon after his appointment, and he did speak out in defence of the public fast held at Stamford in 1580 in defiance of Burghley and of Bishop Scambler.[14] All of Sheppard's successors were well known to, if not related to, the bishops appointing them, but only John Buckeridge, archdeacon from 1604-11, was of the calibre to get promotion. He was certainly no friend to the

Puritans and was one of the associates of Lancelot Andrewes, having been an influential tutor to the young William Laud at Oxford. Buckeridge's theological antipathy to Puritanism may not have been matched by the other archdeacons, but both his predecessor, William Bayley, and his successor, Richard Butler, had reasons based on personal experience for disliking the Puritans. Bayley had had the misfortune to succeed the deprived Puritan Robert Cawdry as rector of South Luffenham and only got possession of his parsonage after lengthy legal proceedings, going as far as Star Chamber, to eject Cawdry. Richard Butler, substitute for the vicar-general of the diocese from 1590–1610, had been the chief object of Puritan wrath during the crisis surrounding the enforcement of the canons of 1604. From 1587 the Puritans got no support from the archdeacons of Northampton, but the holders of that office were in general men of poor administrative ability, so that their antipathy towards Puritanism was not given expression in vigorous action against the Puritans. A harmonious relationship between the bishop and the archdeacon did not make up for the loss of competence resulting from an episcopal policy strongly influenced by family considerations.[15]

The strength of the diocesan judicial machinery was, of course, crucial in determining the effectiveness of the ordinaries in coping with Puritanism. At Peterborough an efficient system had to be created out of nothing at a time when the religious changes of the sixteenth century placed great strain on the diocesan courts of well-endowed and ancient sees such as York and Chichester.[16] This was particularly true when the courts were faced with enforcing uniformity, a problem which was new both in scale and scope. The difficulties facing a poor diocese without even the experience of ancient custom to draw on were far greater. Unfortunately the documents necessary for tracing the early development of the episcopal courts at Peterborough in detail do not survive, but our knowledge of the personnel instrumental in their creation does not suggest that conscientiousness was a feature of administration in the early years. John Chambers, the first bishop, was one of the reformation's survivors. Having been the last abbot of the monastery he succeeded to the new see, where he remained until his death in 1556, having co-operated with whatever authority existed. During Chambers' episcopate John Mountstevinge, the first diocesan registrar, was permitted to accumulate offices and leases from the bishop and the dean and chapter which established his family as important within the soke of Peterborough but was detrimental to the see. Mountstevinge's principal concern was financial gain. Among offices sold by him were the registrarship of the diocese, an action described by Bishop Clavering in 1732 'as being disreputable, if not scandalous', and the registrarship of the dean and chapter, which he conveyed to Bishop Scambler so that the latter could provide employment for his son Edward. As the principal lay officer in the diocese from its inception until the 1570s Mountstevinge had considerable influence on the growth of diocesan institutions, an influence which he did not fail to use to his own financial advantage but which was harmful to the body he served.[17]

During the period in which we are interested the surviving court records do give a comprehensive picture of how the diocesan machinery functioned and show that, in one important respect, the Peterborough courts differed from most other episcopal courts. The bulk of the business transacted in the consistory and correction courts of the diocese was not carried out in the cathedral city but in other towns in the diocese. The unsuitability of Peterborough as a centre for the area was probably responsible for this development. In practice the diocese was divided into two parts, the area to the north and east and that to the south and west, operating from different centres, but the division was never made official and business from parishes in the central area could crop up in courts for either part of the diocese. The cases emanating from parishes in the south and west were generally heard at Northampton at All Saints' church, and those from the north and east were tried at Oundle or, less frequently, at Peterborough.[18] On two separate occasions the court at Northampton was faced for a short period with rival forms of ecclesiastical government inspired by the Puritans; in 1570 the order of Northampton established a short-lived experiment, modelled on the consistory of Geneva, which sought to bring together the religious and civic government of the town; in 1587–8 the *classis* was exercising its own form of censure on clergy of the surrounding district. The effect that these experiments had on the local standing of the diocesan courts cannot be measured but their existence, even for short periods, must have undermined episcopal authority in the area. After the suppression of the order and the deprivation of five clergy from the area in 1574, court sessions for the western deaneries were removed to Wellingborough on a number of occasions in 1575; other towns where sessions were held during the period included Kettering, Uppingham, and Thrapston. From 1615 many sessions of the court dealing with the western part of the diocese were held at Rothwell where the vicar-general, John Lambe, had a residence. Personal convenience was probably the chief motive, but Lambe may well have preferred to operate from Rothwell rather than from Northampton because of the Puritan temper of that town. He had seen at first hand the support for Puritans in Northampton during the crisis years of 1604 and 1605 and his experiences at that time had led him to consider that the town was 'the chief fountain of that [the puritan] humour'.[19]

The peripatetic nature of the Peterborough courts meant that the bishop took even less part than was customary in their judicial functions. The courts were handed over almost completely to the vicar-general. Scambler and Howland sat on rare occasions at sessions held at Peterborough, in the palace, or at Castor, and never elsewhere. Bishop Dove was more active during the earlier years of his episcopate and sat more often than his predecessors at sessions held at Peterborough. During the crisis surrounding the enforcement of the canons in early 1605 Dove took it upon himself to make the episcopal presence felt at Northampton where he was locked out of All Saints' church by the Puritan incumbent. Dove, however, withdrew from his courts after the arrival of John Lambe as vicar-general and chancellor of the diocese in 1615 and left their supervision to that haughty but determined opponent of the Puritans.[20]

Four vicars-general were active between 1570 and 1630, the first of whom was James Ellis. It was Ellis who was most active in the first crisis of the reign involving Puritan clergy of the vicinity of Northampton in the early 1570s. As a result Puritans accused him to their more influential supporters of malpractice. In April 1573 Scambler was writing to Burghley in defence of

Ellis in the following terms: 'Who standeth against them, the puritans they seek to molest by some means, as lately my chancellor [Ellis], whom by indictments very much and yet by clamours and reproaches openly in the face of the country they disquieted, professing not to be satisfied by any other means but by his departure'. The bishop indicated that the Puritans were emboldened by the support of influential friends: 'when I and mine officers have been to resist them, much further will they proceed if I be destitute of a chancellor'. Clearly the influential friend that Scambler had in mind was the Earl of Leicester, whose correspondence with the bishop in the years following the deprivations certainly reflected 'letters in wild words . . . rather a commandment than a request'.[21]

To some extent the vigorous protests of the Puritans testify to Ellis's diligence in rooting out their activities, but his success in this regard was seriously tempered by two circumstances, one of which was beyond his control and the other his own responsibility. The charges of malpractice made by the Puritans against Ellis were not just the result of rancour but may have had some substance. In one letter Leicester referred to him as a 'covetous commissary' and Ellis was in fact the defendant in a lawsuit, promoted by John Mottershed the diocesan registrar, alleging maladministration of the will of William Binsley, archdeacon of Northampton. The case was eventually heard before the local court of ecclesiastical commission, presumably because it involved personalities closely identified with the diocesan courts, but the verdict is not recorded. The other problem was more fundamental and was common in ecclesiastical courts in other dioceses. Ellis, having diligently uncovered Puritan activity among the clergy of Northampton, brought the matter to a head, with the result that five incumbents were deprived. This represented some success on his part and suggests that the courts were able to enforce their edicts but, having removed the offending clerics from their livings, the courts still could not undermine the local influence of the Puritans in the face of strong support from all sectors of society in the area. Four of the deprived clerics continued to work in the area. Thurston Moseley retired to Sywell and attended services at the adjacent parish of Overstone, where a famous exercise was held; Eusebius Paget was identified as one of a 'rank of rangers and posting apostles that go from shire to shire' and became a leading figure at the celebrated Southam exercise just over the county boundary; Arthur Wake retained his mastership of the Hospital of St John in Northampton and, through family connections, remained an important local figure; and William Dawson emerged as a Puritan schoolmaster at Northampton a few years after his deprivation from Weston Favell. The net result of the episode, even when the court was successful in enforcing the law, was that the system of church law was subject to censure by its opponents without being able to destroy the influence of those condemned by it. The courts could not enforce uniformity even when they were able to enforce discipline because their only sanction, excommunication, became less of a deterrent both spiritually and socially as the sixteenth century progressed.[22]

The strong reaction of the Earl of Leicester to the affair may have resulted from his close association with Thurston Moseley, the deprived vicar of Hardinstone, on whose behalf Leicester had already intervened in the affairs of the diocesan courts. Moseley had earlier been restored to his cure and the sequestration on the living relaxed by Scambler at a special session of the court held before him at Peterborough on 23 December 1572 because 'the Earl of Leicester, by his letters, required the same'. The effect of the pressures put on the bishop by powerful patrons of the Puritans are amply illustrated by this episode. Just as Scambler was subject to pressure from above so his officials were criticized from below. William Smith, one of the surrogates appointed by Ellis, was vicar of All Saints', Northampton, in the years following the deprivations and had to struggle against a congregation unafraid of voicing its opposition. The court records of the 1570s are full of incidents involving disputes between Smith and his congregation and, in some cases, the ecclesiastical commission was called on to intervene. Among Smith's earnest opponents was Henry Sharpe, the bookbinder later to figure in the Marprelate scandal, who was presented before the commissioners because 'he rageth against Mr Smith & speaketh evil of his doctrine, commenteth upon his sermons & libelled him'.[23] With discontent being expressed from the mighty in the land and by the ordinary members of the congregations it was clear that the diocesan courts and their officials needed the support of institutions with greater powers of enforcement. The ecclesiastical commission for the dioceses of Peterborough and Lincoln established in 1572 had such powers.

The activities of the ecclesiastical commissioners are recorded in an act book of 56 folios, covering the period from March 1574 until 28 March 1579, which survives among the diocesan records. Although much of the business of the commission was routine and did not differ significantly from causes heard in the diocesan courts, there were some cases of particular importance which were brought before it. The commissioners met at Peterborough and the bishop was usually on the bench, as was William Latimer, dean of the cathedral. In general the clerical representation was greater than the lay, one layman making up the necessary quorum. Among the laity the Wingfield family, both father and son, who had a residence at Upton near Peterborough, were most regular in attendance, but others who sat on the bench included Sir Thomas Cecil, Sir Edward Montague, Edmund Brudenell and Edmund Elmes. The greater powers given to the commissioners, who could imprison and take bonds for good behaviour, meant that some of the more intractable cases were referred thither by the diocesan courts. Among them was one involving the Puritan supporter Edward Caswell of Collingtree, who withdrew from the sacramental life of the parish after the deprivation of George Gilderd. Caswell and his wife had been cited before James Ellis for refusing to receive the communion in accordance with the Book of Common Prayer but 'being thereto enjoined by Doctor Ellis' they neglected his strictures, stood excommunicated for over one year and were brought before the commission on 23 September 1577 where they received a similar admonition. The commission also dealt with the more vociferous Puritan opponents of William Smith and with Francis Merbury, a Puritan preacher in Northampton, who was eventually tried before the High Commission in London. These were cases which would have been particularly troublesome in the diocesan courts, but there is no evidence that the commission was any more successful in intimidating the Puritans. The scanty survival of its records makes it difficult to assess the impact of the commission in bolstering the normal disciplinary procedures of the diocese as did its counterpart in Gloucester. Presumably it was planned that the commission should have a permanent part in diocesan affairs but the act book at Peterborough suggests that the local commission was primarily concerned with the crisis of the years following 1574 and, although other business came into the court, spent most of its time on these matters. No records survive after 28 March 1579.[24]

If the local commission did cease to function at that date, as seems likely, then discipline was once more in the hands of the normal diocesan courts assisted by episcopal visitations. It was the visitation of 1573 which had originally revealed the extent of puritan activity in the diocese and led to the deprivations of the following year. Very little positive evidence of puritan activity was uncovered in the visitations of 1577 and 1582, but it is likely that this owed more to lack of co-operation from the parochial authorities rather than to a decline in the number of Puritan adherents. In 1577, of the seven clergy recorded as not appearing at the visitation, five had already come to the notice of the diocesan courts for nonconformity and by 1582 the coincidence of Puritanism with failure to appear at the visitation became more marked among the clergy and even extended to the laity.[25] The crisis provoked by Whitgift's three articles in 1584 was averted with only one deprivation, largely due to the intervention of Burghley and Sir Thomas Cecil on the Puritans' behalf and to the translation of Scambler to Norwich.[26] A metropolitical visitation of 1589, following the Marprelate scandal and at the height of governmental proceedings against the *classes*, was more successful in uncovering Puritan activity than earlier visitations. The same is true of the early seventeenth century when the determined onslaught of the government in enforcing the canons undermined the local position of Puritan clerics and encouraged, or intimidated, hitherto unco-operative churchwardens and parishioners to make presentments against the Puritans. The visitorial procedures of the diocese responded to a lead from London and, at times of concerted action nationally, were successful in uncovering pockets of Puritanism. Although it is arguable that the crisis of the years 1588–90, involving as it did the dissolution of the *classes*, marked a watershed in the *nature* of Puritan activity, neither that crisis nor that surrounding the enforcement of the canons were anything more than temporary set-backs to the *growth* of Puritanism in the diocese. Episcopal and metropolitan visitations could highlight the problems facing the bishop and act as a spur to the court machinery, but their effect was generally shortlived and it was the latter which had to provide continuity in the policing of the diocese.[27]

In 1587, after the death of Ellis, Bishop Howland appointed as vicar-general Henry Hickman, who had been to his old college of St John's, Cambridge. Hickman, who resided at Northampton, sat in the courts for both the eastern and western deaneries of the diocese, but also delegated a considerable amount of work, much more than his predecessor, to surrogates.[28] The most important and busiest of these was Richard Butler, rector of Aston Le Walls in the west of the diocese, where many of his colleagues were Puritan protégés of Sir Richard Knightley. Butler acted as deputy at most of the centres in the diocese, but was chiefly active in Northampton where he came into conflict with Robert Catelin, Puritan vicar of All Saints'. Their opposition came to a head in the early years of James I's reign. At the end of 1603 a letter from eight of the parochial clergy was addressed to the king claiming that practices customary in their parishes for over 20 years were now being declared illegal and that they were now harassed by a 'surrogate holding and preaching popish positions'. The accusation of preaching false doctrine was endorsed by other Puritan clergy who sought to have a diocesan conference similar to that at Hampton Court. The Puritans encouraged Catelin to 'draw a letter to the bishop, chancellor, and official to require of them that he [Butler] may recant publicly those doctrines . . .', in which Catelin suggested that he 'make choice . . . of such as shall join with him in the conference offering to the adversary that within the diocese he may make his choice number for number excepting none, the place, & the hearers & moderators being indifferently chosen'.[29]

The demands of the Puritans and the determination of Bancroft and the government both acted on Dove to force him to make his presence felt at Northampton and to take affairs out of the hands of his hard-pressed officials. Dove did enter into some sort of conference or disputation at Peterborough with the

Puritans about the canons, but the inhabitants of Northampton were treated to the unedifying spectacle of the bishop being locked out of the pulpit of the parish church of All Saints' by the Puritan incumbent.[30] This reflection upon the status of the bishop among his Puritan subordinates testifies to the extent of feeling which the enforcement of the canons encouraged in the locality, but it also indicates the danger inherent in delegating responsibility for order in the diocese to surrogates drawn from the ranks of the parochial clergy. The authority of the courts was bound to be diminished when one incumbent sat in judgment upon another. The problem was likely to be accentuated when the official was attempting to enforce religious uniformity upon a group of nonconforming clerics who enjoyed a great deal of support among the laity. Surrogates had to be employed, but their appointment called for a discretion which was not always found during the period. Both William Smith and Richard Butler found themselves in trouble with their Puritan colleagues; others were also attacked. Among the surrogates appointed by Hickman were Edward Baker, forger of capitular leases, and Walter Baker, presented to the living of Barby in 1594. Barby had been disturbed by a Puritan faction prior to Baker's arrival and he was soon defending an action for simony brought against him by the Puritan Lord Zouche, patron of the living. He was inhibited from preaching but appealed to Robert Cecil to allow him to minister in the parish until the case before the High Commission was completed. The decision went against Baker, who was convicted of simony and removed, whereupon the Puritan Simon Rogers was presented to the living. The right of men like these to sit in judgment on their colleagues was questionable and their presence as surrogates only served to undermine further a system already under attack.[31]

Not all surrogates were disreputable and one in particular provided some hope of dialogue between Puritans and diocesan officials in the early seventeenth century. Among the surrogates appointed by Hickman on 6 February 1604 was Robert Williamson, rector of Tichmarsh. Williamson had been a member and a leader of the Kettering *classis* in the late 1580s but had withdrawn from close association with the Puritans after the trials of the *classis* leaders. He had been appointed to a prebendal stall in

the cathedral by Howland prior to his appointment as a surrogate, in which capacity he became involved in the task of
enforcing the canons. His reputation and presence provided the
only suggestion of compromise during that crisis. Williamson
undertook, or was delegated to, the task of attempting to reconcile
those clergy who refused to subscribe, and a number of them
made submissions similar to that of Robert Baldock who, on 23
May 1605, promised 'to confer with Mr Doctor Williamson in
matters of ceremony and I will never refuse to acknowledge and
yield to any truth which I shall therein hear warranted from the
holy scriptures'. A few of the Puritans had their suspensions lifted
as a result of such submissions but their intentions were open to
question as several of them, including John Rogers of Chacombe,
soon reappeared before the diocesan courts for nonconformity.
Whether Williamson achieved anything of substance in these
discussions remains open to question, but his case is of interest
in being the only example during the period of using a man with
known Puritan sympathies to mediate between the bishop, his
officials and their Puritan opponents.[32]

From a legalistic point of view the enforcement of the canons
of 1604, as a result of which 16 Puritan clerics were deprived,
marked the most successful campaign against the Puritans by the
diocesan courts. It was a campaign which drew great strength
from being part of a national enterprise designed to root out not
only the Puritan leadership but the rank and file parochial
clergy. Unfortunately, by the early seventeenth century success
in enforcing the church law carried with it social and political
consequences which both reflected the decline in the status of
the church courts and contributed further to that decline. A
decline in status afflicted the church courts in general and, at
Peterborough, inefficiency, maladministration and poor leadership had contributed to that state of affairs. Since 1560 the
diocesan courts had been unable to launch a concerted and
persistent campaign against the Puritans with the result that, by
James's reign, nonconformist worship had become vested with
the respectability attendant upon long-established practice in
several parts of the diocese. Therefore, when the diocesan
authorities attempted to enforce the canons, it was not the
Puritans who were charged with nonconformity but the courts

who faced charges of innovation from several influential quarters in the diocese. The corporation of Northampton appealed to Robert Cecil saying that forms of worship unchallenged for 40 years were suddenly being called in question and a petition to the Privy Council was drawn up by 45 gentry of the county on behalf of the deprived ministers. The signatories to this petition included such hardened campaigners in the Puritan cause as Sir Richard Knightley and his son, but also included members of families who had not previously shown a marked preference for Puritan ideas.[33]

The opposition of the gentry mitigated the effect of the government policy because in several parishes where Puritan clerics were deprived the lay patrons replaced them with men of similar views who had not yet been before the courts. At Ridlington, for example, Thomas Gibson was deprived after a ministry of 20 years, during which he had been a strong supporter of the local Puritans, but the patron of the living, John, Lord Harington, simply appointed Gibson's son, also Thomas, to the living. The younger Thomas had recently taken his degree from Emmanuel College, Cambridge, having been a scholar at the equally Puritan Sydney Sussex College. In this, as in other parishes, the bishop removed an older generation of Puritan clerics only to find that a newer generation stepped into the vacancies.[34] The intervention of the gentry not only undermined episcopal policy but also highlighted a fundamental weakness in the diocesan machinery, a weakness which bedevilled the bishops throughout the country. However much they were able to make cognisance of recusant gentry and proceed against them in their courts, the bishops of Peterborough were never able to summon the Puritan gentry in their courts during the sixteenth century. The Puritan laymen styled gentlemen who did appear before the diocesan courts were not the country gentry but belonged to that class which has come to be known as the parish gentry.[35]

Because of their social position the country gentry were immune from harassment in the diocesan courts for their religious views, even if their matrimonial or economic difficulties sometimes resulted in their appearance. The success of the Puritan clergy in attracting the support of many of the leading gentry families ensured that the bishop always had to face awkward social consequences if he sought to act against the parochial clergy. Although on occasion the government sought the advice of the bishops about the religious temper of the neighbouring gentry, none of them at Peterborough held much sway with that group. Direct lay intervention in diocesan affairs was not limited to potentates like the Earl of Leicester. Late in 1591 Bishop Howland could not prevent the institution of William Kitchin to the living at Cranford St Andrew despite the fact that Kitchin, at his appearance before the bishop on 10 December 1591, refused to subscribe to the articles because of his scruples about the use of the sign of the cross in baptism, the ring in marriage, and the wearing of the surplice. Kitchin's patron was Margaret, widow of John Fosbrooke, gentleman, whose son had himself been a *classis* member, and she ensured that Kitchin was secured in the living where his persistent nonconformity continued to trouble the bishop's officials.[36]

The social limitation on the bishop's power to enforce uniformity was obvious to a wide sector of society by the early seventeenth century. This knowledge further demoralized a system already under strain, and the final decline of the courts as authoritative agents of enforcement came when the institutions themselves became identified with partisan policies. Without adequate sanctions against miscreants the church courts could only retain their authority when the law which they enforced was endorsed by a wide section of the population. To the committed Puritan the policies enforced in the church courts were always partisan and the system was under constant attack by the Puritan press. Nevertheless to the uncommitted observer the church courts were embedded in the fabric of local society and had a legitimate authority, even if it was an authority in decline. The attempt to enforce uniformity became less acceptable as the years went by and, with the arrival of John Lambe as vicar-general in 1615, the identification of the courts with the essentially clerical Arminian policies of the following years made their edicts even less acceptable. The early years of James's reign marked the last serious attempt to deal with the problem of Puritanism through the ecclesiastical courts until the 1630s, when Laudian bishops had been appointed in many dioceses. During Lambe's period of office as vicar-general, from 1615 until

1629, the key struggle was not fought out in the courts. Lambe himself was a capable administrator with a vigorous surrogate in Samuel Clarke, incumbent of St Peter's, Northampton, but his power was limited by the inheritance of a discredited system with ineffective sanctions. He could harass the Puritans and, by endorsing the policy enshrined in the 'beauty of holiness' ideal, he could cause them temporary financial difficulties. However, the policy he pursued was a policy of a faction within the established Church and, as such, its strictures were often ignored by Puritan defendants or their patrons. The result was that by 1633 the Puritan John Dod could refuse to read the sentence imposed in the archdeaconry court on a young couple convicted of fornication because the young man 'had taken penance in the church . . . without authority from any ecclesiastical jurisdiction and thought it quite sufficient'. The identification of the church courts with the policies of the Arminians became complete after the appointment of Lambe's successor, Thomas Heath, in 1629. Heath was a thoroughgoing Laudian who was forced to flee to the Netherlands during the Civil War, after which he confirmed the worst suspicions of the opponents of Arminianism by his conversion to Rome.[37]

Many of the problems faced by the bishops of Peterborough in enforcing conformity were also faced by their contemporaries, most of whom were no more successful than Scambler, Howland and Dove. The crucial problem was the decline in the authority of the ecclesiastical law which resulted from the religious changes of the sixteenth century. All bishops had to operate through a discredited system; the best that most could hope for was to mitigate the effects of this fundamental flaw. The circumstances surrounding the creation of the see of Peterborough made this a formidable task, and, although their difficulties were shared by their colleagues, the bishops here had to face the problem in a particularly acute form. Unlike the dioceses of Chester and Chichester, where the early growth of Puritanism owed much to the support of a sympathetic bishop, none of the bishops or dignitaries of Peterborough, with the exception of Nicholas Sheppard, showed any disposition to favour the Puritans. Nevertheless the organizational abilities and missionary zeal of Puritan clerics supported by influential members of the laity meant that the diocese became a notorious centre of Puritanism in which all the weaknesses of the establishment were exposed.[38]

As a poorly-endowed see governed by a bishop from a cathedral city situated at one extremity of the diocese, Peterborough had disadvantages from the start. The bishops, none of whom were of high quality, had to spend much of their energy coping with the problems concomitant with a poor endowment; the result was that the bishops settled for short-term economic advantage and impoverished their successors. In acting in this way they were no worse than colleagues in well-endowed sees. The principal defect deriving from the poor endowment of the see was the failure to attract men of ability to the diocese. Therefore, in the early years of the period when the ecclesiastical law still retained some authority, the diocesan courts had not established a tradition of competence and their status was undermined by maladministration resulting from the delegation of authority to unsuitable officials. During that period of weakness the Puritans made such inroads among the gentry of the diocese and the urban oligarchs of Northampton that, by the time the officials had put their house in order and the courts were well administered, the social and political consequences of vigorous action against the Puritans reduced the courts to the status of a harassing agent able to act against individuals but unable to enforce its edicts on determined groups of opponents. The bishops of Peterborough were not responsible for the decline in the status of the ecclesiastical courts in general but their supervision, or lack of it, over their own courts hastened that decline in the diocese. Their problems were considerable because of the economic and administrative disadvantages inherent in the establishment of the see, but the bishops and officials did little to prevent the diocese becoming 'from time to time the nest and nursery of factious ministers'. The growth of Puritanism in the diocese resulted from a combination of several circumstances, one of which was the fact that the see 'but for the title of a bishop' was not one to attract the ambitious or able. The diocese of Peterborough had not the means in its revenues, its institutions, or its personnel to combat the growth of Puritan activity.[39]

# The Courts Christian

# 8

## The Prerogative Court of Canterbury
## from Warham to Whitgift

## Christopher Kitching

### I

Few aspects of church administration in the sixteenth century aroused more persistent accusation of profiteering than its testamentary administration.[1] The impeachment of Sir John Bennet, M.P., judge in the Prerogative Court of Canterbury, in the 1620s on charges of extortion provided common lawyers and the Church's Puritan critics with useful ammunition: it suggested that attempts to reform the ecclesiastical courts in the previous century had achieved precisely nothing and that corruption had become progressively more deeply rooted.[2]

Was the system itself at fault or was it merely shown in a bad light by the notorious failings of individuals? With the exception of the diversion of appeals to the Delegates of the Crown in Chancery in 1534, reforms imposed on the court by Parliament and Convocation or archiepiscopal statute brought no major structural change in probate administration.[3] By and large the same courts granted probate in 1600 as in 1500, and in much the same way. There was a steady tightening up of court procedures in reply to critics and in attempts to reinforce the professional status of court officials. But in this sphere of church administration one is struck rather by the continuity than by the change.[4]

### 2

From at least the thirteenth century, archbishops of Canterbury had claimed some prerogative authority to grant probate and administration in cases where persons died with property or debts in more than one diocese. Until Morton's archiepiscopate there is no clear mention of a separate court handling such prerogative jurisdiction; it seems rather to have been the responsibility of the Court of Audience.[5]

A great deal of research has been done on the implementation of probate jurisdiction at both diocesan and provincial levels, demonstrating the relative rights of bishops, archdeacons, deans and other ecclesiastical officials who, by delegation or by virtue of a peculiar jurisdiction, exercised the right of probate.[6] That the Church had acquired the right from the secular authorities was the talking point of common lawyers, who occasionally contemplated retrieving it from the Church.[7] Yet it was generally accepted in the sixteenth century that, even if a secular jurisdiction, such as a manorial court or town corporation, could demand to prove a will which touched upon its own interests, further probate by a church court would automatically follow.[8]

As regards legacies and debts, however, there was a considerable overlap between the jurisdictions of ecclesiastical, equity and common law courts. The Church had never been entitled to regulate the disposal of real estate, but was restricted to movable goods and debts. However, the distinction was not always clear-cut, and close liaison with other courts was often necessary. The growing tendency of equity courts in the sixteenth century to attract disputes over legacies removed some business from the ecclesiastical courts, but apparently encountered little opposition until well into the next century.[9] The use of prohibitions from the 1590s must also have affected the P.C.C., but the loss of the court's filed records from this date makes quantitative assessment impossible. It may be that the P.C.C. was not as badly affected as its neighbours.[10]

At the beginning of our period the P.C.C. was fully fledged, though it was still variously styled as the 'Court of the Prerogative', and the 'Prerogative Court', the former title being redolent of its evolution from the archbishop's household, exercising his prerogative. This 'prerogative' was ill-defined. Whilst from an early date the archbishops made compositions with the diocesans to establish their respective rights to grant probate, these left the Canterbury claims quite unimpeded by explicit limitations, save that the deceased should have movable goods in several dioceses. The qualification *notable* goods was later added but was scarcely more specific. Protests were frequently made about archiepiscopal interventions in testamentary affairs on the pretext of the Canterbury prerogative. Morton was challenged by the bishop of London on the matter of *bona notabilia*, but triumphantly secured two papal bulls confirming Canterbury's rights, without even mentioning the terms in dispute.[11] It is clear from the wording of the appointment of apparitors that no fixed value had yet been set on the goods which the deceased must have held in a second diocese before the P.C.C. might intervene.[12]

In the North, probate jurisdiction was rather different. There was no Prerogative Court at York until 1577 when Sandys became archbishop. Until then the Exchequer Court, the senior probate court for the diocese of York, had little occasion or desire to deal with cases in which the deceased had property in more than one diocese. Problems of communication may be sufficient explanation for the concentration of the archbishop's courts upon purely diocesan affairs and for the late arrival of the prerogative concept. Dr Marchant has noted that in the first few years of the Prerogative Court of York's existence it handled little business.[13]

3

The history of the P.C.C. down to the Elizabethan settlement is punctuated by a series of challenges to the court's authority led successively by the bishops, Wolsey, Parliament, Cromwell and by the crown itself during the three royal visitations of 1535, 1547 and 1559.

The disputes over the prerogative under Warham have been repeatedly described although some of the finer details have been overlooked. When Warham became archbishop, the diocesans were still smarting from the blow they had received at Morton's hands and were bent on revenge. In 1512, the bishops of London, Winchester, Lincoln, Exeter, and Coventry and Lichfield spearheaded a move in Convocation against the Canterbury prerogative, demanding at least a rational explanation of its basis.[14] They reaffirmed that probate was rightly an ecclesiastical matter, but implied their concern to handle the affairs of their own flock. They said that Warham had intervened when the deceased had *bona notabilia* of £5 in divers dioceses, but had neither justified the P.C.C.'s right to intervene nor explained how the figure of £5 was arrived at. The constitutions of Ottobon and, for that matter, of Archbishop Stafford, mentioned nothing of this prerogative, yet Morton had asserted it *crebris suspensionibus et excommunicationibus censurarumque fulminationibus.* Warham, who as bishop of London had fought and contravened these claims, now fully endorsed and enforced them wearing his new hat!

Attacking the basic premise that it was cheaper for executors to have a will proved in London than to appear before various local courts, the bishops pointed out the costly nature of a trip to London and maintained that there were cases where the deceased was subsequently found to have insufficient *bona notabilia* to justify P.C.C. intervention. A more careful scrutiny of the case was called for.

Another vexed question was that of debts. The presence of a creditor or debtor living in a diocese other than that of the deceased was used to justify P.C.C. intervention. Was this reasonable: were debts really *bona notabilia* of assignable location?

The case presented by the bishops may be studied on two levels. As diocesans they were attempting to preserve as much of the deceased's property as possible from diminution by excessive fees and costs of probate, and thus to ensure sufficient remainder to fulfil the obligations of the deceased to his family and to promote charitable benefactions for the good of his soul. On the other hand, as ordinaries they were attempting to preserve their own jurisdiction (and financial interests) against encroachment by Canterbury. Warham was alleged to be claiming more than any of his predecessors and, if the ordinaries were cited to appear in his courts for their defiance, it was the archbishop who was both judge and party in the cause.

The issues raised were important enough to warrant a protest to Rome, instigated by Foxe of Winchester.[15] Warham, aided no doubt by the presence in Rome of the other English primate, Cardinal Bainbridge, succeeded in having the matter referred back to Henry VIII. After heated exchanges in which Warham defended the moderation of his claims, the matter was allowed to rest with no change in the status of the P.C.C.[16] Nor does there seem to have been any further significant challenge from the bishops, although the £5 *bona notabilia* rule, extended to £10 where it concerned goods within the diocese of London, may have been more clearly defined as a result of these clashes, and it continued until the nineteenth century.[17]

The restoration of peaceful relations with his diocesans did not mark the end of Warham's probate problems. Wolsey, as *legatus de latere*, established a court at York Place to which he began to summon would-be executors and administrators, in definance of the rights of diocesans and southern primate alike.[18] This was not just a resurrection of the old struggle for supremacy between the two English provinces, but rather one manifestation of the Cardinal's bid to assume all-effective power over the courts, temporal as well as spiritual.

Warham, remembering something of his tactics as bishop of London fighting Morton, naturally protested, stressing the uncertainty and extra costs besetting testators and executors faced with yet another probate court.[19] Yet in January 1522 he signed the infamous composition which effectively gave way to Wolsey's demands.[20] By its terms, Wolsey was to maintain an unspecified number of commissaries throughout the southern province, the chief of whom was to sit in London. To the latter were to come all persons seeking probate or administration when the value of the deceased's estate exceeded £100 in any one diocese. Executors of lesser estates were given the option of approaching the Cardinal's commissary instead of their own ordinary. The proceeds of the commissary's probate jurisdiction were to be divided equally between the two archbishops. Estates of those having *bona notabilia* in several dioceses were to be under the joint purview of Wolsey's London commissary and Warham's own commissary of the prerogative. Again, no £5 limit was specified.

Very few records of this legatine jurisdiction have survived. Opposition was immediate and predictable. There were soon complaints that Wolsey was attracting causes which were prerogative matters and which should have been judged jointly with Warham. Yet in the absence of the necessary registers it is impossible to assess the real extent of Wolsey's encroachment on other jurisdictions.[21]

There is slightly more evidence of the joint administration by the two commissaries in prerogative cases: John Alen and later John Oliver for Wolsey, and John Cocks for Warham. They met mainly at St Paul's, with some minor sessions at one or other of the commissaries' houses, until Wolsey fell from power in October 1529.[22] Cocks then sat unchallenged as keeper of the prerogative and much of the business was transferred to Lambeth.

The third crisis concerning the prerogative under Warham was the attack on the church courts which began in the Parliament of 1529 and exploded with the Supplication against the Ordinaries. Tension between Warham and his diocesans was reduced as they sought to present a united front before the onslaught first of Wolsey and then of Parliament. Parliamentary complaints were not new – they reiterated old grievances against probate fees and excessive delays.[23]

Grievances against the Prerogative Court must be seen in the context of a general flood of protests against the courts Christian. Recent writers have demonstrated that many of the complaints in the Supplication lacked substance and were more the product of general unrest against the Church than a true reflection of a worsening situation within its courts. Warham's retort to Parliament's claim that delays and expense were often caused by bishops and archbishops citing executors and others to attend at far distant courts was that Parliament itself had recognized the circumstances in which the P.C.C. had the right to act. Moreover, in the great majority of cases executors only had to go to the nearest official of the bishop or archdeacon.

Most of the protesters wanted merely a tightening up of the existing system rather than any seizure of power from the Church, and they had already demonstrated their intentions at the beginning of the Parliament in the Probate Act, which sought to control fees in the church courts.[24] In many respects the Supplication was already out of date; Warham had taken steps to reduce fees, and was engaged in further deliberations to see what stood in need of reform. In defending the Church, he pointed out that the civil lawyers, whose livelihood was threatened by any attack on the church courts and their fees, had served the state in many capacities, notably as diplomats, and that it was important not to erode their already limited vocational opportunities.[25] His firm lead did much to save the church courts and particularly the P.C.C. from further serious attack, but it also sapped his remaining strength, for he died shortly afterwards.

The great Reformation changes which took place in the early years of Cranmer's episcopate largely eclipsed the problem of the church courts. The procedure of the church courts was altered only to the extent that appeals were now directed to judges delegate of the Crown in Chancery.[26] The need to recognize the royal supremacy explicitly in the titles of officials led to some ugly and lengthy styles of address. While they reflected the important change in the nominal source of authority for the court's practice, they in no way altered basic procedure.[27]

The main challenge to the prerogative jurisdiction in these years came from Cromwell's inhibition of 1535 which heralded the first royal visitation and the subsequent establishment of a vicegerential probate court,[28] which in several respects can be seen to have been modelled on Wolsey's probate jurisdiction. Cranmer raised no known objection to this activity, which must have withdrawn some business from the P.C.C., but he was under no pressure since Petre as Cromwell's commissary employed advocates, proctors and registrars of the Court of Arches in his court, so that any loss of fees resulting from their reduced business in the P.C.C. was offset by their earnings in the new court. There was no threat to the ecclesiastical lawyers and, as it happened, no long-term threat to the P.C.C.

Evidence of the operations of the royal visitation is scattered and fragmentary. One of the visitors' tasks was to grant probate, or at least to inspect probates granted by the church courts. Thus the will of Robert Modye of Nottingham was granted probate by the dean of Nottingham in April 1537 under licence from the commissary of the Exchequer Court in York; three days later the probate was inspected by commissaries of the crown, assisted by a notary public. This chance survival must have been typical of many wills proved by the royal visitors.[29]

Despite Cromwell's court and the visitation, the P.C.C. handled plenty of business in the late 1530s. Whereas citations from

Cromwell's court were issued in chancery style in the king's name, returnable to the commissary, those of the P.C.C. continued to run in the archbishop's name, recognizing the royal authority in a later clause, until the death of Henry VIII. The theory that episcopal authority then lapsed and had to be renewed by letters patent from Edward is probably sufficient explanation for the chancery style of P.C.C. citations for Edward's reign and the first few months of Mary's.[30]

Edward VI's visitation hardly seems to have affected the P.C.C. at all. If the general inhibition was ever served on the court, as seems likely, it was soon lifted, for there is no noticeable diminishing of probate business during the visitation. The visitors' duties still included probate and evidence of their activity in this sphere has survived for London, Kent, Essex, Middlesex, Norfolk, Suffolk and Cambridgeshire but not elsewhere.[31]

Under Mary there may have been some temporary anxiety as to the fate of the P.C.C.'s lay commissary, William Cooke. Happily Mary confirmed all previous acts of lay judges in the spiritual courts and absolved Cooke, permitting him to continue in office provided that he consulted a cleric when passing judgments involving spiritual censures.[32] The Acts of Court confirm that excommunications were passed for the rest of Cooke's life only in the presence of an advocate in orders, John Kennall.[33]

The autumn of 1559 saw the third and last royal visitation. As in 1547, the visitors within the dioceses of London, Norwich and Ely kept a register of their probate proceedings.[34] No register of testamentary business on the other circuits has survived.

The remainder of the century saw no further serious obstruction of the work of the P.C.C. by higher authority. Certainly in matters of mere probate it was unchallenged, although as has already been suggested, the growing power of the equity and common law courts in the related business of legacies and debt cannot be ignored even if it cannot be quantified. Parliamentary pressure for reform continued down to the end of the century, though with no major impact on the P.C.C. beyond a general increase in the alertness of its officials to the need for reform in certain points of practice.[35]

4

The calibre of the court officials was of paramount importance. Successive archbishops showed themselves willing to order reforms in their courts, but more often than not it was the practising officials who pointed out faults and suggested reforms. Clearly the court could scarcely afford to relax the standards of professionalism required of its officers. What sort of men were appointed to posts of responsibility and what were their various duties?

The officials of the court were not amateurs but highly skilled civil lawyers and notaries at the peak of their profession. The judge and advocates of the P.C.C. were doctors of the civil law who, from 1511, had to be members of the newly founded college of advocates in Paternoster Row before practising in the principal church courts. Theoretical law taught at the universities was no substitute for practical experience in the courts. New advocates therefore had to spend a year observing before they could practise, and the college provided a useful forum for the exchange of ideas and discussion of points of law. In 1567 Henry Harvey, dean of Arches, acquired property in Knightrider Street, some of which he sub-let to the college of advocates to provide more spacious accommodation for what became known as Doctors' Commons.[36]

For the office of judge (otherwise called Master, Keeper or Commissary) of the P.C.C. it was fitting that only men of considerable distinction should be chosen. Preferment was in the hands of the archbishop himself or, *sede vacante*, of the prior/dean and chapter of Canterbury, though appointments by the latter had to be confirmed by the incoming primate. Tenure was lifelong, provided that the incumbent conducted himself fittingly. Rarely was the P.C.C. let down by the archbishop's choice of candidate. Most of the commissaries had already achieved fame by their learning and legal prowess when they were appointed. They had begun with outstanding careers at one of the universities. John Cocks (1522–32 and 1543–7),[37] William Cooke (1547–58),[38] Walter Haddon (1559–71),[39] and William Drury (1571–89)[40] had gone on to become professors of civil law. Cocks and Haddon had become vice-chancellors of their universities. Cocks, Richard Gwent (1532–43),[41] and Cooke all held

the more senior post of dean of Arches before becoming judge of
the P.C.C., a post which they seem to have held concurrently.[42]

The heavy demands of Church and state on the time of senior
civilians meant that a system of deputies had evolved to keep the
church courts functioning even in the absence of their senior
officials. The commissary delegated his authority to one or more
advocates whose skills were compatible if not equal. At times the
system was essential. For example, the death of Cooke on 25
August 1558 initiated an unsettled period for the commissary-
ship. Pole – determined to restore a clerical régime – made the
strange choice of his chaplain, Maurice Clennock, as commissary.[43] Clennock was merely an LL.B. and not a member of
the College of Advocates. This was within the letter of the law
but cannot have been well received within the profession; it is
probably no coincidence that he abandoned the post in October.[44]
Clennock then delegated his responsibility to William Mowse,
an advocate, and Thomas Darbyshire, another civilian who was
archdeacon of Essex. Together they held the fort until 4 November when Pole repented of his former folly and granted the com-
missaryship to Henry Cole, dean of Arches.[45] But Cole was also
dean of St Paul's and too busy to attend the P.C.C. regularly.
The death of Mary and Pole on 17 November actually brought
the court to a temporary standstill. As usual, clerks prepared the
pages for forthcoming sessions in advance, but noted against
two sessions that there was no meeting *ob defectu commissarii*.[46]
Cole nevertheless did not resign, and the dean and chapter,
*sede vacante*, simply appointed as deputy the archdeacon of Canterbury, Nicholas Harpsfield.[47] It was not long before Elizabeth
intervened to order the dean and chapter to appoint, instead of
these firm adherents of the old religion, her loyal supporter and
close friend Walter Haddon, whom she had already made a
Master of Requests. At first they demurred on the grounds that
Haddon was a layman, but on 27 December the Council dispatched a letter citing the precedent of Cooke to show that such
an appointment was possible and noting that Haddon had expressed willingness to consult William Mowse or another cleric
when passing censures.[48] The dean and chapter yielded and from
the beginning of Hilary term 1559 Haddon was nominal commissary of the P.C.C. He may have been regularly present at

sessions for granting probate, but the Acts of the Court suggest that he was normally absent from the judicial sessions until Michaelmas, being presumably preoccupied with parliamentary and other business.[49] The bulk of the judicial work was carried by Mowse and Cole until June when their religious convictions finally drove them out, and thereafter by Kennall and Thomas Huyck.[50]

The commissary's function was to grant probate and administration; to act as judge in testamentary matters arising; and, after due deliberation, to pass sentence. A more controversial duty was to advise on the disposal of the goods of intestates, but, except for occasional registrations of decrees in Mary's reign,[51] there is never enough evidence for the historian to make a reasoned appraisal of this aspect of his work.

The function of the advocates in a P.C.C. cause is unclear.[52] One or two were certainly present during most contested causes, as is attested by the surviving bills of cost which include their fees.[53] Yet the majority of the routine business was in the hands of the proctors, who submitted the necessary documents. It may reasonably be assumed that advocates were the senior legal advisers for clients and proctors alike, assisting in the drafting of important legal documents, especially the sentence – at the reading of which they were present – and intervening on points of law with oral argument, and, where necessary, summing up. A comparison with barristers in the common law courts (with reservations) seems fair.[54] As doctors of civil law, they, like the commissary, were in considerable demand in other church courts. While the advocates deplored such practice, it appears that proctors sometimes handled cases on their own without the help of an advocate.

The principal session days of all the courts in London were fixed to enable judges, advocates and proctors to plan their busy timetables. The courts observed four terms, but session days were calculated according to the incidence of convenient saints' days. The saints' days chosen for the calendar were not themselves session days: the Court of Arches sat in the morning of the first day following the feast (unless this were a Sunday), with Admiralty in the afternoon, Audience the second morning, and the P.C.C. in the second afternoon. Certain days between the feasts were not accounted for in this way and were used by the courts to handle adjournments and catch up with registration. The P.C.C. regularly met outside the principal session days.[55]

Did the archbishop himself ever grant probate? Examples from the sixteenth century cast doubt upon such a theory: the commissary himself is sometimes called *dominus commissarius* so that the phrase *coram domino* could equally well mean 'before the commissary'. After Clennock's appointment, the register notes that the wills were proved *coram dicto magistro*, yet the entries immediately following the heading say *coram domino*. After the death of Pole some wills were proved *coram decano et capitulo Cant'*, although *apud London*, yet it cannot be assumed that the chapter was present. Therefore, we may justifiably treat with caution even the occasional statement that probate was granted *coram domino Cant' Archiepiscopo*. Probate was probably entirely delegated to the commissary and his deputies.[56]

As against the responsibilities of commissary and advocates, it is more difficult to assess the importance of the registrar or scribe of the acts. Recording the business of the P.C.C. was an onerous and important responsibility entrusted only to skilled notaries. The frequent holding of minor sessions of the court in the registrar's house suggests that he was *regarded* as second only in importance on the grounds that his name and rank appear frequently and boldly in the court records – what else would we expect from the official who was keeping the records?

The personal services of the registrar were dispensable. Deputies could and did carry much of the work. Thomas Argall (1534–63*d*.), was absent from many of the judicial sessions; he was also registrar of Petre's court, of the Court of First Fruits and Tenths, and of other special courts.[57] For many of his inevitable absences, William Walker deputised,[58] yet we cannot assess how much work Argall did for the court outside court hours, both by ordering the records and by disciplining and supervising the junior clerks and notaries of his department. One of the clerks (the judge's clerk or seal keeper) was accorded a fee for each document he sealed,[59] but the other clerks (an uncertain number) were paid from the proceeds of the registrar's own office. From 1534 until 1588 the office of registrar was held in Argall's family;

he was succeeded by his son Lawrence (1563–84) who in his turn was succeeded by Richard Argall.

The responsibilities of the proctors are easier to catalogue. A person due to appear to prove a will or seek administration or to be party to a cause could appoint a proctor in his stead.[60] An analysis of proxies on the complete file for 1541 shows that, while the skilled body of notaries who had been admitted as proctors of the Court of Arches took the great majority of proctorial business in the P.C.C., other persons occasionally appeared in this capacity – regional notaries public; members of the clients' families; persons of unspecified status. The Arches proctors, therefore, did not have the monopoly of business in the P.C.C. which they had in both Arches and Audience despite parliamentary protests at their closed shop. Nevertheless, it is probable that other persons appeared only in strictly routine business: in contested causes the parties would surely require the skilled services of an Arches proctor.[61] Parker's Statutes of 1573 ordered the P.C.C. to come into line with the other courts, and debarred non-Arches proctors from practising therein.[62]

To enlist the aid of a proctor the client applied to an archdeacon for a sealed written instrument or 'proxy' naming the proctor he wished to appoint or several of the notaries currently practising in the P.C.C. The proxy was transmitted to the court and one of the named proctors would undertake to perform the business, first appearing before the registrar to record his proxy (*constitutio*). If he later became too involved with other work, he might appoint a substitute (*substitutio*). If the client were not satisfied with his services he might withdraw the proxy (*revocatio*). Sessions of the P.C.C. for this type of business were quite informal, sometimes being held in the registrar's house or office. The proctors themselves probably had a rota to allocate business equitably and presumably had an office in or near the advocates' commons.

Like the apparitors, the proctors incurred some odium for their capacity to begin proceedings by entering *caveats* and petitioning the judge, on behalf of their clients, to cite an opposing party to appear before the court. The Supplication of 1532 maintained that the archdeacons did not scrutinise the applications for proxies.[63] Yet a proctor could only instigate proceedings on behalf of a client and, while litigation was some-times contrived by a party to put his adversary to trouble and expense, it must be said that this happened regularly in all courts of law and was not specific to the church courts.

There was some truth in the parliamentary claim that the proctors wanted a closed shop. The proctors of Arches made repeated attempts to get archbishops to restrict their numbers to ten to ensure all a reasonable living. Archbishop Winchelsea suggested ten as an optimum in 1295 but, despite Warham and Cranmer's confirmation of his order, it is doubtful whether the number ever fell so low.[64] The archbishops did not oust existing proctors but ruled that no more should be appointed until numbers had fallen. There were parliamentary protests that such a restriction was not in the public interest on the grounds that ten proctors were insufficient to handle speedily all the available business; this would cause vexatious and expensive delays.[65] In 1541, 14 proctors were practising and both Cranmer and his successors turned a blind eye to growing numbers, perhaps in the light of parliamentary pressure.[66] When Whitgift reviewed the situation in 1587 there were 25.[67] Despite an inflation in the amount of business, Whitgift sought to restrict numbers to 15. He devised a scheme whereby existing proctors should specialize in particular courts, with vacancies in the 15 senior posts being filled from among the junior proctors until the desired number of 15 proctors *in toto* was reached. At this point new recruits would be admitted. It is doubtful whether the target was ever reached.[68]

In court the proctor defended the interests of his client. He prepared the necessary documentation and advised his client on the wording of allegations and answers; he was also allowed to petition the judge to act in a particular way or to make counter-representations to similar petitions put by the opposing proctor.

The duties of the respective court officials were the source of much friction within the P.C.C. Proctors, registrar and deputy registrars were all notaries public with wide experience in drafting and copying documents. In the 1580s Lawrence Argall took strong exception to encroachments by the proctors on the registrar's duties, particularly in the matter of engrossing wills and inventories.[69] His argument was based upon precedent and dictated less by concern for income than for the rightful work-

load of the two departments. He reasonably asserted that, whereas proctors and advocates had the right to draw up documents
necessitated by the initiation of causes and to represent their
clients, it was the registrar's right to 'write all such things as are
enacted and to be sealed with the Seal of the Office, and whereto
his hand or consignation is required'.

But rivalries and professional jealousies did not always dominate the scene. There were often strong family ties between the
officers and signs of mutual respect. Christopher Middleton,
a proctor making his will in 1527, appointed as his executors
two advocates, William Middleton his cousin and John Tregonwell his son-in-law, and left his son Stephen in the custody of
another advocate, Dr Incent.[70] In 1597, Dr William Lewin, the
commissary, entrusted the arrangements for his funeral to his
friend John Law, 'actuary' of the P.C.C. Lewin admitted to
being something of a task-master. After bequeathing to the
advocates £10 for a dinner in his memory and the purchase of
some plate, and to the registrars and proctors £5, he added:
'I do heartily pray the advocates and proctors of the Arches that
if in the execution of mine office I have seemed somewhat strict
unto them, that they impute it to the desire I had that causes
might proceed in a just, orderly and speedy course'.[71] Thomas
Argall left money to his colleagues for a funeral breakfast. To a
less lavish extent the proctors also followed this custom.[72]

Such evidence confirms that the world of the civil law courts
was that of a small, close-knit élite, bound together by professional
and family ties. Officers inter-married and offices were often held
in the family for generations.[73] Was this, or the restriction of
numbers, detrimental to the public interest? It may be significant that we never find advocates or proctors complaining of
over-work, and they would surely not petition for a reduction in
their numbers if they felt unable to handle existing business.

Yet it was not the skilled professionals just considered who
incurred the greatest public odium, but rather the apparitors.
They came face to face with the public as the agents of communication between the P.C.C. and the province at large. They
were relatively few but, as they were concerned solely with
testamentary business, they covered a wide geographical area,
making themselves known to the diocesans and, to some extent,

co-operating with local apparitors. It was their responsibility to see that applications for probate and administration were made, in appropriate cases, to the P.C.C. within a reasonable time of death; to do this they had to have some means of ascertaining both who had died and whether the goods left would warrant P.C.C. intervention. If such application were not made, it was they who had to report to the judge and obtain citations against the next of kin or principal creditors of the deceased, which suggests that apparitors were the main instigators of *ex officio* proceedings in the court – a fact not likely to enhance their popularity. They had to deliver citations and excommunications personally. They had to sequestrate the goods of those dying intestate (within the P.C.C. jurisdiction) and often helped to appraise the goods. The ordinaries probably saw them as spies of the court, for it was their responsibility to report suspected infringements of the prerogative by lesser jurisdictions. Apparitors were empowered to bring in wills to save the executor a trip to London on payment of a fee for securing probate. Both this fee and the apparitor's travelling expenses were recoverable from the executor; the costs of delivering citations were chargeable to the persons cited. By the early seventeenth century the registrar kept a seal book of citations issued, as a check on the accounts presented by the apparitors every term. A further precaution against abuse was the oath and bond demanded from apparitors.[74]

Under Wolsey and Warham the province was divided into 27 areas, each of which had one or two P.C.C. apparitors.[75] The territories covered varied in size and status, but the resulting distribution averaged out at effectively one apparitor per county, although one appointment only was recorded for Wales and one only for Exeter diocese. There were some 42 posts, including one for Calais. The appointees were usually described as *litteratus*; the fact that several were styled gentleman or even esquire suggests that this was not regarded as a menial occupation. After Wolsey's demise the same distribution of apparitors appears to have been necessary for the work of the P.C.C. alone. An analysis of the staff of the P.C.C. towards the end of the century records one general apparitor, the most senior, and under him 'many apparitors in every shire of the province'.[76]

5

In considering attacks from laymen upon the church courts historians have neglected to remark that in the face of Puritan attacks under Grindal and Whitgift the archbishops invited the opinions of ordinaries and other ecclesiastical judges in London and the provinces as to what still needed reform. Grindal's projected reforms did not materialize,[77] but Whitgift inherited many of the suggestions and incorporated some of them in his statutes for the central courts of the southern province in 1587.[78] Annexed to these was a set of regulations specifically designed for the P.C.C. These established no new principles, merely serving to pinpoint those weak points in the system where the judges felt that justice was not always being done. Administrations were not to be granted until at least 14 days after death, in order to give relatives time to make sure that there was no will among the effects of the deceased. If a caveat were entered, a grant of administration was not to be passed to the original party until the objections had been thoroughly investigated. An invalid administration had to be formally revoked before a fresh admin- istration could be granted. The orders urged the P.C.C. not to rush to an instant settlement of probate but rather to be sure that the parties involved had a fair deal. Speed, so often regarded by outsiders as the main criterion of efficiency, was not always compatible with justice.

Discussions and criticisms of the church courts in both Parlia- ment and Convocation provoked the crown to commission Whitgift in 1594 to conduct a thorough survey of ecclesiastical jurisdiction.[79] The resulting memoranda from the bishops reflect a growing anxiety even outside the P.C.C. at the tendency to grant probate or administration too soon.[80]

Some of the proposed reforms concerned matters which could not easily be regulated by statutes, and were best left either to the discretion of individual officers or to be discussed in Doctors' Commons before gradual implementation. It was important to retain a certain amount of discretionary power for the judge in testamentary matters – for example, over what constituted a valid will; too rigid a definition of the way it must be written, the number of witnesses and so forth, would invalidate many a document which evidently expressed the last, sincere wishes of the deceased. In pondering the answers received from his ordinaries, therefore, Whitgift was careful not to issue restrictive orders on the minutiae of court procedure, although several reforms were promulgated in the convocation of 1597, most notably the 'table of fees'.[81] Thereafter Whitgift addressed successive letters to his diocesans urging them to implement the reforms in their dioceses.[82] It was 1604, however, before the results of Whitgift's inquiry were fully codified. The canons demanded that judges ensure that wills came within their jurisdiction before proceeding to grant probate;[83] executors were to be reimbursed for unnecessary expenditure incurred by a resulting dispute between jurisdictions. Penalties for abuse of practice by court officials were laid down. A regulation of 1587 that no proctor might undertake a case without advice of an advocate was reiterated. The table of fees of 1597 was to be implemented.

6

It is difficult to analyse the levying and control of fees and the payment of officials in the P.C.C. during the course of the century because all the principal documentation recording fees actually levied has perished.[84] The fees laid down in the Probate Act of 1529 remained operative for the rest of the century and are repeatedly cited as the guiding authority in the memoranda submitted to Whitgift.

This Act proposed a new scale of fees for probate and administration in proportion to the value of the estate, fixing the maximum sum which the judge and registrar could levy.[85] This may have appeased some of the anti-clerical M.P.s but there were several major loopholes in the Act which weakened its practical impact, and it made no mention of fees for litigation. The Act's failure to spell out exactly what was covered by the probate fee left registrars a good deal of discretion. If his fee was only for actual registration, then he could presumably charge extra for a parchment exemplification of the will, the wax for sealing it, or the certificate of probate. Dealing with the most valuable estates, the Act accorded the registrar discretion to charge a flat rate for registration or a variable sum depending

on the length of the document. The same charges were author-
ized for copying wills as for registering them. Registrars, therefore, had ample opportunity to raise the same money as before
the Act while adhering to the letter of the law.

By the later seventeenth century executors were being urged
to provide a parchment exemplification of the will drawn up by
a notary public as well as the original will. If this practice (as is
suggested by the 1529 table of fees and Lawrence Argall's
memoranda of 1580) was current in the sixteenth century,
expense to the executor was increased.[86] The court's rights in
this matter were uncertain. An important judgment was passed
in Common Pleas in Michaelmas term, 6 James I.[87] The commissary of the archdeacon of Huntingdon had been charged
with extortion for exacting a fee for making an engrossment of a
will to which he attached the grant of probate. The court ruled
that the certificate of probate could be attached to either the
original will or a parchment exemplification. The fee for the
certificate could only be charged once, and a judge could not
compel an executor to have an exemplification made for this
purpose. However, if the executor requested that an exemplification be made or if he accepted the court's recommendation
that this be done, he was responsible for the costs. Sixteenth-
century practice is obscure because most executors retained the
original wills; by the seventeenth century the originals were
remaining with the court and the executors were retaining an
exemplification with attached certificate of probate.

A register of fees for the diocese of Rochester shows that the
1529 table was adopted there,[88] although it appears that the
apparitor was paid out of the judge's fee;[89] that the registrar
made a supplementary charge of 1s. for every will registered;
that wax cost 1d. and every administration bond 1s.; and that
apparitors received an additional 1s. for every executor or
administrator warned to appear. The actual cost for a simple
probate or administration, then, could far outstrip the set
probate fee.

It seems probable that in the 1520s a P.C.C. apparitor received 1s. 8d. for bringing in a will.[90] The Elizabethan fee
was probably 1s. with 2d. a mile permitted for travelling expenses
when serving citations and excommunications.

Litigation costs varied considerably according to the complexity of the case, but they were relatively more expensive in the P.C.C. than in the lesser jurisdictions, both on account of the seniority of the officials to be paid and the distances to be covered by both parties and apparitors alike. Nevertheless, the surviving evidence suggests that P.C.C. court fees remained static throughout the century. Since Dr Marchant has inferred the same for the northern province, this may have been generally true of the church courts.[91] There was evidently no attempt to keep pace with inflation by raising fees – in real terms the official's income probably fell unless he found new fees to levy.

Even from the few surviving bills of costs a good deal of information on the cost of litigation can be gleaned.[92] Table 2 abstracts a simple bill produced at the end of a fairly modest cause in 1548. Expenses of this kind were at best annoying and at worst positively damaging to the parties concerned, though the judge did not necessarily allow all that was asked. Proctors and advocates received a termly fee for each case they undertook.[93] For proctors this was 3s. 4d. and for advocates 6s. 8d., 10s. or 13s. 4d. depending upon the extent of the work involved. The judge received a fee for each major decision taken in the form of a decree, order or sentence, and also for hearing or reading the examination of witnesses. Practically all the other costs were clerical. In most causes the final sentence was by far the most expensive item. The basic costs outlined in the table, of course, could be greatly swollen if there were complications, such as the need to examine witnesses in the provinces. When the regional commissioners submitted their expenses the tally might reach £6 13s. 4d.

Did the officials exact higher fees than were warranted? In his defence of the registrar's office in the 1580s, Lawrence Argall proudly boasted that there had never, to his knowledge, been any complaint of extortion laid against the registrar and his clerks. He added that any profiteering was more likely to be perpetrated by the proctors.

Whitgift's table of fees of 1597 almost certainly did not apply to the central courts. It was nothing like as comprehensive as the Elizabethan P.C.C. fee list and therefore could not have served as a model for it. It is probable that it was designed solely for the lesser jurisdictions. Recently it has been doubted whether it was ever regularly enforced in view of the continuing criticisms of the rapaciousness of the church courts. Even if the P.C.C. was not subject to this control, it is clear that its fees, though high, were sufficiently inflexible to prevent officials exacting much more than the amount laid down. All had to be accounted for in the bill of costs and at this stage the proctors were watching the registrars; the registrars the proctors; and the judge all of them to guard against charging of excessive fees. If unreasonable profits were made from under-the-counter payments or bribes, they have not come to light so far.

A study of the amount of business coming before the P.C.C. reveals that, despite inflation, the officials of the court were probably maintaining their real level of income. For a while in the 1540s and 1550s the registrar's clerks were in the habit of counting the number of probates granted per month, and also of providing occasional yearly totals.

*Approximate yearly totals, 1549–59*

| 1549 | 320 | 1553 | 310 | 1557 | 630   |
|------|-----|------|-----|------|-------|
| 1550 | 425 | 1554 | 300 | 1558 | 935   |
| 1551 | 520 | 1555 | 180 | 1559 | 1,090 |
| 1552 | 410 | 1556 | 330 |      |       |

*Lawrence Argall's totals for 1575–80*

| 1575 | 586 | 1577 | 603 | 1579 | 594 |
|------|-----|------|-----|------|-----|
| 1576 | 616 | 1578 | 612 | 1580 | 577 |

The last years of the 1550s were years of epidemic and this probably explains the huge increase in P.C.C. business at that time – an increase which put the court under severe pressure but also meant that it earned considerable revenue. During the later period the yearly average of business was far greater than in the early 1550s. This increase probably reflects the fact that inflation was often raising the level of a man's debts above the £5 *bona notabilia* level and bringing his will before the P.C.C.[94]

Figures for administrations are more rough and ready, but a quick count, using as a guide the indexes to the first Administration Act books, beginning at the end of 1559, suggests a yearly average of about 200 in the 1560s, 300 in the 1570s and almost 400 in the 1580s. The court, therefore, was never short of business, and as the number of probates and administrations increased so did the number of contested causes, all of which brought in yet more revenue. Despite (or perhaps because of) the impact of inflation, therefore, it is unlikely that the livelihood of the officers of the court was seriously threatened, even taking into account the pegging of the probate fees in 1529.

As one of the central courts Christian, the Prerogative Court of Canterbury received its full share of the continual contemporary criticism being levelled at the Church during the sixteenth century. Did the court change significantly as a result? It has been shown that the professional officials of the P.C.C. were continuously aware of the need for reform and willing to implement sensible proposals. No radical changes resulted, but there was a general tightening up of procedure. Although they were interested in their own professional position and livelihood, the officials also showed due concern for the public interest – which sometimes led them to resist external pressures to speed up the administration of probate within the court. On the whole the leading officials believed a fair application of the law to be more important than speed. Although the exercise of Canterbury's prerogative in the matter of probate jurisdiction had been contested in the early years of the century, the danger in which the court lay was soon removed with the necessity for both archbishops and bishops to present a united front in the face of parliamentary attack. Warham's plea that the central courts provided a livelihood for state servants seems to have quashed the mainstream of opposition to the actual existence of the court. Later criticisms were levelled rather at the functioning of the courts and the corruption of their officials, but there is no reason to suppose that the church courts were any worse than their secular counterparts in this respect.

Inflation would have seriously undermined the income earned by officials of the court, given the fixed nature of fees, had not the business coming before the court so increased. As it was, so many more men were dying with property or debts in a second county worth more than £5 that the P.C.C. was under greater pressure of work than ever before – a factor which prevented the further reduction of officials proposed by successive arch-bishops!

During the course of the century, therefore, the existence and role of the probate court had been accepted. Indeed the importance of its role escalated during the period of inflation. In the face of contemporary criticism, and because of a genuine desire for justice and high professional standards, the court inaugurated minor reforms (generally of a tightening-up of procedure) and demanded that its officials be honest. Yet probate was granted in 1600 in much the same way and by the same court as in 1500. The transference of authority signalled continuity rather than change. The willingness of the court to implement modest reforms and minor procedural adjustments throughout the period just considered helped to postpone the real day of reckoning for the church courts well into the next century, and to maintain stability and continuity amid the clamour for more radical change.

Table 1    Probate fees according to the statute of 1529

| | Value of estate | Judge's fee | Registrar's fee |
|---|---|---|---|
| Probate | up to £5 | nil | 6d. |
| | £5 to £40 | 2s. 6d. | 1s. 0d. |
| | over £40 | 2s. 6d. | 2s. 6d. or 1d. per 10 lines |
| Administration | up to £5 | nil | 6d.* |
| | £5 to £40 | 2s. 6d. | 6d.* |
| | over £40 | not mentioned | not mentioned |

* for the certificate of administration

Table 2    Cowper v. Cowper, Bill of Costs, 1547–8

In a cause concerning the alleged will of Richard Cowper, deceased. The expenses of John Cowper, instigator of the cause

*Michaelmas Term 1547*

| | | |
|---|---:|---:|
| Proctor's fee | 3s. | 4d. |
| Proxy (sealed) | 1s. | 4d. |
| Copy of an alleged will | 1s. | 8d. |
| Acts of court | | 8d. |
| Interlocutory decree citing another person to appear | 2s. | 0d. |
| Execution of the decree | | 8d. |
| Certificate of execution of the decree (sealed) | 1s. | 4d. |
| Advocate's fee | 6s. | 8d. |
| | 17s. | 8d. |

*Hilary Term 1548*

| | | |
|---|---:|---:|
| Proctor's fee | 3s. | 4d. |
| Advocate's fee | 6s. | 8d. |
| Drafting of sentence | 3s. | 4d. |
| Acts of court | 1s. | 0d. |
| Promulgation of sentence | 26s. | 8d. |
| Beadle's fee | 1s. | 0d. |
| Further interlocutory decree to show cause why sentence may not be passed | 2s. | 0d. |
| Execution of the decree | | 8d. |
| Certificate of execution of the decree (sealed) | 1s. | 4d. |
| | 46s. | 0d. |

# 9

## Church courts and the Reformation in the diocese of Chichester, 1500–58

### Stephen Lander

It was largely through visitations and the regular sessions of his courts that a bishop sought to maintain the standards of the clergy and the religious life of his diocese, and to settle disputes over ecclesiastical matters. The state had also assigned to the Church the right of providing wills and of administering the goods of those who died intestate. Consequently, the spiritual welfare of a diocese depended to a large extent upon the efficiency and authority of its church courts, especially those of the bishop. It has long been known that these courts were left constitutionally untouched by the Reformation, and it has even been suggested that they actually had their jurisdiction strengthened by the legislation of the time of Henry VIII. It is the argument of this article, however, albeit on the basis of the evidence for one diocese, that the courts were undergoing reform in the last decades before the break with Rome, but that officially-inspired attacks upon them during the 1530s undermined their authority permanently.

In the diocese of Chichester, as in nearly every other diocese, the multiplicity and complexity of jurisdictions had come during the later Middle Ages to present a limitation upon the bishop's authority. In the city of Chichester, for example, archbishop, bishop and dean exercised ecclesiastical as well as temporal jurisdiction, while across the bishop's park, the diocesan of Exeter had jurisdiction over the royal college at Bosham.[1] It is hardly surprising that most bishops of Chichester, like other diocesans whose authority in their cathedral cities was limited, chose normally to reside at one of their episcopal manors outside the city.[2]

At the end of the fifteenth century there were as many as nine different ecclesiastical courts at work in the county of Sussex, which, apart from peculiar jurisdictions, was at that date very nearly coterminous with the diocese of Chichester. Of the diocesan courts, the most important was the consistory court of the bishop. This court, which usually sat in the cathedral, dealt with the whole range of ecclesiastical jurisdiction.[3] Theoretically it acted for the whole diocese, but the majority of its cases were from the archdeaconry of Chichester. Like the consistory courts at Ely, it had developed a wider scope than consistory courts in a number of larger dioceses which only dealt with instance cases.[4] Probably because the office of commissary at Chichester was of comparatively late development, its bishops do not seem to have been regularly active in the correction of offenders, and the business arising from its small number of parishes was usually light.[5]

In the two archdeaconries of Chichester and Lewes, the bishop's commissaries and the two archdeacons shared jurisdictional rights, and both commissaries made regular trips away from the city, usually to the ruridecanal churches, to hold courts.[6] Commissaries had probably first been appointed at Chichester as elsewhere, to contest the monopoly of first instance jurisdiction claimed by archdeacons, and their activities had made a settlement of archidiaconal and episcopal rights essential.[7] It is not clear whether the agreement that had been reached at Chichester before the end of the fifteenth century had come about as the result of a dispute, like those between the archdeacons of Ely and Lincoln and their bishops, but it strongly favoured the bishop.[8] Archdeacons were unable to act in any case which involved the goods of those who died intestate, they could not deprive priests of their benefices, and were unable to decide matrimonial, incest or heresy cases, or those arising on any of the bishop's 13 Sussex manors.[9] In those cases that were not specifically reserved to the bishop, however, the archdeacons and commissaries exercised concurrent jurisdiction with the

result that confusion and competition were likely. The fact that
the settlement reached between the archdeacon of Chichester
and the bishop was still thought worthy of note as late as 1481,
moreover, probably shows that there was still rivalry between
the two at that date. In curtailing archidiaconal rights which
represented a limitation upon his own, therefore, Robert Sherburne, the last pre-Reformation bishop of Chichester, was to
have a profound effect upon the spiritual administration of his
diocese.

The peculiar jurisdictions within the see also presented
limitations to episcopal authority, and were often particularly
badly administered. In the city of Chichester, the dean exercised
ordinary jurisdiction over the Close, all the parishes of the city,
except All Saints in the Pallent, and over the parishes of Fish-
bourne and Rumboldswyke in the suburbs. This peculiar was
only subject to episcopal control during triennial visitation and
during a vacancy of the deanery, the usual administration of its
parishes being exercised by the dean or his official in a peculiar
court. It is known that such a court, dealing with all types of
cases from the city, was active during the last 25 years of the
fifteenth century. In the archdeaconry of Chichester, archiepiscopal manors formed the peculiar of Pagham and Tarring,
and in the archdeaconry of Lewes, the exempt deanery of South
Malling. Exercise of ordinary jurisdiction over these two deaneries belonged to their dean or his commissary and was subject
to the archbishop of Canterbury as diocesan during a vacancy
and not to the bishops of Chichester.[10]

Finally, of monastic exemptions from episcopal jurisdiction,
that claimed by Battle Abbey seems to have been a source of
extended conflict with the see, not the least because it gave the
priest who served the parish of Battle, called the dean, jurisdiction over his parish. He had the right, which was retained
until the nineteenth century, to decide all cases, except for
matrimonial disputes which were reserved to the bishop, who
otherwise could only correct offenders from the parish of Battle
if the dean failed to do so.[11]

The limitations placed upon the bishop's authority by this
variety of jurisdictions are clear. To bring a persistent offender
to justice, which was never an easy task with the poor roads over

the South Downs cutting off the city of Chichester and the consistory court from most of the diocese, was rendered harder still, since the culprit could remove himself from the bishop's jurisdiction to escape the attentions of his apparitors. If he lived in the Selsey peninsula, for example, he was within easy reach of the diocese of Winchester, of the dean of Chichester's peculiar, and of the exempt deanery at Pagham. Rivalry between courts, moreover, could be dangerous to the spiritual welfare of the parishes, since where there was competition for business, judges and proctors tended to treat instance cases far more seriously than disciplinary cases, because the former brought in far higher fees. The official of the archdeacon of Canterbury, for example, only began to ferret out offenders when instance business declined sharply after 1500.[12] In the diocese of Chichester during the first years of the century the dean's peculiar court, the archdeaconry of Chichester commissary court, and the consistory court all spent a disproportionate amount of time in dealing with instance cases. Between September 1506 and September 1507, in fact, the last two courts tried nearly four times as many instance as office cases, and this was at a time when the former invariably took at least three months to complete, and the latter seldom more than two or three weeks.[13] What this meant in practice is only too clear. Clerical incontinence appears to have been quite a serious problem at this date with some 15 per cent of parishes in the archdeaconry troubled by it, but the courts spent little time in dealing with offenders, did not press charges against some, and treated the majority of those who were convicted with great leniency. In one notorious case the judge actually respited the penance of an incumbent who had confessed fornication with one of his parishioners. Only when there were aggravating circumstances were offending priests removed from the churches they had profaned by their conduct.[14]

It is not known how active the archdeacons' courts were at the turn of the century in this diocese but in some areas such courts were particularly inefficient at correcting offenders. This may have been because archdeacons were even more likely to be absent from supervising their courts than a bishop was from his, and their officials were often of a lower calibre. The official of the archdeacon of Chester, whose principal held a prebend at

Lichfield and usually resided there, for example, seems to have been particularly ineffective, and was regarded with contempt in his archdeaconry. Since most archdeacons of Chichester and Lewes were also absentees, the situation may well have been little better in Sussex. However, it would be dangerous to argue too much from this evidence as in other areas archdeacons' courts may have been inactive where the bishop's consistory was active and *vice versa*.

It seems likely, therefore, that any attempts at reform in the diocese of Chichester at a parochial level which were to be carried out through visitations and the regular sessions of the courts would have been seriously handicapped had Sherburne not gone some way towards eliminating the diversity of jurisdictions in his diocese, and coming to terms with those that remained. His reforms were chiefly concerned with the jurisdictional rights of the two archdeacons. No proceedings have survived for either of their courts, but a few references show that the archdeacon of Chichester or his official, at least, was still active judicially during the vacancy following the translation of Bishop Fitzjames to London in June 1506.[15] Moreover, a comparison of episcopal income from probate fees in 1506–8 with the very much larger sums received during the 1520s, when it is known that virtually all probate was granted by episcopal officers, leads to the inescapable conclusion that both archdeacons had ordinary rights as late as 1508.[16] Sherburne was not slow in realizing that the concurrent jurisdiction of archdeacon and commissary no longer fulfilled a useful purpose, and, on the collation of his former receiver general, William Norbery, to the archdeaconry of Chichester in April 1512, he appointed him commissary for that archdeaconry, thus in effect amalgamating the two jurisdictions. A similar process was in operation at this time in a number of other dioceses, such as Lincoln, where, perhaps significantly, Sherburne had been an archdeacon.[17]

This partial reorganization of the courts in the archdeaconry of Chichester continued in force until October 1518 when Sherburne brought a number of new men into the diocese to reform and revitalize his spiritual administration. Pre-eminent amongst these new officers were John Worthial, William Fleshmonger and John Stilman, who were to be at the centre of the bishop's administration at Chichester throughout the remainder of Sherburne's episcopate and beyond. Worthial, a B.Cn.L. in 1508, was principal of New Inn Hall at Oxford from 1510 to 1520, and proceeded to his doctorate in 1525. He appears to have started his career as an ecclesiastical lawyer in the Lincoln courts, being a proctor in the audience court of Bishop Atwater in 1517. It may have been on the recommendation of Atwater, whom Sherburne much respected, or because of his standing at Oxford that the bishop chose to bring him to Chichester, but he eventually monopolized the posts of commissary general, official principal and chancellor, and proved a trustworthy and industrious servant who reaped his reward in livings from a grateful bishop. Surviving letters show just how important he was thought by contemporaries to be in the diocesan administration.[18]

William Fleshmonger, who became dean of Chichester in 1518 and was Sherburne's chancellor and official principal until the mid-1520s, was also from the diocese of Lincoln. A doctor of civil and canon law by 1514 and a member of Doctors' Commons by 1522, he was, like Sherburne, a Wykehamist, and it is probable that he came to the bishop's notice through New College where he had been a fellow. That Sherburne was eager to have him as dean may be indicated by the fact that the previous incumbent, Thomas Larke, resigned on the large pension of £42 to make way for him. Sherburne's hopes were justified, for the fruitful co-operation that followed between them stands out in comparison with the troubled history of relations between the Chichester chapter and see, and Fleshmonger provided added authority to Worthial's pronouncements in the consistory court during the latter's first years as an ecclesiastical judge.[19]

John Stilman, a public notary, was from the diocese of Bath and Wells, a married man with a family like others of his profession. He was active as both episcopal and capitular registrar by August 1518, and, until his death or retirement in 1543, was a crucial figure in the administration of the cathedral and diocese. With the judge of an ecclesiastical court, the registrar was the most important official both in the regular sessions of the courts and at visitation. He was responsible for issuing citations, for taking depositions, recording visitation presentments and collecting evidence, for keeping a note of the proceedings of the courts and for registering wills, for compiling and preserving the records of the bishop's administration, and for ensuring that the judge's instructions and orders were obeyed.[20] Stilman's industry is much in evidence in the records that survive. He made fresh copies of both of Sherburne's registers, in which he included records of four episcopal visitations, a complete list of subsidy exemptions, and a large collection of vicarage ordinations and similar documents. He sat in the commissary court for the archdeaconry of Chichester as well as the consistory court for over 20 years, took part in all the episcopal and probably all the Chichester archidiaconal visitations in this period as well, and in an elegant book hand transcribed copies of episcopal statutes.[21] After his death, the diocese had to wait until the 1570s before it had another registrar who approached his experience and industry, and whose work was of the same quality.

The arrival of Worthial, Fleshmonger and Stilman, and of a number of less important officials such as the proctors Richard Gybon, William Bolton, William Frende, Laurence Woodcock and William Draper, and the appointment of larger numbers of apparitors, shows that Sherburne made a thorough reorganization of his spiritual administration at this time.[22] These men provided him with the tools to carry out a more far-reaching reform of the courts than had previously been possible. No compositions or commissions survive to bear witness to the changes that took place, although it is reasonably clear what happened. Both archdeacons were induced to surrender all of their jurisdictional rights, except those exercised summarily at visitation, in return for a proportion of the fees accruing to the episcopal courts.[23] The ground had been well prepared for such a change in the archdeaconry of Chichester with Norbery as commissary and archdeacon, and it seems probable that a similar arrangement had been made under Mr Oliver Pole, the archdeacon of Lewes, who was for a time the bishop's chancellor.[24] It is not known what proportion of fees was reserved to the archdeacons, although it seems from the evidence about probate fees that they struck a good bargain, sometimes receiving as much as half of the sums collected.[25]

Although the most important union of jurisdictions begun at this time, this was not the only one. Probably from as early as

Fleshmonger's election as dean in 1518, although certainly from 1520, jurisdiction over the dean's peculiar was exercised through the consistory court.[26] This was not the result of a formal composition, but of fortuitous appointments, for Sherburne appears to have appointed Worthial to preside in the consistory court at the time, as Fleshmonger was using him to act as his official.[27] Deans had before, like Fleshmonger, acted as episcopal officers, but it had not led to a union of their respective jurisdictions.[28] That it did in this case is a clear indication of the trust between Fleshmonger and Sherburne, a trust that was advantageous to both. It brought the bishop control over the city which was the centre of his diocese, and increased the power and prestige of his consistory court on the one hand, while on the other it brought greater authority to bear upon offenders in the peculiar than the dean alone could muster. That it was a success is evident from the fact that it survived, for a time, both Sherburne's resignation in 1536, and Fleshmonger's death in 1541.[29]

This period saw one further jurisdictional development, although it was one that could be paralleled in other dioceses. It became the practice of the dean of Pagham and Tarring to appoint a proctor of the consistory court at Chichester to sit in his peculiar court in the church of All Saints, Chichester.[30] This appears to have happened for the first time, perhaps significantly, while Thomas Milling was dean. Like Sherburne and a number of the proctors whom he appointed as commissaries, he had been at New College, and it is probable that he was known to Sherburne before he was collated to the deanery in August 1513. Such an arrangement had advantages for both of them. The dean could in this way attract to his court a better-trained and more experienced canon lawyer than might otherwise have been possible, for the evidence shows that when a proctor was not acting, Milling had to depend on such humble figures as Simon Oxley, the vicar of Tarring, or the notoriously immoral Alexander Shawe, vicar of Pagham. On the other hand, the bishop through his officers was able to bring influence to bear upon the peculiar jurisdiction. This was especially true, when, for a time, Worthial himself acted as commissary for Milling.[31]

These jurisdictional changes and reforms were accompanied

by a remarkable improvement in the efficiency and effectiveness of the episcopal courts, in the archdeaconry of Chichester at least. The consistory court which had sat on only 19 court days in 1507, sat on 36 in 1520, and 45 in 1524, and, until the number of sessions declined again during Sherburne's last years at Chichester, this increase was accompanied by a growth in business before the courts.[32] The authorities were able to speed their dispatch of probate and instance business, and, most importantly for the spiritual life of the diocese, to deal in greater numbers with those, whether cleric or lay, who offended against the Church's teachings. The evidence shows that it was in this last field that Sherburne's reforms had the most significant results, and also where the efficiency of his courts stands in sharpest contrast with the situation under the Reformation bishops who were his successors at Chichester.

Between September 1506 and September 1507, the consistory and archdeaconry of Chichester commissary courts had dealt with 220 instance cases, but only 65 office cases, while in the year 1520, soon after the jurisdictional changes, they dealt with a very similar number of instance cases, 227, but with as many as 195 office cases.[33] This remarkable increase in activity, which was maintained during the 1520s, was, in part, caused by the union of jurisdictions which brought cases formerly heard by the archdeacon to the episcopal courts, but it was also undoubtedly the result of new and extensive attacks on abuses that were made by Bishop Sherburne and his officers through the courts.[34] They were active in many fields, but most noticeably in attempts to improve the repair of church fabric and the performance of the clergy in the parishes. During 1507, the authorities in the archdeaconry of Chichester had only brought six cases against those responsible for disrepair of church fabric, but in 1520, Sherburne's officers brought 71 such cases, and this was at a time when the problem of dilapidations was less serious than previously, if the evidence of visitation *comperta* is to be believed.[35] Moreover, during 1520 the authorities were apparently successful at getting repairs carried out, and fragmentary evidence shows that they continued to lavish attention on the problem until the early years of the Reformation Parliament.[36] They were also busy correcting beneficed clergy who were absent from their livings without licence. In February 1521, a diocesan official was sent to London to report on the behaviour of a Chichester priest who was thought to be disporting himself there, and he reported to Worthial that the priest was 'fussing and croaking in London', and only 'serveth his benefice by a canon'. By the time his parish was visited in September of that year, he had been forced to reside.[37] Others who were absent without leave were treated severely. John Williamson, the vicar of Binsted, was threatened with deprivation if he did not appear at his benefice within five days, the vicars of Houghton and Amberley were threatened in their absence with large fines, and the eight incumbents who were found to be absent without licence at the episcopal visitation of 1521 had the fruits of their livings sequestered. A similar severity, which had not been shown hitherto, was accorded to incontinent priests, even though clerical incontinence was also less of a problem than previously.[38]

These were not the only fields in which the courts were used extensively and successfully under Sherburne. They were also used, to an extent hitherto unknown, to coerce inefficient monastic heads, for example; and in a concerted effort to resist attempts by parishioners to withhold from their parish church or priest what they owed them in tithes, offerings, or church dues.[39] Furthermore, it was in the regular sessions of the courts that judicial enquiries were undertaken into the endowments of unserved chantries and of inadequately endowed parish benefices, as a prelude to action being taken to re-use the former and improve the latter – a feature of Sherburne's episcopate.[40]

The courts could not have been used to such an extent had they not been able to deal with cases very rapidly, so it is not surprising to find that office cases against both laymen and clerics were being dealt with more quickly, and offenders were being made to appear before the courts more easily, during the 1520s than previously, as the table opposite makes clear. This was not, however, because unjustified charges, which had subsequently to be dropped, were being brought against laymen, as was later alleged of church courts, for the evidence seems to show that a majority of defendants were guilty.[41] The difficulty of making an assessment of guilt or innocence from the surviving records is well illustrated by the case of Thomas Moreland, the vicar of Bosham, who in 1536 was alleged to have confessed fornication with Agnes Pers. When proceedings began in the consistory court, he claimed that the woman was honest and that he had made no confession and it was subsequently established that one of his parishioners had made up the whole story.[42] Moreover there is stray evidence from elsewhere that the process of compurgation was unreliable and open to severe abuse.[43] It does still seem possible to make a reasonably accurate assessment of the guilt or innocence of those laymen who were cited to answer charges *ex officio*, however, by analysing the number of cases dropped after a preliminary hearing. The table on page 226 gives the results of such an analysis.

The duration of office cases in the courts of the archdeaconry of Chichester[44]

| | Number of office cases before courts | | Number of appearances sought by courts in these cases | Average number of appearances needed to deal with one case |
|---|---|---|---|---|
| Nov. 1506–Nov. 1507 | (77) | 43 | 95 | 2.2 |
| Jan. 1520–Jan. 1521 | (78) | 195 | 279 | 1.4 |

The ease with which the authorities were able to secure the appearance of those cited during the 1520s meant that they were also able to provide a less costly and time-consuming service for plaintiffs in instance cases, and a quicker dispatch of the probate of wills. In instance cases it was very common for plaintiffs to give up their suit because of the costs involved before an agreement or a definitive sentence had been reached, so it speaks well of the courts over which Worthial presided that definitive sentences were far more common in the 1520s than at other times. Between September 1506 and December 1507 only one case was concluded in this way, but between January and July 1520, six definitive sentences were promulgated, and a number of others are to be found among proceedings that survive for 1524–6.[45] Sherburne's courts were able to provide a service for plaintiffs in which the conclusion of suits, where no interim agreement had been reached, was financially feasible. This did not mean, however, that his officers pushed cases to this expensive conclusion,

The results of office cases against laymen during the 1520s[46]

| Probable results | Consistory court Jan. 1520 to Jan. 1521 | Commissary court Jan. 1520 to Jan. 1521 | Consistory court Jan. 1524 to Jan. 1525 |
|---|---|---|---|
| Confessed | 14 | 8 | 7 |
| Guilty (injunctions issued or failed in purgation) | 16 | 24 | 11 |
| Probably guilty (not admitted to purgation or often absent from court) | 11 | 8 | 10 |
| Total | 41 | 40 | 28 |
| Innocent (succeeded at purgation or dismissed) | 5 | 11 | 8 |
| Probably innocent (no action taken against defendant) | 9 | 4 | 2 |
| Total | 14 | 15 | 10 |
| Result uncertain | 24 | 27 | 5 |
| Total number of cases | 79 | 82 | 43 |

for they often used arbitrators to try to settle disputes away from the courts. During 1520, for example, it is known that Worthial introduced arbitrators to settle 15 cases.[47] The speed with which instance cases passed through the courts, however, and their outcome, depended as much upon the parties involved as upon the authorities. When executors came to the courts with wills to prove, on the other hand, official efficiency was of the greatest importance, and the speed with which wills were dispatched during Sherburne's episcopate was remarkable, for the majority of them were proved within eight weeks of being written, and over 80 per cent were proved within 12 weeks.[48] Obviously Dr Kitching's warning against confusing speed with efficiency and justice must be heeded here, although the circumstances were probably somewhat different in diocesan probate. Moreover, the complicated processes involved in dealing with the goods of deceased bankrupts were carried out reasonably quickly at this time also, and the courts were proving wills very cheaply.[49] The preamble to the 1529 Probate Act accused ordinaries of taking as much as £2 or £3 for the probate of a will, and the new scale introduced by the Act provided for fees of 6d. for goods valued under £5 rising to 5s. for those valued over £40. At Chichester, however, except for those who were granted probate *in forma pauperis*, the standard fee was 10d.[50]

The church courts at Chichester were clearly particularly busy and efficient in the years that followed Bishop Sherburne's jurisdictional reforms. This seems to have been because he retained a personal interest in them, and made efforts to protect and expand their activities. Sherburne was himself a respected and experienced ecclesiastical judge and monastic visitor, and, like some other bishops who showed a lively concern for the maintenance of their episcopal rights, was active on a number of occasions in defending the jurisdiction of his courts from the depredations of outsiders. In 1516, he had availed himself of the occasion of the dispute over probate jurisdiction in the southern province to win from the archbishop of Canterbury a number of minor concessions over the extent of the Prerogative jurisdiction as it affected his diocese, for example.[51] In 1520–1, he successfully defended his recent reorganization of the courts from an attempt by a former archdeacon of Lewes to recover the archdeaconry and the jurisdictional rights that had previously gone with it.[52]

Probably more important than either of these successes, however, was the agreement made with Wolsey during the 1520s which kept his legatine court, one of 'the most aggressive and powerful tribunals in the history of the English Church', from interfering with the work of the Chichester courts. The details of the settlement do not survive, although Sherburne was accused in 1530 of allotting half the value of his casualties to Wolsey for the right to retain his jurisdiction unchecked, and a damaged draft of a dean and chapter document seems to indicate that in 1527 Sherburne was paying over to him as much as £20 a year. The evidence so far adduced of actual payments of such a sum, however, seems highly unreliable. It is clear that Sherburne was prepared to pay for independence, an independence moreover, which appears to have been maintained, for the meagre surviving evidence reveals that Wolsey's legatine court took cases from many dioceses, but not from Chichester.[53]

Sherburne's interest in his courts was not limited to jurisdictional matters. Although Worthial usually presided, the bishop retained and exercised the right to hear important cases himself. The evidence of his own judicial activity is almost certainly incomplete, but he clearly dealt with a wide range of cases. He sat to decide the augmentation of two vicarages in 1513–14, for example, to grant pensions from livings, to hear a difficult matrimonial dispute between members of local gentry families in 1533, and in 1534 to try a notorious heretic.[54] Moreover, he clearly exercised a close control over the everyday work of the courts. Their activities, especially with regard to clerical residence and church finance, reflect the bishop's own preoccupations, for example, and he appears to have intervened in cases that interested him. He was involved in the expulsion from the diocese of the curate of Cowfold, for example, showed interest in the proceedings over the bankrupt Robert Toprat's estates, and on occasions initiated charges against offenders.[55] A letter that survives from Sherburne's registry gives a good indication of his close control over quite minor matters. A local landowner, one of whose servants had been before the courts, wrote: 'Whereupon and at my special desire your said commissary respited the penance *which was only by your commandment*, and therefore I heartily thank your good lordship and glad I shall be to redress my servant in all things that your lordship shall think necessary'.[56]

Sherburne was clearly fortunate in finding able and industrious officers, but it appears to have been his jurisdictional reforms and protection of the courts, and his continuing interest in their activities, that were ultimately responsible for their effectiveness. Unfortunately for the future history of the diocese, however, his jurisdictional reforms and judicial activity were not developed or continued by his successors, and the church courts at Chichester were never again as effective as they had been during the 1520s.

This decline in effectiveness was largely the result of influences from outside the diocese which began to be felt during Sherburne's episcopate – though Bishop Richard Sampson's later neglect of his see for work in London was also important – for the evidence shows that national events after 1530 had a direct and dismal effect upon the exercise of spiritual jurisdiction at Chichester. There is little doubt that the church courts were unpopular with some of the laity in the years preceding the 1529 Parliament, perhaps because of their very efficiency, but the violence of anti-clerical feeling in the Commons in 1529, and the extent of the attacks upon ecclesiastical jurisdiction made in Parliament in the next five years, were unprecedented.[57] The scope and purpose of these attacks have been the subject of much debate, but their actual effect upon the courts in the localities has not. They cannot be judged in isolation, however, since this period also saw a number of potentially more serious threats to the exercise of ecclesiastical jurisdiction by the bishops. Plans for far-reaching reform of the courts were clearly circulating during the Reformation Parliament, for example, and a draft bill, possibly connected with the agitation of 1532, proposed the prohibition of all *ex officio* actions except in heresy cases. This could have destroyed at a stroke the ability of the bishops to maintain ecclesiastical discipline in their dioceses or carry out reforms through their courts. Other plans went further, and Richard Pollard, one of Cromwell's servants, even proposed the abolition of the separate spiritual jurisdiction altogether. The courts had their defenders, however, and in the event nothing came of these plans. The threat of change, however, especially to the important office jurisdiction, and the knowledge that reform of the canon law was being discussed during this period, clearly hung over the courts. At Chichester this undoubtedly contributed to a dramatic decline in their activity.[58]

Cranmer's metropolitical visitation of 1534–5, which was undertaken with royal support, was the first of the southern province for over a century, and represented a direct challenge to episcopal authority. Mr Richard Gwent, one of the visitors, came to the diocese of Chichester in the summer of 1535. He visited Chichester cathedral in July, and at the start of August wrote to Cromwell to report what he had found. While the visitation lasted, Sherburne's jurisdiction was inhibited, and no episcopal court sat between 10 April and 24 July 1535. For this bishop who had kept Wolsey's commissaries from interfering in his diocese, this must have been a severe blow, even though it was an indignity to which other bishops were also subjected. It must have been the more so for Sherburne since its purpose was to enforce the royal supremacy to which he was opposed.[59] Potentially more serious threats to episcopal power and prestige followed, for the inhibition for the famous royal visitation was issued in September 1535, Layton, one of the visitors, was in Sussex during September and October, and Cromwell's vicegerential court was at work by the middle of October if not before.[60]

In the event, however, although the royal visitors did come to Sussex, and the vicegerential court was active in London until 1540, the threat posed by the inhibition and the court, in the diocese of Chichester at least, proved more theoretical than actual. Sessions of the consistory court continued uninterrrupted throughout the period, and only one Chichester case appears among all the surviving records of the vicegerential court, and that involved a will which would probably normally have come before the Prerogative Court of Canterbury rather than a diocesan court.[61]

The threat of change and the damage caused by these events was real enough, however, and their effect upon Sherburne and upon the ecclesiastical officers of his diocese was profound. The office jurisdiction which they had used so effectively during the 1520s was under attack in Parliament and seemed on the point of abolition. Their right to settle tithe, perjury and defamation cases was contested, and the cherished independence of their courts had been destroyed by the archiepiscopal and royal visitors who had descended upon the diocese. It is not surprising that they took fright and drastically reduced the much abused *ex officio* activity of their courts. Nor is it surprising that potential plaintiffs were far less willing than before to use the Chichester courts to settle their disputes.[62] Moreover, they now had less opportunity to do so, because the authorities also reduced the number of court sessions, in the case of the consistory court from 45 in 1524 to 24 in 1534 and 23 in 1536.[63] As a result, there was a very sharp decline in office and instance business during Sherburne's last years at Chichester, and only the probate business of the courts remained unaffected, as the following table shows:

Cases before the courts of the archdeaconry of Chichester[64]

|  | Jan. 1520 to Jan. 1521 | July 1533 to July 1534 | Feb. 1537 to Feb. 1538 | Oct. 1556 to Oct. 1557 |
|---|---|---|---|---|
| *Office cases* | | | | |
| Consistory court | 90 | 27 | 31 | Not separate |
| Commissary court | 105 | 58 | 47 | Not separate |
| Both courts | 195 | 85 | 78 | 122 |
| *Instance cases* | | | | |
| Consistory court | 136 | 31 | 30 | Not separate |
| Commissary court | 91 | 53 | 43 | Not separate |
| Both courts | 227 | 84 | 73 | 73 |
| *Probate cases* | | | | |
| Consistory court | 50 | 16 | 20 | Not separate |
| Commissary court | 71 | 85 | 80 | Not separate |
| Both courts | 121 | 101 | 100 | 287 |
| *All cases* | | | | |
| Consistory court | 276 | 74 | 81 | Not separate |
| Commissary court | 267 | 196 | 170 | Not separate |
| Both courts | 543 | 270 | 251 | 482 |

The table also shows that the business of the courts only recovered slowly and that even in the 1550s office and instance business had not returned to pre-Reformation levels. There were reasons within the diocese for this. The preamble to the 1536 Tithe Act stated that many people 'have attempted in late time past to disobey condemn and despite the process, lawes and decrees of the Ecclesiastical courts of this realm, in more temerous and large manner than before this time hath been seen',[65] and it is clear that under Sherburne's successors the courts had greater and greater difficulty in ensuring the appearance of those cited, and in getting their orders obeyed. This was particularly unfortunate, for it meant that office proceedings were often ineffectual, that potential plaintiffs were deterred from starting proceedings, and that the courts declined in authority and effectiveness. In the 1520s few office cases had required more than one session to complete, but by the 1550s many took two or three sessions, and some dragged on and on.[66] The case of Robert Fowler of Albourne, who was cited to all the consistory court sessions between December 1556 and June 1557, was one that did, and other cases before the courts of both archdeaconries during the 1550s show that his was by no means exceptional.

The main reason for the courts' difficulties was the growing disrespect that was shown to spiritual sanctions, a legacy of the denigration heaped on the courts during the 1530s and a reflection of the unsettled times. In the 1520s, the Church's censures, as used in this diocese, had had a telling force. People actually fled the diocese to escape a suspension, and this lesser penalty was usually perfectly adequate to enforce obedience. The large numbers of those suspended in office proceedings who sought an absolution before the next session of the court shows how serious this lesser penalty was considered before 1530, and the fact that the threat of excommunication or merely of being judged contumacious without censure often had the desired effect, indicates how strong the authorities' position then was.[67] After Sherburne's death, however, the situation changed very noticeably, although it did not reach dire proportions in Sussex until Catholic recusants challenged the Elizabethan settlement.[68] The following table, by showing the marked rise in the use of excommunication and decline in that of suspension at Chichester over the early Reformation, gives a clear indication of the debasement of both penalties, and seems to show that the change had occurred by 1537:

The use of ecclesiastical censures in office cases by the courts of the archdeaconry of Chichester[69]

| Date | Total office cases | Excommunications | Suspensions |
|---|---|---|---|
| Jan. 1520–Jan. 1521 | 195 | 1 | 41 |
| July 1533–July 1534 | 85 | 1 | 21 |
| Feb. 1537–Feb. 1538 | 78 | 10 | 16 |
| Oct. 1556–Oct. 1557 | 122 | 13 | 20 |

There were also more specifically local reasons why the courts at Chichester did not recover from the shocks of the 1530s.

Richard Sampson left his spiritual officers virtually unassisted, and, without episcopal guidance, Worthial proved a less industrious servant. He had been nearly 30 when he first came to the diocese, so that by 1540 he was over 50, and by then had clearly lost some of his early energy. He was also more heavily involved elsewhere than he had been in the 1520s. He became a residentiary of the cathedral in 1530, and by Fleshmonger's death in 1541 he became the senior, and acted as president of the chapter. From then until his death in 1554, chapter business took up more and more of his time. It is not, therefore, surprising that he left the city of Chichester for the peripatetic sessions of the commissary court considerably less often during the 1540s than he had during the 1520s.[70] This meant that judicial activity for the archdeaconry became more concentrated on the consistory court at Chichester, an unfortunate process which was to be taken considerably further by Worthial's successor as commissary and official principal, Richard Brisley.[71]

This was not all, however, for after 1543 Worthial was having to preside as judge without the help of a long-standing and able assistant, for it was in that year that John Stilman died. It is not surprising that he now showed less vigour in hunting out and dealing with offenders, or that the attacks on abuses made under Sherburne were not resumed.[72]

Structural changes to the courts after Worthial's death in 1554, however, were far more detrimental to the effectiveness of episcopal jurisdiction. In the very month in which Worthial made his will, a dean's peculiar court began to act again apart from the consistory court.[73] Consequently, the parishes of the cathedral city of the bishops of Chichester were once again outside episcopal control, except during triennial visitation, and it seems probable that the difficulties experienced by Bishop Curteys in the city in the 1570s were one result. Moreover, the dean's court provided far less efficient justice for the city than had the consistory court. It met so infrequently, was so taken up with the administrative acts involved in instituting and inducting priests to benefices, and in proving wills, that there was little inclination or opportunity to correct offenders or to try ecclesiastical disputes.[74]

Steps even more detrimental to the courts were taken by

Worthial's successor as judge, Richard Brisley. He was often dilatory in proceeding with offenders, and dealt with cases outside the proper court sessions in his own house. On one such occasion, moreover, a penance was commuted to a money payment at the request of the defendant. He also received irregular fees. Thomas Hide and Alice Davie, who had consented to marry after being prosecuted for fornication, for example, were required to pay the judge 4s., and for a will proved in London, Brisley personally received 3s. 4d. These few references do not show corruption as serious as that later found in the diocese of Gloucester, but there had evidently been a decline in standards since the 1520s.[75] Consequently, it is not surprising to find that although the authorities attacked heresy and witchcraft during Mary's reign, they made none of the efforts of Sherburne's officers to root out the more widespread problems of clerical non-residence and poverty, and of dilapidated churches.[76]

More serious for the future work of the courts was Brisley's amalgamation of the commissary court for the archdeaconry of Chichester and the consistory court. Throughout Worthial's dominance at Chichester these two courts had functioned separately, even though the judge, registrar and proctors were usually the same in both, and regular, although latterly declining, numbers of circuits were undertaken into the deaneries each year. Brisley, however, was so involved in heresy trials that he made no effort to distinguish between his activities as commissary and official principal, and between March 1556 and November 1557 made only four trips into the deaneries.[77] This meant that judicial activity for the archdeaconry away from Chichester became very infrequent, and in the 1560s it became more infrequent still, being limited to summary hearings at visitation.[78] This had two most unfortunate results. First, it became more inconvenient for potential plaintiffs, for those with wills to prove, and for those cited to the courts to answer charges or at the instance of a third party. When there had been regular sessions in each rural deanery, no parish was more than a day's travel from the hearings of an ecclesiastical court, but now that the vast majority of cases were dealt with at Chichester, the cost and inconvenience involved must have increased considerably. This was especially so since the city where the consistory court sat was particularly badly placed as a judicial centre for the archdeaconry, let alone the diocese.

Second, and perhaps of even greater importance for the office jurisdiction of the courts, the removal of court sessions from the localities placed the burden of detecting faults more squarely upon episcopal and archidiaconal visitations, and therefore on the shoulders of the already harassed churchwardens, whose reliability had always been in question. This was one reason why the Elizabethan authorities had such difficulty in detecting and stamping out recusancy in the diocese in the 1570s and 1580s, and why Bishop Curteys recommended the establishment of a branch of the Ecclesiastical Commission in Sussex.[79]

It was in this context, therefore, equally unfortunate that the commissary court in the archdeaconry of Lewes was also becoming settled, in this case in one of the parish churches in Lewes. Courts were still being held regularly in outlying areas by Mr Robert Taylor, the commissary of Lewes, as late as 1557, but after his deprivation in 1559, this occurred only at visitation. By the early 1560s, in fact, the ecclesiastical courts in both archdeaconries of this diocese had taken on the form they were to retain until the nineteenth century.[80] It was a form, moreover, the inadequacy of which was to be ruthlessly exposed by the resistance of papists and Puritans.

It could reasonably be argued that the picture here presented of the Chichester courts at the Reformation, one of reform and efficiency during the 1520s, but of decline thereafter, owed more to specifically local circumstances, such as the presence of an active resident bishop during the 1520s and early 1530s, or the failings of Worthial and Brisley in the 1540s and 1550s, than to national events, and that, consequently, the diocese was something of a special case. There are enough parallels between the changes at Chichester and developments in other dioceses, however, to cast doubt upon such a conclusion. Bishop Foxe of Winchester noted with approval the efficiency of his chancellor during the 1520s, and boasted to Wolsey in 1527 that there was 'as little openly known sin or enormous crimes, both in persons spiritual and temporal' in his diocese, 'as is within any diocese of this realm'.[81] Historians have noted an upsurge of business in the 1520s, similar to that at Chichester, in the Lichfield and Canterbury courts, and the latter were also using excommunications with care at this date.[82] Moreover, episcopal courts were clearly not the only ones that were flourishing. At Chester, where the archdeacon's authority was virtually episcopal, for example, the official made an unsuccessful attempt to broaden the activity of his court in the early 1520s by holding some sessions elsewhere than in Chester, and the efficiency of some archdeaconry courts in the Lincoln diocese at this date has received special mention.[83] Furthermore, it is clear that Sherburne was by no means the only bishop in the last decades before the break with Rome who was interested in his diocesan courts. Bishop Atwater of Lincoln presided in person over something like regular sessions of an audience court, Bishop Stokesley is known to have tried London cases in person, and many of Sherburne's contemporaries on the bench were active visitors.[84] Also it seems inconceivable that bishops West of Ely, Nykke of Norwich, Booth of Hereford and Foxe of Winchester, like Sherburne, should have gone to the trouble and expense of resisting the interference of Wolsey's commissaries had they attached no importance to the work of their diocesan courts and considered them as little more than a source of revenue and prestige, and the same may, to some extent, be said of the resistance shown by bishops Longland, Gardiner, Stokesley, Reppes and Veysey to Cranmer's metropolitical visitation.[85] To these bishops on the very eve of the Reformation, ecclesiastical courts were still an essential and effective part of diocesan organization. Their reform might be discussed in Convocation, as it was in 1532, but they must be defended from interference from above or resentment from below.

There were also later parallels with the situation at Chichester. The most notorious example of corrupt and inefficient courts is probably that provided by the Gloucester evidence for the early years of Elizabeth's reign, and, although the Gloucester experience was probably extreme and untypical, there were certainly other inefficient courts in the decades after 1540. For example, those of another Henrician diocese, that of Chester, in the 1540s and 1550s, were presided over first by a man who was a frequent litigant in his own court, and then by another who fathered, by three different women, one bastard under Henry

VIII, five legitimate children under Edward VI and another bastard under Mary.[86] Their court could hardly have commanded respect. At Lichfield in the 1560s, moreover, Bishop Bentham had considerable difficulty in enforcing the 1559 Injunctions and in making any headway against Catholic recusants, and the same could be said of almost every diocese.[87] Church courts in general revived during the latter part of Elizabeth's reign as litigation increased, but even then the continuing use of ecclesiastical commissions indicates contemporary recognition of the inability of the old episcopal courts to deal with those, whether Catholic or Puritan, who repudiated the jurisdiction of the Church. Moreover, even if recusants are excluded from calculations, the same pattern emerges, as at Chichester, of failure to enforce obedience to court procedures and of numerous excommunications. This was true of the comparatively well-administered diocese of London, for example, of archdeaconries in the dioceses of York, Norwich and Chester, and of certain deaneries in the archdeaconry of Taunton.[88]

The Chichester courts may present an especially clear picture of reorganization and reform in the 1520s and of decline in business and efficiency over the early Reformation, but it was a picture, especially with regard to the 'rapidly growing contempt of the laity' for the Church's 'strictures and fulminations', that is apparently applicable in varying measure to other dioceses.[89]

It is clear that in Chichester as elsewhere the decade or so before the Henrician Reformation witnessed the efforts of an energetic bishop to breathe fresh life into the diocesan administration. Sherburne sought to bring the control of his diocese into his own hands, defying the attempts of rival jurisdictions. Meeting with success, he then tried to turn the attention of the courts away from their preoccupation with instances cases and towards the business of discipline. There is every sign that this bishop made the consistory effective where correction cases were concerned and the work of the court in all its aspects was rendered more efficient (although whether more just we have no means of knowing). It has been possible to demonstrate that the years 1530 to 1557 saw a weakening of the consistory's effectiveness and authority – presumably as a result of the shocks administered to the system by the Reformation and its unsettled aftermath.

# 10

## The decline of ecclesiastical jurisdiction under the Tudors

## Ralph Houlbrooke

Not until comparatively recently was the jurisdiction of the courts Christian in England restricted to the cognisance of matters of doctrine, church organization, clerical discipline, and the fabric and contents of church buildings. In the nineteenth century their attentuated jurisdiction in cases relating to marriage, probate and slander was finally taken from them. This long survival of temporal jurisdiction may at first sight appear paradoxical in the European country where religious division and lay emancipation from clerical control had probably progressed furthest. Yet the business before the church courts was affected during the Reformation century and a decline in ecclesiastical jurisdiction in many areas was apparent.[1]

### 1. *Attacks upon ecclesiastical jurisdiction prior to the Reformation*

For most of the Middle Ages there had been intermittent friction between lay and ecclesiastical jurisdictions. During the twelfth century a writ of prohibition had become available to parties in certain types of dispute who wished to prevent determination of the case by ecclesiastical judges.[2] This writ was used to take from the church courts cases relating to real property, rights of presentation, and debts and chattels. By the mid-thirteenth century the last two were giving rise to fierce controversy. The fourteenth century saw the forging of a lethal new weapon, originally designed to guard the crown against papal encroachments but before long turned against the church courts within England. Between 1353 and 1393 three statutes of *praemunire* were passed to prevent the pope entertaining causes properly determinable in the king's courts and to deal with those promoting papal bulls in such cases. By the 1430s *praemunire* was being used against the courts Christian in England. The mid-century saw Convocation fruitlessly petitioning against this use.[3]

Despite the evolution of *praemunire* and hierarchical complaints that it was impeding the exercise of ecclesiastical jurisdiction, the consistory court of Canterbury, for example, was enormously busy in the 30 years 1463–93, when it never heard fewer than 400 cases a year and sometimes more than 800. What is more, the great majority of these cases were concerned with breach of faith in failing to fulfil contracts or pay debts – the focus of controversy in the thirteenth century.[4] The immunity of the church courts in this sphere may have been due to Edward IV's charter of ecclesiastical liberties of 1462, as it was at almost exactly this time that Canterbury began its 15-year-long expansion of business. The charter mentions *praemunire* explicitly only in connection with tithe suits, but it appears that A. F. Pollard was correct when he suggested that it gave added protection to other areas of ecclesiastical jurisdiction.[5]

The common lawyers once again took up the weapon of *praemunire* in Henry VII's reign. There was a rapid decline in the number of cases of breach of faith dealt with by the consistory at Canterbury.[6] No such suits were entertained in the consistory at Norwich after 1509, when the surviving records begin, although they had certainly been dealt with there in the fifteenth century.[7] At Durham where the bishop controlled the issue of writs of *praemunire*, cases of breach of faith made up the biggest category of the consistory's business until the 1530s but the court ceased to entertain them after the crown gathered up the palatine jurisdiction in 1536.

The use of *praemunire* during Henry VII's reign enjoyed official approval. Professor Storey has recently underlined the leading part played by Sir James Hobart, who as attorney general (1486–1507) initiated prosecutions in King's Bench and as Justice in Norfolk and Suffolk encouraged the laying of informations at quarter sessions. Dr Kelly has shown that a trickle of prosecutions in King's Bench grew to a spate after Henry's last Parliament of 1504 and that a high proportion of the writs were directed against clergy and ecclesiastical officials in Norwich diocese.

The ecclesiastical lawyers and bishops regarded the more aggressive attitude of the royal courts towards their jurisdiction with resentment and foreboding. The lawyers saw their livelihood disappearing. Eight or nine proctors were active in the Canterbury consistory court in the 1480s, a maximum of five after 1500. The bishops were less directly affected but they probably felt that crown encroachments dealt a blow to their prestige and authority. The resentment of Richard Nykke, bishop of Norwich and formerly a diocesan administrator, is amply illustrated in a letter of his to Warham shortly after the 1504 Parliament, 'The lay men be more bolder against the churche than ever they were. If your lordship help not, having the great seal in your hand, I and other your subjects can no thing do. If your fatherhood would favour me, I would curse all such promoters and maintainers of the praemunire in such cases as heretics and not believers in Christ's church.'[8] His complaint lends authority to the accusations made against ecclesiastical judges in Henry VIII's reign that they denounced as heretics those who threatened to impede their jurisdiction.[9]

## 2. *The weakening of the fabric*

The sentiments expressed in Nykke's letter may have sprung from a deeper groundswell of clerical reaction towards the end of Henry VII's reign. Soon after Henry VIII's accession there were signs of clerical hopes that the threatening policies of the immediate past would be abandoned. In 1510 the bill 'for the liberties of the English church' was introduced in the Lords, although it disappeared from sight after being mangled by the Commons.[10] Church lawyers took significant initiatives of their own. In 1511 the ecclesiastical judges of Canterbury began once more to order unsuccessful defendants in cases of breach of faith to pay restitution of debts. In the same year Richard Bodewell, dean of Arches, founded the association which later became Doctors' Commons.[11] Whether by accident or design, the

measures taken to defend ecclesiastical jurisdiction coincided
with the vigorous repression of unorthodoxy. The years 1510–12
saw the biggest persecution of heretics witnessed for nearly a
century.[12] At least nine dioceses were affected; over 160 suspects
were compelled to abjure and 10 were burned. The well-known
case of Hunne fused the explosive elements of heresy prosecution
and disputed jurisdiction. Charges of heresy against Hunne were
weak and it was popularly believed that the diocesan authorities
had determined to punish him because he had embarked on a
*praemunire* suit against his parish priest. When the chancellor of
London was faced with trial for Hunne's murder in King's
Bench, the bishop of London appointed as preacher at the
opening of Convocation in 1515 Richard Kidderminster, who
argued that proceedings against clergy in lay courts were contrary to the law of God. All this must be viewed against the
background of the Commons' attempt to revive a statute of
1512 limiting benefit of clergy and of a papal pronouncement of
1514 that no layman had authority over clerics. Shortly afterwards, Convocation called Friar Standish, Kidderminster's
opponent, before it to answer interrogatories concerning papal
authority and the immunity of clergy from secular prosecution.
The chief temporal judges were to decide that by this action the
hierarchy had incurred the penalties of *praemunire*.[13]

Thus the doctrine of *praemunire* made its most dramatic
appearance to date. This was but a foretaste of what was to
happen when, after the interlude of Wolsey's rule, the issues
were revived. In December 1530 the whole body of the clergy
was indicted of *praemunire* and the two convocations only obtained
the royal pardon on payment of nearly £119,000. In the statute
of pardon of 1531 their offence was baldly stated to have been
the exercise of ecclesiastical jurisdiction. The purpose behind
this statement was tactical. In 1534 the Act for Submission of the
Clergy confirmed ecclesiastical jurisdiction and laws insofar as
they were not repugnant to the laws of the realm.[14] This did not
entail the demise of *praemunire*, which remained in force against
ecclesiastical judges who acted contrary to statute or who held
certain pleas determinable at the common law. Bishop Nykke of
Norwich, bitter opponent of *praemunire* 30 years before, became
its first major victim after 1534.[15]

During Elizabeth's reign, however, the more ancient writ of prohibition was the main weapon used by the temporal against the spiritual courts. The doctrine had developed that a prohibition would lie in a cause which, although spiritual, the church courts were nevertheless barred from entertaining – that is, for example, a suit for tithes on products exempt from tithe. An action of *praemunire*, however, would result if the plea itself was temporal, as for instance in the case of a suit in a church court for recovery of a debt. It is unclear how this distinction developed. St German stipulated that a writ of either prohibition or *praemunire* would lie in a temporal cause brought before the church courts.[16]

During the years of the Reformation Parliament the church courts were subject to a good deal of rather imprecise abuse. About half the heads of the 1532 *Commons' Supplication against the Ordinaries*, so often cited in this context, related to the conduct of the clergy and had little to do with the courts. Some practices were indicted as customary whereas they were extremely rare: imprisonment and *ex officio* citations without presentment come under this category. Mrs Bowker's analysis of local material has shown that hardly any of the points in the Supplication apply to the lower church courts.[17] Certain categories of highly articulate people (common lawyers, M.P.s, heretics etc.) had good reason to dislike the courts spiritual, but they amounted to a tiny minority of the population. Most probably benefited from the simple, speedy procedure of the courts. The fact that these had been able to expand their business enormously in the fifteenth century in a disputed area testifies to their basic popularity.

After the enactment of the royal supremacy the common lawyers hoped that they might profit from a drastic pruning of ecclesiastical jurisdiction. A radical paper of 1534/5 argued the advantages of common law procedure, the partiality of ecclesiastical judges in tithe and probate litigation, and the need to determine marriage and defamation cases in temporal courts.[18] In August 1535 Thomas Cromwell's servant, Richard Pollard, wrote that the temporal judges should be given the whole ecclesiastical jurisdiction.[19] The civilian William Petre was also in favour of taking most of the ecclesiastical courts' work from them, leaving them with nothing but the settlement of matrimonial causes and the probate of small wills.[20] All these schemes came to nothing because of Henry's determination to keep his Church as nearly papal as possible.

In formal terms the Reformation restored ecclesiastical jurisdiction to the crown almost intact. Yet statutes were passed affecting almost every area of its jurisdiction, some of them limiting the competence of the church courts. The scale of probate fees, levy of mortuaries, pluralism and non-residence, appeals, procedure in heresy cases, marriage and tithe law, scope of testaments, doctrine – all were affected by parliamentary legislation. Heresy procedure was subjected to safeguards in 1534; after 1539 an important role in the maintenance of religious uniformity was assigned to mixed lay and clerical commissions. Benefit of clergy was whittled away by statute and the abolition of minor orders occurred in 1550. From 1576 clerks convict ceased to be handed over to the ordinary.[21] Determination of tithe causes in London was transferred from the episcopal to the mayoral court.[22]

What would the royal supremacy mean for the church courts in practice? Reform of the ecclesiastical laws was envisaged and a draft was ready by 1535 but neither Henry nor Cromwell took an interest in it.[23] A second draft prepared in Edward's reign did not receive royal or parliamentary sanction before the king's death. The vicegerency was set up for a time but dropped after Cromwell's death.[24] Cromwell inhibited the bishops from exercising their jurisdictions in autumn 1535 (although the inhibition did not affect at least one diocesan consistory), supervised a royal visitation, issued injunctions, and diverted some of the more profitable testamentary business into the vicegerential court. Litigation dealt with in the diocesan courts shrank to a trickle. Meanwhile, some of the mud thrown in the continuing anti-papal campaign stuck to the courts and their personnel.

### 3. *Post-Reformation ecclesiastical jurisdiction*

The years of greatest apparent danger past, business began to revive. The structure of ecclesiastical jurisdiction was intact but weakened. The merely provisional sanctioning of ecclesiastical laws had given the common lawyers a formidable weapon to wield.

The most damaging moral effect of the Reformation upon the church courts was, of course, to weaken respect for their sanctions – suspension and excommunication. During Elizabeth's reign a growing hard core of recusants and of Puritans lost spiritual fear of these sanctions. Before the Reformation excommunication was rarely resorted to; suspension was the normal sanction. By the 1560s suspension had practically disappeared and excommunication was employed ever more frequently, until it was used to punish even contumacy. Absolution became a mechanical process. Large numbers of people failed to seek it – it has been calculated that hardened excommunicates and their families constituted nearly one-sixth of the population of York in the seventeenth century. It was impossible to ostracize so large a body of people and disciplinary proceedings against those who consorted with excommunicates were therefore few.[25] Writs of *de excommunicato capiendo*, revived in the 1550s, were rarely employed in the late sixteenth century, presumably because they had proved ineffective.[26] Certainly temporal judges hampered the procedure by setting excommunicates at liberty without bail bonds. Whitgift believed that the sanction was now only useful in preventing the pursuit of actions at law but it was rarely urged in bar by defendants in the church courts.[27] Corporal punishment, still fairly common on the eve of the Reformation in some dioceses (such as Winchester) for the punishment of sexual offences, ceased to be used also. In 1576 J.P.s were empowered to whip the parents of bastard children – a tacit acknowledgment of the failure of sexual discipline by the church courts?[28]

Individuals were now readier than before to flout ecclesiastical laws; judges were less inclined to initiate prosecutions in certain spheres. This explains in part the enormous increase in litigation between parties in the church courts during and after the Reformation, much of it concerned with matters which had previously been uncontentious or which had been settled by means of correction procedure. This development is clearest in the field of tithe disputes. It was said that tithe payers were now bolder than ever before in withholding payment. Even Sir Edward Coke, deeply suspicious of the ecclesiastical courts as he was, conceded that the 'noise of the dissolution of Monasteries ...

(Laymen taking small occasions to withdraw their tithes)' had led to the statute of 1536 which empowered J.P.s to assist the ordinary against those who obdurately refused to pay tithe.[29] The biggest increase in tithe litigation at Norwich took place in the late 1540s at a time when prices were rising rapidly. Clergymen and their farmers were now going to law in order to secure payment of tithe in kind or a commutation which represented full value of the tithe at current prices. Tithe payers were also under severe economic pressure and extremely reluctant to see favourable customs reversed.[30] Before the Reformation a diocesan judge sometimes declared such customs void without the expense of a suit.[31] Fifty years later the issue would give rise to a protracted and expensive suit. Economic pressures could make tithes hard to levy even when the case was not complicated by a disputed custom. Thus during the period 1549–59 an exceptionally large proportion of disputes over tithe of grain came before the Norwich consistory, although there had never been any doubt about the manner in which such tithes should be levied.

The same influences were at work, though perhaps to a lesser extent, in the rapidly increasing litigation over testaments and alleged defamation. The expansion of testamentary litigation in the courts of Norwich and Winchester from *c.* 1545 far outpaced any increase in the number of testaments made. Declining respect for the probate administration was partly responsible. It was alleged in the 1570s by Bishop Parkhurst of Norwich and by his successor's chancellor that probate of wills and letters of administration were granted far too quickly.[32] Men were supposedly more willing to suppress or forge wills because they were not required to swear an oath upon them. This neglect of the prescribed safeguards allowed false testaments to be proved and made genuine wills more vulnerable to subsequent attack. In either case litigation was likely to ensue. Available evidence does suggest that probate was being granted too quickly on the eve of the Reformation, although it may have slackened in the following period.[33] Allegations of undue delay in probate, unfounded in all but a small number of cases concerning large estates, made it more difficult for those who administered the courts to implement reforms of abuses caused by over-rapid administration.

Defamation had a strong criminal element.[34] What mattered was the malicious breach of Christian charity, whether or not the accusation was true. In mid-sixteenth-century Norwich very large numbers of 'common defamers' and 'sowers of discord' were presented in disciplinary sessions. During Elizabeth's reign the trend was in the opposite direction – defamation became an instance matter. Only one defamation suit between parties is known to have been introduced in the York consistory court in 1561. Over the next 20 years the number grew with astonishing rapidity; from 1580 to 1640 they regularly made up nearly half the business of the court, while common scolds formed but a tiny proportion of the offenders dealt with in the archidiaconal courts. A similar development seems to have taken place in Norwich by the early seventeenth century.

The correction work of the courts, however, also increased during the Reformation. The main concern of the inferior courts was with sexual misdemeanours, payment of ecclesiastical dues, probate, punishment of common defamers, and the maintenance of church fabric. With the Reformation some of these tasks became more formidable and a number of new ones were added to the courts' workload. The end of auricular confession meant that penance could no longer be enjoyed extra-judicially for 'secret' sins. The problem of maintaining church buildings probably became more serious – perhaps because of the brutal disruption of parochial finances under Edward VI. The responsibility for enforcing payment of poor rates fell initially upon the archdeaconry courts. The purchase of a whole range of new items – poor box, register, Great Bible, pulpit, homilies, prayer books, *Paraphrases*, chalice – had to be enforced. Quarterly sermons were first widely enforced in the early years of Elizabeth when clerical morale sank to its nadir, many benefices stood vacant, and only a tiny minority of the clergy was actually licensed to preach. The early Elizabethan bishops made some attempt to enforce the new requirement that the people participate in the eucharist three times yearly. The problem of enforcing attendance was a large one – either because standards were raised or because attendance had declined during the Reformation.[35]

Officials of the courts benefited most from the upsurge in business transacted. For the court proctors the lengthier process of instance causes was much more lucrative than the enforcement of discipline. One of Bishop Parkhurst's most revealing complaints against his court was that citations were often made out by scribes without authorization by the judge, 'who upon hearing thereof might and ought to move the parties to quietness'.[36] Reconciliation of the parties outside the court was decreasingly important to court officials. All court personnel made more work for themselves, not less. Depositions, for which scribes were paid by the line, grew longer and more detailed as the century progressed. Recorded acts in causes reveal increasing procedural ingenuity and suits tended to take longer to settle than previously. The number of proctors increased. In the 1520s three practised at Norwich; in the 1560s, five; and in the 1590s, eight. In the 1560s, apparently for the first time, the idea of employing an advocate at Norwich was mooted. The chancellor opposed the suggestion, saying that 'I would rather departe than to give the county occasion to be burdened with an unnecessary member; for if we had more ravens we must have more carrion'.[37] Ecclesiastical lawyers were presented with a comfortable living in the post-Reformation years. This explained in part the increase in the number of those being granted degrees in civil law at the universities between 1551 and 1590.[38]

In the archidiaconal courts before the Reformation the majority of business concerned social and moral offences, in whose punishment the judge was assured of popular co-operation. After the Reformation the greater burden of official requirements made upon the laity through the courts probably shifted the balance from consent to coercion. Reports of abuse of the parochial representatives who made presentments in the courts became commoner in the post-Reformation records at Norwich. The situation encouraged official spying and this was precisely what apparitors of the courts were accused of.[39] His offices were no substitute for co-operation. In the diocese of Canterbury, so it has been claimed, a different development took place. Presentments in visitations were relied on more, the reports of apparitors less, after the Reformation. In any event, the workload of the archidiaconal courts by the 1560s was probably larger than could be effectively discharged under the existing system, even given co-operation. Hence the call for the reinvigoration of a smaller unit of jurisdiction – the rural deanery.[40] The J.P.s, already overworked, but with more effective sanctions at their disposal, assumed some of the responsibilities of the church courts, for example, the supervision of poor relief.

### 4. *The independence of ecclesiastical lawyers*

The cumulative effect of certain of the Reformation changes was to render ecclesiastical lawyers much less amenable than previously to hierarchical control. The profession had already been laicized and lawyers been given greater security of tenure. The registrar, for example, was customarily appointed for life from the fifteenth century onwards.[41] Many of those appointed were laymen. Later on the combined office of chancellor/vicar-general/official principal developed in the same way. A statute of 1545 enabled married laymen to exercise ecclesiastical jurisdiction.

After the Reformation lawyers were no longer appointed to the episcopal bench. A man of exceptional vigour such as John Hooper or Thomas Bentham might overcome this disadvantage and intervene as ordinary to enforce the settlement of causes by arbitration and cut back the luxurious growth of litigation.[42] But Bishop Parkhurst of Norwich, although a great admirer of Hooper's, showed a pathetic helplessness in the face of his lawyers' activities. Although he had the patronage of the chancellorship in his hands, his first appointment was of a clergyman without legal qualifications whom Parkhurst himself described as 'unskilful'. During this period Parkhurst himself (possibly following Hooper's example) sat as judge, but he never repeated the experiment. His third chancellor felt as impotent in the face of the entrenched consistory proctors and registrar as the bishop himself did. He accused them of prolonging causes and accepting bribes, and looked forward to the time 'when it shall please the lord to cause the highest power to search the doings of lawyers and to perceive their pettyfogging, juggling and hypocrisy'.[43] Parkhurst's chancellors stayed too short a time effectively to master the court personnel. On the other hand, a chancellor who held a life patent might well come to identify his interests with those who administered the courts rather than with those of the bishop. Eventually the evolution of the post of bishop's secretary enabled bishops to get a better grip on diocesan administration.

## 5. *Revival of authority: the High Commission*

The Reformation set in train or accelerated a series of changes which gravely undermined the authority and the efficiency of the church courts. With one exception, the courts gained nothing from their new relationship with the crown. The exception was a major one, however, for it was what many churchmen came to regard as the mainstay of ecclesiastical jurisdiction: the High Commission. Elizabeth's first ecclesiastical commission of 1559 was mainly concerned with the maintenance of religious uniformity, although it was also empowered to deal with any causes falling into the sphere of the courts spiritual – adultery and fornication being specifically mentioned. By the later years of the reign, settlement of private suits (many of them concerned with marriage and testaments) made up the bulk of the commissioners' work. They were empowered to fine and imprison and it was these penalties, not available to other ecclesiastical courts, which gave their jurisdiction its bite.

Membership of the commission meant that certain temporal judges exercised ecclesiastical jurisdiction, but this was compensated for by general harmony between the two jurisdictions during the first half of Elizabeth's reign – major conflicts did not develop until temporal judges had ceased to sit on the commission. It is true that the High Commission did divert a certain amount of business from the diocesan courts, but this fact was offset to some extent by the intermittent granting of local commissions covering a given diocese to bishops, church lawyers, divines, J.P.s and others. The confidence of all ecclesiastical judges was probably strengthened by the knowledge that even if their own sentences proved unenforceable they could transfer the cases to the High Commission for effective prosecution. 'The whole ecclesiastical law', Archbishop Whitgift was to claim, 'is a carcasse without a soul, if it be not in the wantes supplied by the Commission.'[44] The effectiveness of the commission was first seriously jeopardized in the 1580s when Whitgift used it to enforce uniformity upon Puritan ministers who had the sympathy of men of influence. It was Puritan refusal of the *ex officio* oath which first gave the common lawyers a pretext upon which to oppose the commission.

## 6. *Reform*

Puritan criticisms of the courts Christian were probably more damaging than those made during the Reformation years. Many of the Elizabethan bishops themselves, in contrast to their predecessors, had serious reservations about the jurisdiction exercised by the courts. On doctrinal essentials they agreed with the Puritans. The Puritan attack, moreover, was cogent, systematic, sustained and practical. The judicial hierarchy and the law it administered were, they claimed, taken directly from the 'Pope's Shop'. No part of the machinery was more 'popish' than the archbishop's court of faculties, which sold dispensations. The marriage law in particular contained many objectionable 'popish' features. The Church's matrimonial and testamentary jurisdiction were even held by some to have been usurped from the lay magistrate, who could discharge the responsibilities involved more efficiently. The church courts negated in principle the godly discipline which the Puritans wanted to see installed in the English Church. Laymen, without vocation, had at their disposal excommunication, the ultimate sanction of the Church, which they employed not only in correction cases but to punish and humiliate the godly, to settle instance disputes, and in trivial matters. Papists and neuters, who staffed the courts, punished trivial offences against religious uniformity more severely than they punished evil livers. In the event, of course, such well-publicized and articulate attacks also affected the attitudes of unsuccessful litigants in the courts, even though they had no ideological sympathy with the Puritans.[45]

Throughout Elizabeth's reign the bishops sought to tackle the more glaring abuses encountered by means of gradual reform. Their main weapons were synodal and visitation articles. Reform of the ministry and the solution of pressing pastoral problems came at the head of the episcopal agenda. Overhaul of diocesan administration and procedure in litigation came lower on their list of priorities. Excessive use of excommunication and too frequent commutation of penance was dealt with in canons and articles from 1571 onwards: sentence of excommunication was to be pronounced only by a learned clergyman; commutation of penance was to be reserved to the bishop; commutation money was to be spent on specified objects; notorious offenders must express repentance publicly.

These important provisions went some way towards meeting Puritan criticisms but they did nothing to reduce litigation or facilitate closer control of court underlings. The qualifications of judges were stipulated in the canons of 1571 but the most important measures taken to limit litigation and vexatious *ex officio* suits were not taken until after Whitgift's elevation to Canterbury. The articles and canons agreed upon by him in 1597 subjected dispensation for marriage without banns to new safeguards, tightened up divorce procedure, facilitated curtailment of appeals by insufficient clergy against bishops who had refused institution, limited fees, and curtailed the number of active apparitors, forbidding their employment as informers or promoters. The success of the last-named would have gone some way to make the courts more popular with humble people. The canons of 1604 provided the fullest statement of the Church's administrative and disciplinary regulations to have emerged since the break with Rome. There were new controls on court personnel. A comprehensive canon dealt with fraud, deceit, neglect and disobedience on the part of registrars. These canons certainly came nearest to tackling the evils afflicting the church courts at root, but unfortunately they came at a time when the temporal courts had already launched a fiercer, vigorous attack upon ecclesiastical jurisdiction *per se*. Moreover, the canons were probably insufficiently harsh and precise, in particular with respect to control of the registrar and chancellor.[46]

The probability is that the canons did strengthen the hands of vigorous individual bishops and diocesan judges, but that improvement in standards was slow and piecemeal. The High Commissioners complained to Bishop Jegon of Norwich in 1603 that divers constitutions agreed upon to control court officials had been so little regarded 'as that the former complaints are now again more earnestly renewed than at any time heretofore'.

Commutation of penance without the bishop's knowledge and the indiscriminate granting of marriage licences were both stipulated. All bishops received this letter but probably few acted upon it with Jegon's promptitude. He directed a detailed questionnaire to judges and registrars in the diocese dealing with points raised in the letter and others besides. Subsequently all diocesan apparitors were suspended, some sacked, and all were administered a new oath promising honest discharge of duty. Jegon's efficiency is impressive but the fact that he had to undertake this purge suggests that the canon of 1597 along these same lines had not previously been implemented in the diocese.

### 7. *The encroachments of the common law*

During the second half of Elizabeth's reign, an increasing number of discontented litigants before the church courts sought the intervention of temporal judges in their suits through writs of prohibition. The determined and resourceful litigant, increasingly contemptuous of the ecclesiastical courts, saw the writ as simply one more means of carrying on the legal battle. The initial impetus came from parties in suits before the church courts; it is thus highly misleading to talk of an *attack* upon ecclesiastical jurisdiction by common lawyers before the very end of Elizabeth's reign.

The efficiency of the church courts did decline during the Reformation. Weakened episcopal control and the cultivation of litigation by court officials created conditions in which it was natural for parties to seek outside aid. But despite their deterioration there is no evidence to suggest that the church courts, even after the Reformation, were inherently more inefficient or oppressive than their temporal counterparts. Had the ecclesiastical courts had a weapon equivalent to the writ of prohibition, they might well have drawn business from the common law courts.

Contemporary churchmen sometimes suggested that there had been a sudden explosion in writs of prohibition towards the end of the century after a long period in which they had been rarely used. But in fact the writ had never gone right out of use.[47] Sir Edward Coke was able to cite 24 prohibitions concerned with the one issue of the tithe of great trees which had issued from King's Bench between 1542 and 1557. The number of prohibitions increased, gradually at first, as litigation in the ecclesiastical courts itself increased. The consistory court at Norwich apparently received no prohibitions at all between 1519 and 1551 and received one each year in 1552–4. The average rose to two a year in the 1560s; three were received for the first time in 1569. These prohibitions, however, did not halt the steady increase in litigation before the court.

Despite the growth of a more litigious spirit during the century, the great majority of cases before the church courts in the later sixteenth century were abandoned or peacefully settled before reaching sentence. Only a very small minority of litigants were determined enough to go to the lengths of seeking a writ of prohibition. Hence the apparently paradoxical situation which obtained at the beginning of the seventeenth century: the business of the English courts Christian reached their post-Reformation peak at the very moment when the writs of prohibition had made almost every field of ecclesiastical jurisdiction open to encroachment by the temporal courts. The issue of prohibitions to church courts dealing with a particular type of case, however, did not remove that sort of suit from their cognisance immediately.

The greatest number of prohibitions were granted in two types of suit very prominent in the great expansion of church court business in the late sixteenth century – those concerned with tithes and testaments. At the end of the century some 75 per cent of prohibitions were issued in tithe cases alone.[48] Long before the sixteenth century it had been established that church courts could not entertain pleas relating to tithes amounting to a quarter of the value of the benefice; to tithes already separated from the other nine parts; or to tithes claimed on a wide range of exempt products.[49] Numerous prohibitions were still issued on these grounds in the sixteenth century. Doubts about exemptions still remained. As late as 1598 the bishops regarded the exact limits of the exemption of great trees as a matter of dispute. A number of new grounds for the issue of prohibitions were established in the years after the break with Rome. By far the most important of these was that the spiritual court was entertaining a suit for full tithe despite the existence of a contrary tithing custom. But what constituted a custom? In the ecclesiastical law the validity of some prescriptions depended upon their being proved to have existed for 40 years; a statute of 1549 stipulated that tithes of a number of important products, including grain, were to be paid as they had been for 40 years past.[50] In respect of other tithes, the common law rule that a prescription must have existed 'time out of mind' remained valid. In addition, a number of statutes passed during the Reformation confirmed exemptions from tithe or created new ones on certain monastic possessions, lands covered by compositions, and barren land brought under profitable cultivation for seven years after conversion.[51] Suggestions that church courts were entertaining pleas aimed at destroying these statutory exemptions gave rise to numerous prohibitions. Yet prohibitions which interrupted suits related to tithing customs were the most important.

Temporal judges placed the largest share of the blame for the increase in tithe litigation upon the shoulders of ministers who would not accept time-honoured customs. Yet the temporal courts were ready enough to entertain the pleas of tithe-owners seeking to recover what they claimed was due to them. In 1587 a pretext in the Tithes Act of 1549 was found which enabled them to do so and to make further large inroads into the ecclesiastical jurisdiction.[52]

The Act of Wills of 1540 greatly increased individual freedom to devise land by will and may, therefore, have made a higher proportion of wills worth going to law over.[53] Attempts to force an executor to prove a will, or sections of a will dealing exclusively with the devise of land, were, however, regarded as good grounds for prohibition. As early as 1557 it was held that a prohibition would lie if an executor were sued for legacies which were to have been paid out of the proceeds of a sale of land; the principle was reaffirmed in James I's reign.[54]

By 1605, however, the doctrine of prohibitions had been so distorted as seriously to threaten every branch of ecclesiastical jurisdiction. The ecclesiastical judges feared in particular attacks on their conduct of cases in three respects: that they failed to observe their own procedural rules; that they insisted on testimony of two witnesses where the temporal courts required that of one only; that they dealt with matters covered by statute, whose interpretation belonged properly to temporal judges. The bishops pointed out that should this last be upheld, the spiritual courts could be deprived of their jurisdiction even in matters relating to faith and religious uniformity.[55]

The bishops in 1605 directed their complaints largely against King's Bench, Common Pleas and Exchequer. Despite the claims of Professor Jones, the Elizabethan Court of Chancery seems to have been careful not to infringe ecclesiastical jurisdiction.[56] But parties often did turn to Chancery if they wished to get their business settled in one court and avoid recourse to both the spiritual and the secular forums.[57] This was clearly the case with much testamentary litigation. Very seldom can Chancery intervention be described as 'encroachment' upon ecclesiastical jurisdiction.

If the early encroachments of the temporal judges can not fairly be described as an attack it is true that very gradually the temporal judges became more actively hostile towards ecclesiastical jurisdiction. From about 1580 onwards common lawyers withdrew from the work of the High Commission. Whitgift's proceedings against the Puritans and the subsequent dispute over the *ex officio* oath focussed attention once more upon procedural differences. In 1593 there appeared the fullest and ablest defence of ecclesiastical jurisdiction written since the Reformation – Richard Cosin's *Apologie of and for sundrie proceedings by Jurisdiction Ecclesiasticall*. The aggressiveness of the temporal judges increased as the resistance of the ecclesiastical lawyers hardened; their main attack followed the bishops' petition to the Privy Council in 1605 for reform of abuses connected with prohibitions. The crown did nothing to stem the flow of prohibitions. In James I's reign prohibitions began to interfere with proceedings by the High Commission itself.[58] The flow of prohibitions was stemmed after Coke's dismissal in 1616 and greatly reduced during the personal rule of Charles I. No king since Edward IV had been as tender of ecclesiastical jurisdiction.[59]

## 8. *Conclusion*

The church courts emerged from the Reformation with their jurisdiction almost intact, but morally weakened. The system resembled a house shifted from its foundations by heavy bombing. Lack of respect for the courts, slacker control over their personnel, the unwillingness of judges to enter into certain disputed spheres, all created conditions favourable to an explosion in litigation. A small but gradually increasing number of litigants began to see the potential of the writ of prohibition. Cautiously and at first indecisively the temporal judges responded to their demands. This process of *ad hoc* unplanned nibbling into the jurisdiction turned into an attack inspired by conscious hostility to the courts Christian only after the status and bounds of the jurisdiction became the subject of open controversy at the end of Elizabeth's reign. Whitgift's offensive against the Puritans brought the conflict to a head.

The Reformation marked an important stage in the long, gradual process by which the spiritual source of ecclesiastical jurisdiction lost its relevance for much of the court's work. A largely secular jurisdiction employing spiritual sanctions was an anomaly, but one which survived into the nineteenth century. Excommunication was dealt a serious blow by the break with Rome; after it, given the support of the common law courts, it could have remained as an effective material deterrent, but the temporal courts withheld their assistance. The courts could have done much with royal support. As it happened, only Charles I rallied to their cause and he was overthrown. Yet it was probably the Civil War which ensured the courts Christian a long and quiet old age, for it made the temporal judges regard their cause more kindly.

# Notes

*Note:* Places of publication are given only for books published outside the U.K.

## Introduction

1. M. Bowker, *The Secular Clergy in the Diocese of Lincoln, 1495–1520* (1968); F. Heal, 'The Clergy of Ely Diocese and the Reformation', *Transactions of the Cambridge and Huntingdonshire Antiquarian Society* (1975).
2. F. D. Price, 'An Elizabethan Church Official – Thomas Powell, Chancellor of Gloucester Diocese', *Church Quarterly Review,* **128** (1939), 94–112.
3. On a lesser jurisdiction controlled efficiently by commissaries see M. Bowker, 'Some Archdeacons' Court Books and the Commons' Supplication against the Ordinaries of 1532', in D. A. Bullough and R. L. Storey (eds), *The Study of Mediaeval Records: Essays in Honour of Kathleen Major* (1971).
4. R. O'Day, 'Thomas Bentham: A Case Study of the Problems of the Early Elizabethan Episcopate', *J.E.H.,* **23** (1972).
5. R. Houlbrooke, 'Church Courts and the People in the Diocese of Norwich, 1519–70' (D. Phil. thesis, University of Oxford, 1970).
6. R. A. Marchant, *The Church under the Law* (1969), 41–2.

## 1. The function of a bishop: the career of Richard Neile, 1562–1640

1. J. Keble (ed.), *The Works of Richard Hooker,* III (1836), *Of the laws of ecclesiastical polity,* Book VII, chapter 3 (1), 180.
2. W. Pierce (ed.), *The Marprelate Tracts, 1588, 1589* (1911), 23.
3. *Ibid.,* 24.
4. P. Collinson, *The Elizabethan Puritan Movement* (1967), 64.
5. W. P. Haugaard, *Elizabeth and the English Reformation* (1968), *passim.*
6. P. Hembry, *The Bishops of Bath and Wells, 1540–1640* (1967); C. Cross, 'The Economic Problems of the See of York: Decline and Recovery in the Sixteenth Century', *A.H.R.,* **18** (1970), supplement; F. Heal, 'The Bishops and the Act of Exchange in 1559', *H.J.,* *17* (1974), 227–46.

Notes

7. C. Cross, *The Royal Supremacy in the English Church* (1969), 142–4.
8. *Ibid.*, 184–5.
9. *Ibid.*, 187–90.
10. P. Collinson, 'Episcopacy and Reform in England in the later Sixteenth Century', in G. J. Cuming (ed.), *Studies in Church History*, III (1966), 91–125.
11. Collinson, *The Elizabethan Puritan Movement*, 201.
12. *Ibid.*, 243.
13. Cross, *The Royal Supremacy*, 199–201.
14. M. Curtis, 'The Hampton Court Conference and its Aftermath', *History*, **46** (1961), 1–16.
15. W. Lamont, *Godly Rule* (1969).
16. H. Trevor-Roper, 'King James and his Bishops', *H.T.* (1955).
17. S. Babbage, *Puritanism and Richard Bancroft* (1962).
18. M. Knappen (ed.), *Two Elizabethan Puritan Divines* (American Society of Church History, II, 1933).
19. See definition of Arminianism, p. 54.
20. N. Tyacke, 'Puritanism, Arminianism and Counter-Revolution', in C. Russell (ed.), *The Origins of the English Civil War* (1973), 119–43; M. Schwartz, 'Arminianism and the English Parliament, 1624–9', in *J.B.S.* (1973), 41–68.
21. G. Ornsby (ed.), *The Works of John Cosin*, I (Library of Anglo-Catholic Theology, 1853), Sermon 4, 85–105.
22. *Ibid.*, 96.
23. W. Prynne, *A Looking Glasse for all Lordly Prelates* (1636); C. Hill, *Antichrist in Seventeenth Century England* (1971).
24. T. M. Parker, 'Arminianism and Laudianism in Seventeenth Century England', in C. Dugmore and C. Duggan (eds), *Studies in Church History*, I (1964), 20–34.
25. J. Hurstfield, 'Church and State, 1558–1612: The Task of the Cecils', in G. J. Cuming (ed.), *Studies in Church History*, II (1965), 119–40.
26. W. Prynne, *The Antipathie of the English Lordly Prelacie* (1641), 222–223.
27. A. Wilson, *The Life and Reign of James I* (1706), 729.
28. W. Haller, *The Rise of Puritanism* (New York, 1938).
29. Rev. D. Parsons (ed.), *The Diary of Sir Henry Slingsby of Scriven, Bart* (1836), 20.
30. W. Prynne, *A Brief Survey and Censure of Mr Cozen's His Couzening Devotions* (1628).
31. E. Topsell, *The Historie of Four-footid Beastes* (1607); and *The Historie of Serpents* (1608).
32. R. Neile, *Marc Antonio de Dominis, Archbishop of Spalato, his Shiftings in Religion* (1624).
33. E. R. Foster (ed.), *Proceedings in Parliament 1610*, I (New Haven, 1966), 111–12.
34. T. Birch (ed.), *The Court and Times of Charles I*, II (1848), 176–9,

being a letter dated 20 September 1632 from Mr Pory to Sir Thomas Puckering.

35. Prynne, *The Antipathie of the Prelacie*, 222.
36. C. Mather, *Magnalia Christi Americana: Or the Ecclesiastical History of New England* (1702), 102.
37. P.R.O., SP 16/312: Neile's report to the king, January 1635/6.
38. P.R.O., SP 16/345: Neile's report to the king, January 1636/7.
39. W. Scott and J. Bliss (eds), *The Works of William Laud*, III (Library of Anglo-Catholic Theology, 1853), 129–255.
40. A. P. Kautz, 'The Selection of Jacobean Bishops', in H. S. Reinmuth, *Early Stuart Studies: Essays in Honour of D. H. Willson* (Minneapolis, 1970), 152–79.
41. William Laud: bishop of St David's 1621, London 1628; archbishop of Canterbury 1633; Augustine Lindsell: bishop of Peterborough 1632/3, Hereford 1633/4; John Cosin: bishop of Durham 1660; Benjamin Laney: bishop of Peterborough 1660, Lincoln 1663, Ely 1667.
42. G. Ornsby (ed.), *The Correspondence of John Cosin . . .*, I, (1853) 61.
43. I owe this information to Pat Mussett of the Prior's Kitchen, Durham.
44. See D. Marcombe, chapter 5, below, pp. 132–5, for discussion of the power and patronage of the bishop which provides a useful background to an understanding of Neile's authority in the seventeenth century.
45. Augustine Lindsell's will, P.R.O., PROB Seager 11.
46. Prynne, *A Looking Glasse*, 9.
47. B. Levack, *The Civil Lawyers in England, 1603–41* (1973), 158–95.
48. R. A. Marchant, *The Puritans and the Church Courts in the Diocese of York, 1560–1642* (1960); *The Church Under the Law* (1969).
49. Westminster Abbey Muniments, The Dean's Book, W.A.M. Book 7.
50. J. Armitage Robinson, *The Abbot's House at Westminster* (1911).
51. P.R.O., SP 16/345: Neile's report to the king, January 1636/7.
52. I. Basire, *A Funeral Sermon on the death of John Cosin* (1673), 77.
53. The statistics are drawn from my D. Phil. thesis in preparation, 'A Biography of Archbishop Richard Neile, 1562–1640'; see also R. A. Marchant, 'The Restoration of Nottinghamshire Churches, 1635–1640', *Transactions of the Thoroton Society*, **16** (1961), 57–93.
54. P.R.O., SP 14/119, 24 February 1620/1, letter from Locke to Carleton.
55. *Eagle*, college magazine of St John's, Cambridge, **17** (1893), 153–4: letter from Neile to the Master, 9 November 1623.
56. Prynne, *A Brief Survey*, a scheme echoed in the Parliament of 1628–9 to which this work was directed.
57. See R. O'Day, chapter 2, below; also 'Clerical Patronage and Recruitment in England in the Elizabethan and Early Stuart Periods' (Ph.D. thesis, University of London, 1972), *passim*; 'The Ecclesiastical Patronage of the Lord Keeper, 1558–1642', *T.R.H.S.*

5 Ser., **23** (1973); see S. Lander, chapter 9, below, for views on the authority of the church courts in the pre-Reformation period.

## 2. The reformation of the ministry, 1558–1642

1. D. M. Barratt, 'Conditions of the Parish Clergy from the Reformation to 1660 in the Dioceses of Oxford, Worcester and Gloucester' (D.Phil. thesis, University of Oxford, 1950), 54–5.
2. J. Strype, *The Life and Acts of John Whitgift*, I (1822), 536.
3. E.g., L.J.R.O., B/V/1/63, Curdworth, Astley, Lee Marston vicarages; D.W.L., Morrice MS. B, pt i, fos. 122–9.
4. See below, p. 88; also see M. R. O'Day, 'Clerical Patronage and Recruitment in England in the Elizabethan and Early Stuart periods' (Ph.D. thesis, University of London, 1972), *passim*.
5. *S.R.*, 21 Henry VIII, c. 13; E. Cardwell, *Synodalia . . .*, I (1822), 290, Canon 76 of 1604.
6. Bodleian, Tanner MS., 50, f. 53; L. Stone, 'Communication: The Alienated Intellectuals', *P. & P.*, **24** (1962).
7. Barratt, *op. cit.*, 7.
8. F. J. Fisher, 'Influenza and Inflation in Tudor England', *Ec.H.R.*, 2 ser., **18** (1965), 120–9; M. R. O'Day, 'The Ecclesiastical Patronage of the Lord Keeper', *T.R.H.S.*, 5 ser., **23** (1973), 90–1; see below.
9. G.L.M.S. 9535/1.
10. J. I. Daeley, 'The Episcopal Administration of Matthew Parker, Archbishop of Canterbury, 1559–75' (Ph.D. thesis, University of London, 1967), 178.
11. G.L.MS. 9535/1.
12. W. P. Haugaard, *Elizabeth and the English Reformation* (1968), 164.
13. Daeley, *op. cit.*, 183; O'Day, thesis, 236–8.
14. J. Bruce (ed.), *Correspondence of Matthew Parker* (Parker Society, 1853), 120–1.
15. Daeley, *op. cit.*, 185–9.
16. Haugaard, *op. cit.*, 165.
17. C.U.L., EDR A.5/1, fos. 67, 70–4, 75–80; O'Day, thesis, 25–50.
18. C.U.L., Ee.2.34, letter 146, f. 123r.
19. O'Day, thesis, 252.
20. *Ibid.*, 280–5.
21. C.C.R.O., EDA 1/3; O'Day, thesis, 258.
22. Bodleian, Tanner MS., 50, f. 35r.
23. O'Day, thesis, 254–5.
24. *C.S.P.D. Addenda, 1547–65*, 505.
25. H. Kearney, *Scholars and Gentlemen* (1970).
26. J. E. B. Mayor, 'Materials for the Life of Thomas Morton, Bishop of Durham', *Cambridge Antiquarian Society*, **3** (1865), 29; G. W. Fisher, *Annals of Shrewsbury School* (1898), 38.
27. H. C. Porter (ed.), *Puritanism in Tudor England* (1970), 186.
28. S. E. Morison, *The Founding of Harvard College* (Harvard, 1935), 96;

but see J. Simon, 'The Social Origins of Cambridge Students', *P. & P.*, **26** (1963), 64.
29. O'Day, thesis, 23–50.
30. C. W. Foster (ed.), *Lincoln Episcopal Records in the time of Thomas Cooper* (Lincoln Record Society, **2**, 1912), 138; C.U.L., Ee.2.34, document 36, f. 64r.
31. O'Day, 'The Ecclesiastical Patronage of the Lord Keeper', *passim*.
32. I.T.L., Petyt MS. 538/38, fos. 71–4.
33. W. P. M. Kennedy, *Elizabethan Episcopal Administration* (Alcuin Club Collections, 3 vols, 1924), III, 161–74.
34. R. O'Day, 'The Law of Patronage in the Early Modern Church of England', *J.E.H.*, **26** (1975), *passim*.
35. G.L.MS. 9535/2.
36. G.C.L., GDR Bishops' Act Books.
37. L.J.R.O., B/A/4A/17 and 18.
38. Bodleian, Oxford Diocesan Papers, C 264, vol. ii; e9; e12; e13; N.R.O., Ordination Books of Diocese of Peterborough, 1570–1642.
39. D. Robinson, *Beneficed Clergy in Cleveland and the East Riding, 1306–40*, Borthwick Paper, **37** (1969), 20–1; R. Donaldson, 'Patronage and the Church: A Study in the Social Structure of the Secular Clergy in the Diocese of Durham, 1311–1540' (Ph.D. thesis, University of Edinburgh, 1955), 315–35.
40. O'Day, thesis, 79–103.
41. *Ibid.*, 153–63.
42. *Ibid.*, 227.
43. *Ibid.*, 270, 312–14.
44. Andrew Clark, *Register of the University of Oxford*, vol. 2, *1571–1622 Matriculations and Tables* (Oxford Historical Society, 2 vols in 5, 1885–9).
45. O'Day, thesis, 275; M. R. O'Day, 'Church Records and the History of Education in Early Modern England, 1558–1642: A Problem in Methodology', *History of Education*, **2** (1973), *passim*.
46. *Ibid.*
47. Richard Baxter, *Reliquiae Baxterianae* (1696), 12.
48. O'Day, thesis, 44–50.
49. For an expansion of this point see O'Day, thesis, 7–20, 308–94.

3. The role of the registrar in diocesan administration

1. R. M. Haines, *The Administration of the Diocese of Worcester in the First Half of the Fourteenth Century* (1965), 133.
2. *Ibid.*, 3.
3. L.J.R.O., B/A/1/10, f. 52v.
4. L.J.R.O., B/A/20.
5. Haines, *op. cit.*, 133. It was also common for them to have practised as proctors: J. Potter, 'The Ecclesiastical Courts in the Diocese of Canterbury, 1603–65' (M.A. thesis, University of London, 1973), 147.

6. See below.
7. L.C.L., Dean and Chapter, Jurisdiction, XVII.
8. See below.
9. L.R.O., COR/R/2, 5, f. 5.
10. *Ibid.*, 12, f. 13.
11. *Ibid.*, 21, f. 22.
12. L.R.O., COR/R/3, 2, f. 2.
13. *Ibid.*, 8, f. 8.
14. *Ibid.*, 16, f. 18.
15. *Ibid.*, 45, f. 49.
16. L.R.O., COR/R/4, 18, f. 21; 35, f. 41.
17. L.J.R.O., B/A/19, Correspondence of Richard Raines.
18. See below.
19. L.R.O., COR/R/4, 54, f. 66.
20. L.R.O., COR/L/1, 23, f. 36; COR/L/2, 1, f. 1; 3, f. 5; 6, f. 10.
21. L.R.O., COR/R/3, 26, f. 29.
22. N.L.W., MS.4919D, fos. 97–8.
23. E. F. Jacob, Review of A. H. Thompson's *The English Clergy and their Organisation in the Later Middle Ages*, *E.H.R.*, **63** (1948), 239–41.
24. See M. R. O'Day, 'Clerical Patronage and Recruitment in England in the Elizabethan and Early Stuart Periods' (Ph.D. thesis, University of London, 1972), 72–195.
25. M. R. O'Day, 'The Ecclesiastical Patronage of the Lord Keeper, 1558–1642', *T.R.H.S.*, 5 ser. **23** (1973), 93–5 *passim*.
26. L.J.R.O., B/V/1/13, rear of volume.
27. L.R.O., COR/R/4, 15, f. 18; COR/M/2, 42, f. 58; 41, f. 57.
28. See M. R. O'Day, 'The Law of Patronage in the Early Modern Church of England', *J.E.H.*, **26** (1975), *passim*.
29. L.R.O., COR/R/3, 34, f. 38.
30. L.R.O., COR/R/2, 5, f. 5.
31. L.R.O., COR/R/3, 35, f. 39; 36, f. 40.
32. L.R.O., COR/R/2, 17, f. 18.
33. *Ibid.*, 15, f. 16.
34. L.R.O., COR/R/4, 48, f. 57.
35. L.R.O., COR/R/3, 14, f. 16; 15, f. 17; 27, f. 30; 46, f. 50.
36. *Ibid.*, 17, f. 20.
37. *Ibid.*, 31, f. 35; COR/R/2, 22, f. 23.
38. L.R.O., COR/R/3, 47, f. 51.
39. *Ibid.*, 51, f. 57.
40. L.R.O., COR/R/2, 18, f. 19.
41. L.R.O., COR/L/1, 35, f. 54.
42. L.R.O., COR/R/4, 5, f. 5.
43. *Ibid.*, 1, f. 1.
44. L.R.O., COR/R/3, 19, f. 22.
45. See above, pp. 47–81; also O'Day, thesis, *passim*.
46. *C.S.P.D., Chas. I*, 1635, 455.
47. P.R.O., PROB 11/73, C.1329: will of James Weston.

48. L.R.O., COR/R/1, 1, f. 1; 2, f. 2; 6, f. 6; 7, f. 7; 13, f. 14.
49. L.R.O., COR/R/4, 17, f. 20.
50. L.R.O., COR/R/3, 48, f. 52.
51. Reinhard Bendix, *Max Weber – an intellectual portrait* (New York, 1962), 452.

## 4. Clerical tax collection under the Tudors: the influence of the Reformation

1. J. J. Scarisbrick, 'Clerical Taxation in England, 1485 to 1547', *J.E.H.,* **11** (1960), 50.
2. *Ibid.,* 49.
3. B. M., Lansdowne MS. 165, fos. 128–9v; 146v–63; P.R.O., SP 12/263/80.
4. *V.E.*
5. D. Wilkins, *Concilia Magnae Britanniae* (1737), III, 594, 645, 659. F. Dietz, *English Government Finance, 1484–1558* (Urbana, 1920), 54.
6. L.P.L., Cartae Misc. I/80, gives detailed listing of amounts paid by various dioceses of the southern province to this grant.
7. *Calendar of Fine Rolls, 1471–85,* **23,** nos. 323, 325, 499, 880.
8. R. L. Storey (ed.), *Registrum Thomas Langley* (Surtees Society, I, 1949), 96–7; E. Hine (ed.), *Registrum Cuthbert Tunstall* (Surtees Society, 1952), 15; A. T. Bannister (ed.), *Registra Caroli Bothe . . .* (C.Y.S., 1921), 104–5.
9. *L.P.,* XX, i, 2.
10. *Registra Caroli Bothe,* 60.
11. R. S. Schofield, 'Parliamentary Lay Taxation 1485–1547' (Ph.D. thesis, University of Cambridge, 1963), 173.
12. *Registra Caroli Bothe,* 104–5.
13. Wilkins, *op. cit.,* III, 594.
14. Dietz, *op. cit.,* 54.
15. Wilkins, *op. cit.,* III, 698–9.
16. *L.P.,* Add. I, 457.
17. C.R.O., Ep./4/1, F.10; *L.P.,* III, ii, 3476.
18. L.P.L., Cartae Misc. I/76.
19. P. Heath, *English Parish Clergy on the Eve of the Reformation* (1969), 146.
20. *L.P.,* IV, i, 1264.
21. *Statutes at Large,* 26 Henry VIII, c.3.
22. Figures for the taxation of Pope Nicholas are taken from B.M., Cottonian MS., Tiberius, CX.
23. *L.P.,* XII, i, 21.
24. *Ibid.*
25. *L.P.,* X, 435.
26. *L.P.,* X, 316.
27. 32 Henry VIII, c.23; 34 and 35 Henry VIII, c.28; 37 Henry VIII, c.24.
28. Scarisbrick, *op. cit.,* 52.

29. *L.P.*, XIX, ii, 778.
30. *L.P.*, XX, i, 882.
31. *L.P.*, Add. II, 1702; *A.P.C. 1542–7*, 451.
32. E.g., bishop of Ely paid £4,130 out of total income of £17,080 between 1540 and 1547; bishop of Hereford paid £1,507 out of £6,148.
33. For growth of arrears see, e.g., P.R.O., E336/27; E347/17/pt 1. Figures for Rochester are in P.R.O., E347/17/pt 1.
34. P.R.O., E336/27; B.M., Add. Rolls, 1248, shows Canterbury £44 in arrears on subsidy of 1540–1.
35. 3 Edward VI, c.35.
36. P.R.O., SP 11/1/2; SP 10/16/91ff.
37. P.R.O., SP 11/1/2.
38. *Ibid.*
39. P.R.O., C 1/File 1326/5–7.
40. P.R.O., E347/1/book 5.
41. 7 Edward VI, c.4.
42. W. Peckham (ed.), *Act Book of the Dean and Chapter of Chichester* (Sussex Record Society, 1952), 20.
43. *A.P.C. 1552–4*, 71, 250.
44. *C.P.R. Mary*, I, 112–13; 389. See C. Haigh, Chapter 6, below.
45. P.R.O., E347/1/book 5.
46. 2 and 3 Philip & Mary, c.4.
47. R. Pogson, 'Revival and Reform in Mary Tudor's Church: a question of money', *J.E.H.*, **26** (1975).
48. Only in 1558 was Pole in a position to begin redirecting these funds from the centre.
49. P.R.O., SP 11/13/f. 114.
50. P.R.O., SP 11/11/40; *A.P.C. 1556–8*, 143.
51. *Ibid.*, 169, 397.
52. This was given in 1563, 1572, 1576, 1582, 1586, 1588 and 1591.
53. William Harrison, *The Description of England* (New York, 1968), 30.
54. 5 Elizabeth, c.29.
55. L.P.L., Cartae Misc. I/72.
56. J. Strype, *Annals of the Reformation* (1820–40), II, i, 330ff. I am grateful to Dr Houlbrooke for allowing me to consult his recent excellent discussion of Parkhurst's troubles.
57. P.R.O., E178/1569.
58. 14 Elizabeth, c.7.
59. P.R.O., SP 12/147/85.
60. P.R.O., E178/2074.
61. P. Hembry, *The Bishops of Bath and Wells, 1540–1640* (1967), 175–81; B.M., Lansdowne MS., 23/6; P.R.O., SP 46/40 f. 81.
62. B. M., Lansdowne MS., 23/6; P.R.O., SP 12/228/15.
63. P.R.O., E178/3451.
64. P.R.O., SP 12/156/51.
65. P.R.O., SP 46/27/f. 191.

66. P.R.O., SP 46/29/f. 256; L.P.L., Cartae Misc. VI/103.
67. B. M., Lansdowne MS., 17/32.
68. *Ibid.*, 18/25; P.R.O., SP 12/131/23.
69. P.R.O., SP 46/39/f. 33.
70. P.R.O., SP 12/149/37.
71. B.M., Lansdowne MS., 36/55; 45/42.
72. *Ibid.*, 20/72.
73. Bodleian, Tanner MS., 79/f. 21.
74. Gonville and Caius College, MS. 53/50, fos. 31–31v.
75. Record of receipts in P.R.O., SP 12/263/80.
76. B.M., Add. MS. 25460, f. 204.
77. P.R.O., SP 46/33, f. 47.
78. J. Ayre (ed.), *Sermons of Archbishop Sandys* (Parker Society, 1842), 199.
79. P.R.O., E178/2074.


## 5. The Durham dean and chapter: old abbey writ large?

1. Canon Fowler (ed.), *The Rites of Durham* (Surtees Society, **107**, 1903), 26, 60–1, 68–9, 75, 77–9, 81.
2. G. Allan, *Collecteana ... Dunelmensis*, 22 parts in 1 vol. (1770), Hegg, The Legend of St Cuthbert.
3. See R. B. Dobson, *Durham Priory* (1974); B. Wilson, 'The Changes of the Reformation Period in Durham and Northumberland' (Ph.D. thesis, University of Durham, 1939); D. Marcombe, 'The Dean and Chapter of Durham, 1558–1603' (Ph.D. thesis, University of Durham, 1973).
4. A. Hamilton Thompson (ed.), *Durham Cathedral Statutes*, Surtees Society, **143** (1929), xxiii–xxiv.
5. D. Knowles, *The Monastic Order in England* (1940), 133, 630–1; A. Hamilton Thompson, *The Cathedral Churches of England* (1925) 153.
6. K. Edwards, *The English Secular Cathedrals in the Middle Ages* (1949), 323–5.
7. *Ibid.*, 251–317, 322.
8. J. Youings, *The Dissolution of the Monasteries* (1971), 27, 84–5.
9. A. G. Dickens, *The English Reformation* (1964), 210–11; D. Knowles, *The Religious Orders in England*, III (1959), 389; Thompson, *Durham Cathedral Statutes*, xxvi.
10. Knowles, *The Religious Orders in England*, III, 390–1; Thompson (ed.), *Durham Cathedral Statutes*, xxvi–xxxiii, xxxix–xxxxi; Thompson, *The Cathedral Churches of England*, 9–10.
11. *Ibid.*; Knowles, *The Religious Orders in England*, III, 391–2. At Durham the dedication of the house was changed from St Mary and St Cuthbert to Christ and the Blessed Virgin Mary.
12. C. Sturge, *Cuthbert Tunstall* (1938).
13. Wilson, *op. cit.*, 73, 92; Prior's Kitchen, Dean and Chapter Register A, f. 95.

14. Wilson, *op. cit.*, 90–2; see e.g. Prior's Kitchen, Dean and Chapter Register A, fos. 201–2, 210–11; Thompson, *Durham Cathedral Statutes*, 233.
15. B.M., Harleian MS. 539, f. 149; Thompson, *Durham Cathedral Statutes*, 4–5.
16. Wilson, *op. cit.*, 95–105.
17. *Ibid.*, 106–7; Marcombe, *op. cit.*, 77, 162.
18. Thompson, *Durham Cathedral Statutes*, 14–63; J. J. Scarisbrick, *Henry VIII* (1968), 514.
19. I.e., between the rivers Tyne and Tees.
20. Thompson, *Durham Cathedral Statutes*, 15–63.
21. Dobson, *op. cit.*, 327–41.
22. Marcombe, *op. cit.*, 115–18.
23. Thompson, *Durham Cathedral Statutes*, 33.
24. R. Brentano, *York Metropolitan Jurisdiction and Papal Judges Delegate, 1279–96* (Berkeley, Cal., 1959).
25. Dobson, *op. cit.*, 218.
26. *Ibid.*, 215–19, 228–9.
27. *Ibid.*, 215–19, 232–41.
28. Wilson, *op. cit.*, 123; Fowler, *op. cit.*, 68–9, 75–7.
29. Prior's Kitchen, Dean and Chapter Register A, f. 28.
30. J. T. Fowler (ed.), *Extracts form the Account Rolls of the Abbey of Durham* (Surtees Society, **103**, 5 vols, 1898 etc.), 103, 286, 701, 720–721, 727, 741–3; *idem, The Rites of Durham*, 103, 285–6.
31. Fowler, *Account Rolls of Durham*, 731.
32. Knowles, *The Religious Orders in England*, III, 392.
33. Thompson, *Durham Cathedral Statutes*, xxxii.
34. Knowles, *The Religious Orders in England*, III, 392.
35. Thompson, *Durham Cathedral Statutes*, 105–9, 109–15.
36. *Ibid.*, 143–7; Marcombe, *op. cit.*, 12–15.
37. *Ibid.*, 162–71.
38. Borthwick I.H.R., High Commission Act Book 1, f. 203; 3, fos. 116–18; Durham Cathedral Library, Hunter MSS., 18a, f. 115, South Road, DR V/6 (1594: *Judge* v. *George Cliffe* – deposition of Robert Swift; G. Hinde (ed.), *Registers of Tunstall and Pilkington* (Surtees Society, **161**, 1952), 172.
39. Thompson, *Durham Cathedral Statutes*, xliii; Thompson, *The Cathedral Churches of England*, 186; Edwards, *op. cit.*, 819.
40. Knowles, *The Monastic Order in England*, 427.
41. Dobson, *op. cit.*, 123–4, 200.
42. *Ibid.*, 302–3.
43. Thompson, *Durham Cathedral Statutes*, 79–81, 89–91, 101–3.
44. Marcombe, *op. cit.*, 243.
45. J. Raine (ed.), *Depositions and Ecclesiastical Proceedings* (Surtees Society, **21**, 1849), 134; Edwards, *op. cit.*, 97.
46. Marcombe, *op. cit.*, 244–6.
47. *Ibid.*; *V.C.H. Durham*, II, (1907) 44–6.

48. Prior's Kitchen, York Book, f. 77.
49. Dobson, *op. cit.*, 222–3.
50. Thompson, *Durham Cathedral Statutes*, 75, 77, 109, 171, 175, 177.
51. Prior's Kitchen, York Book, fos. 77–8; Auckland was the bishop's residence.
52. Dobson, *op. cit.*, 60, 83–4.
53. Thompson, *Durham Cathedral Statutes*, 13; Marcombe, *op. cit.*, 39; Allan, *Collecteana . . . Dunelmensis*, grant of presentation to Tunstall.
54. W. Hutchinson, *The History and Antiquities of the County Palatine of Durham*, II (3 vols, 1785–94), 184–5; Marcombe, *op. cit.*, 77, 271–3.
55. *Ibid.*, 59–60.
56. *Ibid.*, 260–4; Hutchinson, *op. cit.*, II, 153–4; *V.C.H. Durham*, II, 43.
57. Dobson, *op. cit.*, 173, 176–8.
58. *Ibid.*, 187–8, 197–202.
59. R. B. Dobson, 'Richard Bell, Prior of Durham (1464–78) & Bishop of Carlisle (1478–95)', *Transactions of the Cumberland & Westmorland Antiquarian & Archaeological Society*, N.S. **65** (1965).
60. Marcombe, *op. cit.*, 81.
61. J. Bruce (ed.), *The Correspondence of Matthew Parker* (1853), 124; *37th Report of the Deputy Keeper of Public Records*, 79.
62. Marcombe, *op. cit.*, 85–7.
63. See entries in *D.N.B.*
64. Marcombe, *op. cit.*, 111, 120, 245.
65. *Ibid.*, 247–52.
66. P. G. Stanwood (ed.), *A Collection of Private Devotions* by John Cosin, xiii–xviii; G. Ornsby (ed.), *Bishop Cosin's Correspondence* (1869–72), 162. Richard Neile: bishop 1617–27.
67. Matthew Hutton: bishop 1589–95; Toby Matthew: bishop 1595–1606; William James: bishop 1606–17.
68. *V.C.H. Durham*, II, 44.
69. P. Smart, *A Sermon Preached in the Cathedral Church of Durham, 7 July 1628*, 23.
70. *Ibid.*, xxiii–v; *V.C.H. Durham*, II, 44–6.
71. Dobson, *op. cit.*, 58–60, 352.
72. *Ibid.*, 345–6, 368–71, 378–86.
73. P.R.O., SP 10/15 35; Newcastle Reference Library, Raine Testamenta Dunelmensis, B.3 (Robert Dalton); *C.S.P.D. Addenda 1547–65*, XI, 45; Foster.
74. Durham Cathedral Library, Hunter MSS., 18a, f. 115; Dobson, *op. cit.*, 74–7.
75. *Ibid.*, 80; Wilson, *op. cit.*, 90.
76. Marcombe, *op. cit.*, 20–1; Hutchinson, *op. cit.*, II, 176, 187, 201–2.
77. Marcombe, *op. cit.*, 20. The Pilkingtons supplied two prebendaries in our period and the Blakistons three. See Ornsby (ed.), *op. cit.*, 198.
78. *Ibid.*, 21–3.
79. *Ibid.*

80. *Ibid.*, 24–5, 98.
81. Dobson, *op. cit.*, 143.
82. *Ibid.*, 127–9, 134–5.
83. *Ibid.*; Prior's Kitchen, Dean and Chapter Register A, f. 131.
84. Hinde, *op. cit.*, 170; Raine (ed.), *Depositions and Ecclesiastical Proceedings*, 136–7.
85. Dobson, *op. cit.*, 166, 188.
86. Knowles, *The Religious Orders in England*, II, 326; Dobson, *op. cit.*, 184.
87. *Ibid.*, 144–9, 152–4, 156–60.
88. *Ibid.*, 164, 169.
89. *Ibid.*, 172.
90. *Ibid.*, 196.
91. *Ibid.*, 171–2.
92. Marcombe, *op. cit.*, 147, 287.
93. *Ibid.*, 36, 41–3.
94. *Ibid.*, 122–60.
95. Ornsby (ed.), *op. cit.*, xxii, 167.
96. Marcombe, *op. cit.*, 353.
97. *Ibid.*, 88–93.
98. *V.C.H. Durham*, II, 33–4; *C.S.P.D. Edward VI*, vol. 14, 18; Wilson *op. cit.*, 120–2.
99. Marcombe, *op. cit.*, 118, 130–1; P. Collinson (ed.), *The Letters of Thomas Wood, Puritan*, Institute of Historical Research Special Supplement, 5 (1960), 6.
100. Wilson, *op. cit.*, 70; Prior's Kitchen, Dean and Chapter Register C, fos. 191–2; D, f. 4.
101. Dobson, *op. cit.*, 253–5, 291–6, 388–9; Marcombe, *op. cit.*, 98.
102. *V.C.H. Cumberland*, II (1905), 70–2; W. H. Frere (ed.), *Visitation Articles and Injunctions*, III (Alcuin Club Collections, 16, 1908–10), 145–7, 338–9.
103. Edwards, *op. cit.*, x–xi.
104. Thompson, *The Cathedral Churches of England*, 166–9, 171.
105. M. C. Cross, '"Dens of Loitering Lubbers": Protestant Protest against Cathedral Foundations, 1540–1640', in D. Baker (ed.), *Studies in Church History*, 9 (1972), 236.
106. Thompson, *The Cathedral Churches of England*, 210; Edwards, *op. cit.*, xi.
107. Thompson, *Durham Cathedral Statutes*, x–xii.
108. *Ibid.*, lxii; Marcombe, *op. cit.*, 243–4; Frere, *op. cit.*, 146.
109. Thompson, *Durham Cathedral Statutes*, xxxix–xl.
110. Edwards, *op. cit.*, 323–4; Thompson, *The Cathedral Churches of England*, 20, 23–4.
111. Edwards, *op. cit.*, ix, xii; Marcombe, *op. cit.*, 260–7.
112. Thompson, *Durham Cathedral Statutes*, x–xvi, 75–7, 175–7; Marcombe, *op. cit.*, 263; R. B. Manning, *Religion and Society in Elizabethan Sussex* (1969), 16.

113. Edwards, *op. cit.*, 319; Thompson, *Durham Cathedral Statutes*, xlvii; Thompson, *The Cathedral Churches of England*, 190–1.
114. Edwards, *op. cit.*, 323–4; Thompson, *The Cathedral Churches of England*, 190–1; R. B. Walker, 'Lincoln Cathedral in the Reign of Queen Elizabeth', *J.E.H.*, **11** (1960), 189–91; Cross, *op. cit.*, 235.
115. Marcombe, *op. cit.*, 34–5, 293–4.
116. Edwards, *op. cit.*, 251–317; Thompson, *The Cathedral Churches of England*, 184–7; Marcombe, *op. cit.*, 8–9, 44–51.
117. Ornsby (ed.), *op. cit.*, 185.
118. Thompson, *The Cathedral Churches of England*, 191–2.
119. J. Raine (ed.), *Ecclesiastical Proceedings of Bishop Barnes* (Surtees Society, **22**, 1850), 81; Marcombe, *op. cit.*, 350–7.
120. Dobson, *op. cit.*, 9.

## 6. Finance and administration in a new diocese: Chester, 1541–1641

1. P.R.O., SP 12/48 f. 75v; *Salisbury MSS.*, H.M.C., XII, 669.
2. C.C.R.O., Bishop Bridgeman's Register, EDA 3/1, f. 35v; *V.E.*, *passim*; J. Strype, *Annals of the Reformation*, II(1) (1824), 575–6.
3. E.g. R. A. Marchant, *The Church Under The Law* (1969), 114–17, 120–1, 204–27; R. B. Manning, *Religion and Society in Elizabethan Sussex* (1969), 20–5, 85–6, 89–90, 135.
4. *L.P.*, XVI, 1135, g.4; T. Rymer, *Foedera* (1727–35), XIV, 717–24; C. Haigh, *Reformation and Resistance in Tudor Lancashire* (1975), 1–7.
5. *V.E.*, V, 219, 224, 227, 231; W. Dansey, *Horae Decanicae Rurales* (1835), I, 118–19; II, 369–71; C.C.R.O., EDR 6, 53–5; EDA 3/1, fos. 35v, 134v–35.
6. C.C.R.O., EDC 1/8, fos. 64/1, 77v, 78, 179; 1/10, fos. 130v, 140v, 145; *L.P.*, VIII, 496, no. 2; IX, 712; XII(1), 878; A. G. Dickens, *The Marian Reaction in the Diocese of York* (Borthwick Paper, XI, 1957), 8.
7. C. Haigh, 'A Mid-Tudor Ecclesiastical Official: The Curious Career of George Wilmesley', *Transactions of the Historic Society of Lancashire and Cheshire*, **122** (1970), 2–4, 6–10, 15–17; C.C.R.O., EDA 2/2, fos. 52–3; EDA 3/1, f. 35v.
8. A. B. Emden, *Biographical Register of the University of Oxford, A.D. 1501–1540* (1974), 346; Leeds City Library, Archives Department, RD/A/1A, fos. 15v, 36v; *L.P.*, XI, 202, g.8; *V.C.H. Lancashire* (1906–14), VIII, 245, 251; C.C.R.O., EDA 3/1, f. 35v.
9. *Ibid.*, fos. 80–80v, 110–10v, 119, 120v, 123.
10. Haigh, *Reformation and Resistance*, 1–7, 14–15; *L.P.*, VIII, 495–6; IX, 35, 712.
11. C.C.R.O., EDA 12/1, *passim;* EDC 5, 1550; EDA 3/1, fos. 126–6v, 128; P.R.O., DL 42/96, f. 33v; SP 12/48, fos. 73–4, 75; 12/118, f. 103; Borthwick I.H.R., CP.G. 1653.
12. C.C.R.O., EDA 3/1, fos. ix, 99–100v, 101v–2, 108–9v; F. Gastrell,

*Notitia Cestriensis* (Chetham Society, 1845–50), I, 52–3, 55; *Journals* of the House of Lords, I (1846), 112.

13. *L.P.*, XXI(1), 967; XXI(2), 183, 199, nos. 135, 137, 574, 771, g.10; B.M., Harleian MS. 604, f. 82; C.C.R.O., EDA 3/1, fos. 35v, 53–8v.

14. *Ibid.*, fos. 64, 108–23.

15. *Ibid.*, fos. 110–23; E. H. Phelps Brown and S. V. Hopkins, 'Seven Centuries of the Prices of Consumables Compared with Builders' Wage-rates', *Economica*, N.s. **23** (1956), 312–13.

16. C.C.R.O., EDA 3/1, fos. 111–11v, 112–13v, 118–18v, 121–2; *V.E.*, III, 103; Gastrell, *op. cit.*, I, 41–2.

17. P.R.O., DL 42/96, fos. 82v–3v; *C.P.R.*, Philip & Mary, I, 389.

18. J. Le Neve, *Fasti Ecclesiae Anglicanae*, III (1854), 266–7; C.C.R.O., EDC 1/14, fos. 96v, 113, 145v–6; 1/15, f. 165v; EDA 2/1, fos. 99, 103v.

19. Emden, *op. cit.*, 140; *C.P.R.*, Philip & Mary, IV, 260–1; C.C.R.O., EDA 3/1, fos. 64–5v; P. H. Hembry, *The Bishops of Bath and Wells, 1540–1640* (1967), 125–6; C. Cross, 'The Economic Problems of the See of York: Decline and Recovery in the Sixteenth Century', *Land, Church and People, A.H.R. Supplement* (1970), 73–4.

20. P.R.O., SP 12/48, f. 75v; J. Bruce (ed.), *The Correspondence of Matthew Parker, 1535–75* (1853), 100; C.C.R.O., EDA 3/1, fos. 67–9v.

21. *C.S.P.D.*, *1595–7*, 404; C.C.R.O., EDA 3/1, fos. 73–7, 80–80v, 133v–4.

22. P.R.O., SP 12/143, fos. 19, 32v; 12/252, fos. 177–7v; Leeds City Library, Archives Department, RD/A/2, fos. 1v–2v, 33v; *C.S.P.D.*, *1595–7*, 404; C.C.R.O., EDA 3/1, fos. 80–80v; *Salisbury MSS.*, XII, 669.

23. P.R.O., SP 12/48, f. 75v; 12/252, fos. 177–7v; *V.C.H. Lancashire*, IV, 196; *Salisbury MSS.*, V, 210; XII, 669; G. Ormerod, *History of the County Palatine and City of Chester*, II (1882), 19; Gastrell, *op. cit.*, I, 10, 11; G.T.O. Bridgeman, *History of the Church and Manor of Wigan* (Chetham Society, 1888–90), 236, 167; C.C.R.O., EDC 1/30, f. 80; *Commonwealth Church Surveys* (Record Society of Lancashire and Cheshire, 1878), 252.

24. P.R.O., SP 12/1, fos. 85–6; 12/252, fos. 177–7v; C. Hill, *Economic Problems of the Church* (Panther edn, 1969), 205; Borthwick I.H.R., V.1595–6/CB1, f. 22; C.C.R.O., EDV 1/3, f. 6; 1/10, f. 115v; 1/12a, f. 91v; 1/13, fos. 69, 116v; *Kenyon MSS.*, H.M.C., 7.

25. Borthwick I.H.R., V.1578–9/CB3, fos. 63, 77; C.C.R.O., EDA 2/2, fos. 28–30v; EDC 1/20, f. 319v; EDC 5, 1574; EDV 1/12a, f. 121; 1/12b, f. 180; 1/13, f. 205v; *V.C.H. Lancashire*, VII, 42.

26. Haigh, 'A Mid-Tudor Ecclesiastical Official', 9, 16–17, 21; C.C.R.O., EDA 3/1, fos. ix, 33v, 108–9v, 122v–23, 131, 155v, 157v–8, 159v–60; EDA 2/2, fos. 48–9v, 52–3.

27. Borthwick I.H.R., HC. AB 6, fos. 64, 65v, 75v, 82, 119; V1578–9/CB3,

f. 63; VI595–6/CBI, fos. 19r & v; C.C.R.O., EDA 3/1, fos. 131, 170v.

28. C.C.R.O., EDA 2/2, f. 198; EDC 1/30, fos. 359, 361; EDR 6, 71–5; EDA 3/1, fos. 162v–3, 170, 239; Borthwick I.H.R., PN 2, 1599; F. R. Raines, *Fellows of the Collegiate Church of Manchester* (Chetham Society, 1891), 72.

29. C.C.R.O., EDA 3/1, fos. 131, 134v–5, 258–9.

30. Borthwick I.H.R., CP. H.2257; C.C.R.O., EDA 3/1, fos. 131, 134v–5.

31. See R. O'Day, 'Cumulative Debt: The Approach of the Bishops of Coventry and Lichfield to their Economic Problems from the Reformation to the Civil War', *Midland History* (1975), for comparable situation at Lichfield.

32. C.C.R.O., EDA 3/1, fos. ix, 14v, 35, 81–1v, 82–2v, 90, 130v, 131v–4, 135v–7; Gastrell, *op. cit.*, I, 37.

33. S.C.R.O., Earl of Bradford MSS. from Weston Park, 3/1, pp. 153–222 (I am most grateful to Dr S. J. Lander for drawing this volume to my attention); C.C.R.O., EDA 3/1, fos. 131v–3v, 156v–96v; Gastrell, *op. cit.*, I, 36–63; *Commonwealth Church Surveys*, 171–221. For the 1634 order, see C.C.R.O., EDA 3/1, f. 254; cf. Hembry, *op. cit.*, 238–9; Hill, *op. cit.*, 311.

34. *Commonwealth Church Surveys*, 197–201; C.C.R.O., EDA 3/1, fos. 115–16, 130v, 132v–3, 251v–2; W. Scott and J. Bliss (eds), *The Works of William Laud* (Library of Anglo-Catholic Theology, III, 1847–50), 254; Gastrell, *op. cit.*, I, 59; Bridgeman, *op. cit.*, 416–18, 421.

35. C.C.R.O., EDA 3/1, fos. 53–58v, 133v–4, 134v–5.

36. Bridgeman, *op. cit.*, 203–35, 252, 340–64; *C.S.P.D.*, *1631–3*, 578–9, 583; *1633–4*, 7, 8, 10, 16, 38, 39, 51, 56–7, 67, 75, 78–9, 92, 121, 133, 145–6, 163, 169, 291, 339–40; *1634–5*, 404–5; *1635–6*, 61; R. V. H. Burne, *Chester Cathedral* (1958), 98, 120, 130.

37. C.C.R.O., EDA 3/1, fos. 35v, 131v–44v; Hembry, *op. cit.*, 11–13, 143–4; F. Heal, 'The Tudors and the Church Lands: Economic Problems of the Bishopric of Ely', *Ec.H.R.*, 2 Ser., **26** (1973), 199, 207–8; Cross, *op. cit.*, 68, 78; F. R. H. Du Boulay, 'Archbishop Cranmer and the Canterbury Temporalities', *E.H.R.*, 67 (1952), 34, 36.

38. Phelps Brown and Hopkins, *op. cit.*, 312–13; cf. L. Stone in *A.H.R.* (1971), 87, 111; Heal, *op. cit.*, 208–9. There are accounts for Chester for 1541, 1594–5 and 1619–37; on the basis of changes in property, and of rents and fines, income has been calculated for other dates. Individual rents remained stable, 1541–1637, and spiritual revenues varied little, so any inaccuracies will result from fines and any unrecorded sources of income. I have assumed that there was no substantial change in income from fines between 1540s and 1587c; thereafter I have assumed that, on average, one fine could be taken in each year. Gastrell, *op. cit.*, I, 34, an income from fines of £180 p.a.

7. Some problems of government in a new diocese:
the bishop and the Puritans in the diocese of Peterborough,
1560–1630

1. S. Gunton, *The History of the Church at Peterborough* (1686), 57;
   A. Hamilton Thompson, *Visitations in the Diocese of Lincoln* (Lincoln
   Record Society, **33**, i, 1940), ix, xxi; W. T. Mellows, *The Foundation
   of Peterborough Cathedral* (Northamptonshire Record Society, **13**,
   1941), 1–12; cf. R. C. Richardson, 'Puritanism and the Ecclesiastical Authorities: The Case of the Diocese of Chester', in B.
   Manning (ed.), *Politics, Religion and the English Civil War* (1973),
   3–33.
2. W. T. Mellows, *The Last Days of Peterborough Monastery* (Northamptonshire Record Society, **12**, 1947), 4–20; Mellows, *Peterborough
   Cathedral*, 41–8; A. J. Camp, *Wills and their Whereabouts* (1963), 53,
   gives details of division of probate jurisdiction.
3. B.M., Lansdowne MS. 6, f. 143; Stowe MS. 570, fos. 92–3; Mellows,
   *Peterborough Cathedral*, 12–22.
4. *V.C.H. Northants*, II (1906), 473; Mellows, *Peterborough Monastery*, 6.
5. Mellows, *Peterborough Cathedral*, lxii–lxiii; *V.C.H. Northants*, II, 179–
   180; N.R.O., M (T), 1, 11, 41; P.D.R., MD.772; Correction Book
   (hereafter Corr. Book) 15, f. 216; *D.N.B.*, Scambler.
6. Mellows, *Peterborough Cathedral*, xii, xxxi–xxxii; N.R.O., M(T), 1, 4,
   11; B.M., Lansdowne MS. 1025, 263.
7. *D.N.B.*, Howland; H.M.C. Report, *Salisbury MSS.*, V, 11, 333.
8. Mellows, *Peterborough Cathedral*, xxxiii, where Scambler is shown to
   have alienated his patronage on one occasion. He had difficulties in
   enforcing the cathedral statutes on residence by prebendaries:
   B.M., Lansdowne MS. 38, f. 178r and v; Mary made the same sort
   of grant to the bishop of Durham, see above, p. 133.
9. Mellows, *Peterborough Cathedral*, 20; *V.C.H. Northants*, II, 467;
   L.P.L., Cartae Miscellenae, xiii, 56.
10. B.M., Lansdowne MSS. 443–5; N.R.O., P.D.R., Institution Bks,
    I–IV, esp. IV, fos. 14, 16v; cf. W. J. Sheils, 'The Puritans in Church
    and Politics in the Diocese of Peterborough, 1570–1610' (Ph.D.
    thesis, University of London, 1974), 82; for Knightley and Wiburn
    see P. Collinson, *The Elizabethan Puritan Movement* (1967), 141–4,
    172, 369, 394; for Whiston, see Sheils, *op. cit.*, 90, 138–9, 178–80.
11. See M. R. O'Day, 'The Ecclesiastical Patronage of the Lord Keeper,
    1558–1642', *T.R.H.S.* 5 Ser. **23** (1973), 89–109; B.M. Lansdowne
    MS. 443, *passim*, 445, f. 121v; N.R.O., P.D.R., Corr. Books 23,
    f. 98v; 26, fos. 203v., 295; Sheils, *op. cit.*, 55–63.
12. H. I. Longden, *Northamptonshire and Rutland Clergy, 1500–1900*, XII
    (16 vols, 1938–52), 249; N.R.O., P.D.R., Archdeacon's Court
    Book 1, fos. 2, 10, 14, 28, 32, 33; Book 2, fos. 18–28; Richard
    Talentyre was the official in the 1570s, cf. Archdeacon's Court
    Book 4, *passim*.

13. N.R.O., P.D.R., Corr. Book 21, fos. 240–2; Corr. Books 24, 55, *passim.*

14. B.M., Stowe MS. 570, f. 96; Longden, *op. cit.,* IV, 125; VII, 129; the order is printed in *V.C.H. Northants,* II, 44–5; for the fast and Sheppard's intervention see J. Field, *A Caveat for Parsons Howlet and the rest of his darke broode* (1581), esp. sigs G.vii–H.ii.

15. *D.N.B.,* Buckeridge; B.M. Lansdowne MS. 57, f. 172; Sloane MS. 271, f. 25r and v; P.R.O., S.C. 5/C 78/3; C 28/36; C 80/40.

16. R. A. Marchant, *The Church under the Law* (1969), 114–17, 204–27; R. B. Manning, *Religion and Society in Elizabethan Sussex* (1969), 211–17.

17. *D.N.B.,* Chambers; Mellows, *Peterborough Cathedral,* lxi–lxiii; N.R.O. M (T) 4, 41.

18. N.R.O., P.D.R., Corr. and Instance Books; in the north-eastern part of the diocese *c.*66 per cent of the sittings were held at Oundle and 40 per cent at Peterborough, usually in the cathedral.

19. N.R.O., P.D.R., Corr. Books, 8, f. 124v; 10, fos. 12v, 17v; 14, f. lv, 170; 23a., f. 73; 45, p. 186; P.R.O., SP 14/12/96.

20. N.R.O., P.D.R., Corr. Books 33 and 39, and Instance Books 22 and 26, show Dove's activity. Corr. Book 25, fos. 6, 11v: Howland sat personally in case of 1591 involving survival of a Puritan exercise at Oakham, see Sheils, *op. cit.,* 101; *D.N.B.,* Lambe.

21. B.M., Lansdowne MS. 17, f. 55r and v.; Leicester's letters are in Magdalene College Library, Cambridge, Pepys MSS., 'Papers of State', ii, 389–90, 647–8; and B.M., Harleian MS. 398, fos. 51v–53v, attributed there to Nicholas Bacon.

22. N.R.O., P.D.R., Corr. Book 9, fos. 1–4v; B.M., Harleian MS. 398, f. 53; A. Peel (ed.), *The Seconde Parte of a Register* (1915), i, 121–3; Sheils, *op. cit.,* 81.

23. N.R.O., P.D.R., Corr. Books 6, f. 73; 9, fos. 6, 14; for Sharpe and Marprelate see F. Arber, *An Introductory Sketch to the Martin Marprelate Controversy* (1879), 94–104.

24. N.R.O., P.D.R., Corr. Book 9, esp. fos. 1, 4v, 5v, 18, 40, 44v, 52v, 56v; H.M.C., *Various Collections* iii, 1–3; R. G. Usher, *The Rise and Fall of the High Commission* (reprinted 1968), additional bibliography; F. D. Price, *The Commission for Ecclesiastical Causes within the Dioceses of Bristol and Gloucester, 1574* (Bristol and Gloucester Archaeological Society Record Series, X, 1942).

25. B.M., Lansdowne MS. 17, f. 55r and v; Sheils, *op. cit.,* 90–1.

26. Peel (ed.), *op. cit.,* i, 241; ii, 92.

27. Collinson, *op. cit.,* 432–44; N.R.O., P.D.R., Visitation Book 4; Corr. Books 23a, 25.

28. N.R.O., P.D.R., Corr. Book 21, fos. 239v, 239b; see Corr. Book 14, *passim,* for references to Ellis's surrogate, John Bacchus, who often sat at Oundle; for Hickman see B. Levack, *The Civil Lawyers in England 1603–41* (1973), 239.

29. Longden, *op. cit.,* ii, 339; N.R.O., P.D.R., Corr. Books 26–9, give

an idea of Butler's activities; B.M., Sloane MS. 271, f. 25r and v.

30. H.M.C., *Salisbury MSS.*, XVII, 46–7, 58–9; P.R.O., SP 14/12/96.
31. Mellows, *Peterborough Cathedral*, xxxi; Sheils, *op. cit.*, 146; N.R.O., P.D.R., Corr. Books 21, f. 189; 30, f. 31.
32. Longden, *op. cit.*, xv, 111; N.R.O., P.D.R., Visitation Book 7, fos. 57v–60; Corr. Book 21, f. 239b, Corr. Book 40, f. 82; R. Bancroft, *Dangerous Positions and Proceedings* (1593), 79.
33. P.R.O., SP 14/12/69; H.M.C., *Salisbury MSS.*, XVI, 42; XVII, 21; cf. S. B. Babbage, *Puritanism and Richard Bancroft* (1962), 147–232.
34. Longden, *op. cit.*, v, 221; N.R.O., P.D.R., Institution Book IV, f. 14; for Gibson in 1584 see Peel (ed.), *op. cit.*, II, 92.
35. See N.R.O., P.D.R., Corr. Book 38, f. 111v; X648/1, f. 157. The only Puritan member of an important county family to be presented before 1600 was John Wake of Beddington in 1583, but Sir Richard Knightley and Nicholas Dryden were cited in the early seventeenth century.
36. M. Bateson (ed.) 'A Collection of Original Letters from the Bishops to the Privy Council 1564 . . .', *Camden Miscellany*, N.S., LIII (1895), 35–6; J. Strype, *Annals of the Reformation during Queen Elizabeth's Reign*, III (1824), 2, 452; N.R.O., P.D.R., Corr. Book 25, f. 13v.
37. *D.N.B.*, Lambe; Levack, *op. cit.*, 48–9, 177, 182, 238, 246–7; N.R.O., P.D.R., Corr. Book 55, f. 298; Corr. Book 61, *passim*.
38. F. D. Price, 'The Abuses of Excommunication and the Decline of Ecclesiastical Discipline under Elizabeth I', *E.H.R.*, **57** (1942), 51–151; Manning, *op. cit.*, 71–2, 188; Richardson, *op. cit.*, 4–7.
39. H.M.C., *Salisbury MSS.*, V, 333; XVII, 46. See Borthwick I.H.R., Bp. C. & P. 20, for information on Sandys' grants of leases to members of his family.

## 8. The Prerogative Court of Canterbury from Warham to Whitgift

1. E.g. Thomas Wright (ed.), *Political Poems and Songs, 1327–1485* (1859–61), I, 304n., 323.
2. E. Coke, *Institutes*, IV (1797), 335; T. B. Howells, *State Trials*, II (1816), 1145; cf. R. A. Marchant, *The Church under the Law . . . 1560–1640* (1969), 53 n.4, and sources there cited.
3. There was some redistribution of responsibilities with creation of the new dioceses in the 1540s.
4. See P. Collinson, *The Elizabethan Puritan Movement* (1967), 38–42.
5. I. J. Churchill, *Canterbury Administration* (1933), chapter 9; E. F. Jacob (ed.), *The Register of Henry Chichele . . . 1414–43* (C.Y.S., II, 1937), xi; for role of consistory court of Canterbury in prerogative matters see B. L. Woodcock, *Medieval Ecclesiastical Courts in the Diocese of Canterbury* (1952), 73–4, 133–4.
6. E.g. Marchant, *op. cit.*; R. L. Storey, *Diocesan Administration in the*

*Fifteenth Century*, Borthwick Paper, **16** (1959); M. Bowker, 'The Commons' Supplication against the Ordinaries in the light of some archidiaconal acts', *T.R.H.S.*, 5 Ser. **21** (1971), 61–77.

7. E. Coke, *Reports*, IX (1776), 37–8; G. R. Elton, *Reform and Renewal* (1973), 129–38; W. S. Holdsworth, *A History of English Law*, I (1903), 625ff.

8. Jacob, *op. cit.*, II, xii–xiii, on the London Hustings Court; M. Bateson (ed.), *Records of the Borough of Leicester, 1509–1603* (1905), 235; T. P. Wadley (ed.), *The Great Orphan Book and Book of Wills* (Bristol and Gloucester Archaeological Society, 1886); M. A. Farrow (ed.), *Index of Wills proved at Norwich 1370–1550* (Norfolk Record Society, XVI, 1943) i, ix.

9. Penry Williams, *The Council in the Marches of Wales* (1958), 100; W. J. Jones, *The Elizabethan Court of Chancery* (1967), 400–17.

10. Examples of relations with other courts: Coke, *Reports*, V, 27; VI, 23; Holdsworth, *op. cit.*, I, 629. For the impact of prohibitions, see B. P. Levack, *The Civil Lawyers in England 1603–41* (1973), 72, and sources there cited.

11. D. Wilkins, *Concilia Magnae Britanniae*, III (1737), 641; Churchill, *op. cit.*, I, 412.

12. P.R.O., PROB 11/13 f. 12.

13. Marchant, *op. cit.*, 103–7.

14. Wilkins, *op. cit.*, III, 653–57; *H.M.C. 9th Report* I, 56.

15. G. Parrish, *The Forgotten Primate* (Historical Association Pamphlet, 1971), 18.

16. *L.P.*, I, i, 1780; I, ii, 1941.

17. A £10 limit was also negotiated by Lincoln diocese: see M. Bowker, 'The Supremacy and the Episcopate: the struggle for control 1534–40', *Historical Journal*, **18** (June 1975), 240.

18. J. Strype, *Ecclesiastical Memorials*, I (1822), i, 109–12.

19. B.M., Cottonian MS., Cleopatra F II f. 173.

20. P.R.O., SP 1/26 f. 242.

21. But see B.M., Cottonian MS., Cleopatra F II f. 202v.; P.R.O., SP 1/35 f. 193ff.

22. P.R.O., PROB 11 *passim*; Original Wills, PROB 10/May 1529/ Butler has 'in edibus Magistri Joannis Cockes coram eo et Magistro Edwardo Carne, substituto Magistris Johannis Oliver'. Only scattered fragments survive for the joint régime: part of an original file for 1529 (PROB 35/1) is heavily endorsed Warham.

23. Wilkins, *op. cit.*, III, 377–8; S. Lehmberg, *Reformation Parliament* (1970), 84.

24. See below, pp. 208–9.

25. E. Nys, *Le Droit Romain* (Brussels, 1910), 51–3.

26. *S.R.*, 24 Henry VIII, c.12; 25 Henry VIII, c.19; also G.I.O. Duncan, *The High Court of Delegates* (1971).

27. P.R.O., PROB 35/4 no. 8; Special Jurisdictions, Misc., PROB 34/4/5.

28. C. J. Kitching, 'The Probate Jurisdiction of Thomas Cromwell as Vicegerent', *B.I.H.R.*, **46** (1973), 102–6.
29. P.R.O., PROB 34/4/5.
30. S.R., 1 Edward VI, c.2; For Cromwell's citations see PROB 34/4/1.
31. P.R.O., PROB 10/16, bundles for Sept.–Dec.; PROB 11/33, fos. 31–3. The copies are distinguishable from similar PCC documents by means of the annotation and registration marks endorsed.
32. *S.R.*, 37 Henry VIII, c.17; 1 and 2 Philip & Mary, c.8.
33. E.g., P.R.O., PROB 29/9 fos. 31v, 32r.
34. P.R.O., PROB 34/2/1: Testamentary acts for the circuit; PROB 34/1 fos. 63r, 70v, 73r.
35. See below, pp. 245–53.
36. Levack, *op. cit.*, 16ff; E. Nys, *Le Collège des Docteurs en Droit Civil* (Brussels, 1910).
37. Foster, Early Series, I, 296.
38. *Ibid.*, I, 322.
39. Venn, pt I, II, 280; *D.N.B.*
40. Venn, pt I, II, 69.
41. Foster, II, 621; *D.N.B.*
42. Wilkins, *op. cit.*, IV, 274.
43. Foster, I, 290.
44. P.R.O., PROB 29/10 fos. 98r, 100r, 108r.
45. *Ibid.*, f. 121r; Foster, I, 301; *D.N.B.*
46. P.R.O., PROB 29/10, f. 131v.
47. *Ibid.*, fos. 134v, 141v.
48. *A.P.C. 1558–70*, 31.
49. Haddon, like Cooke before him and Lewen after, was an M.P.
50. P.R.O., PROB 29/10, *passim.*
51. E.g. P.R.O., PROB 29/10, f. 47v.
52. See Churchill, *op. cit.*, I, 450–2; Levack, *op. cit.*, 21ff.; C.I.A. Ritchie, *The Ecclesiastical Courts of York* (1956); Marchant, *op. cit.*, 50.
53. Examples in P.R.O., PROB 35.
54. Duncan, *op. cit.*, 198.
55. P.R.O., PROB 29; P. Floyer, *The Proctors' Practice* (1746); cf. C. R. Cheney, *Handbook of Dates* (1945), 73.
56. Churchill, *op. cit.*, I, 405; P.R.O., PROB 11/40 f. 38; 11/41 f. 23; 11/31 fos. 14–5; 11/53 f. 7.
57. P.R.O., PROB 29/1; W. C. Richardson, *History of the Court of Augmentations* (Baton Rouge, 1961), 173n.; J. Foxe, *Acts and Monuments*, VI (1858), i, 94–5: J. A. Muller, *Stephen Gardiner* (New York, 1926), 374.
58. P.R.O., PROB 29/9; cf. PROB 29/5/1 for Walker acting as deputy at an earlier date.
59. Borthwick I.H.R., DR Fees, P.C.C. fee list.
60. Few original files of proxies have survived.
61. Churchill, *op. cit.*, I, 451; Duncan, *op. cit.*, 196.

62. Wilkins, *op. cit.*, IV, 275.

63. C. H. Williams (ed.), *English Historical Documents*, V (1896), 734.

64. Churchill, *op. cit.*, I, 436: Elton, 'The Commons' Supplication of 1532', 518n.; *H.M.C. 9th Report*, 120–1; Wilkins, *op. cit.*, III, 711, 858.

65. J. Strype, *Memorials of Cranmer*, I (1840), 67–8; II, no. 18.

66. Wilkins, *op. cit.*, III, 858.

67. *Ibid.*, IV, 333–5.

68. See archbishops' registers, *passim*.

69. P.R.O., SP 12/144, nos. 67, 68.

70. P.R.O., PROB 11/31 f. 7; 11/24 f. 4; 11/42A f. 53.

71. P.R.O., PROB 11/91 f. 1.

72. P.R.O., PROB 11/46 f. 31; 11/42B f. 34.

73. Walter Haddon left books to his son Clere to further his studies, P.R.O., PROB 11/53 f. 7; cf. PROB 11/91 f. 1.

74. Marchant, *op. cit.*, 23, 31–2; Woodcock, *op. cit.*, 45–9; Jacob, *op. cit.*, II, xxv.

75. P.R.O., PROB 8/1.

76. B.M., Cottonian MS., Cleopatra F I f. 363 (old numbering).

77. J. Strype, *Grindal* (1821), 302–6.

78. Wilkins, *op. cit.*, IV, 333.

79. J. E. Neale, *Elizabeth I and her Parliaments, 1584–1601* (1957), 356–8; Wilkins, *op. cit.*, IV, 347.

80. E.g. I.T.L., Petyt MSS., 538/54 fos. 1–70, and 538/38 f. 188ff.; B.M., Cottonian MS., Cleopatra F II f. 233.

81. J. Ayliffe, *Parergon Juris Canonici Anglicani* (1734), 551–2.

82. Wilkins, *op. cit.*, IV, 366.

83. *Ibid.*, 396, esp. nos. 92, 93.

84. But see Borthwick I.H.R., DR Fees, Probate, for undated schedule (late-Elizabethan) of fees regularly charged in the court with which to compare the few surviving bills of costs of litigation of the earlier period.

85. *S.R.*, 21 Henry VIII, c.5; see table 1 on p. 213 below.

86. See P.R.O., SP 12/144 no. 67.

87. Coke, *Institutes*, IV, 334.

88. B.M., Cottonian MS., Cleopatra F I f. 345.

89. Presumably for bringing in a will, if required to do so.

90. P.R.O., PROB 10/Mar. 1527.

91. Marchant, *op. cit.*, 53.

92. P.R.O., PROB 35.

93. No trace of a *per diem* fee as at York or as recorded in Whitgift's 1597 book of fees.

94. P.R.O., SP 12/44 no. 68: Argall estimated that 200 executors p.a. brought in testaments for probate, requiring no proctorial representation; 200 were brought in by apparitors; more were delivered by solicitors from the common law courts. Approximately 100 p.a. were brought in by the proctors.

## 9. Church courts and the Reformation in the diocese of Chichester, 1500–58

1. H. Mayr-Harting (ed.), *The Acta of the Bishops of Chichester, 1075–1207* (C.Y.S., **56**, 1962), 55–6, 198; J. H. Denton, *English Royal Free Chapels* (1970), 44–6, 113–14.
2. C. Deedes, *The Episcopal Register of Robert Rede, Bishop of Chichester, 1397–1415*, vol. 1 (Sussex Record Society, **8**, 1908), xxiv; *idem* (ed.), *Extracts from the Episcopal Register of Richard Praty, Bishop of Chichester, 1438–45* (Sussex Record Society, **4**, 1905), 89; C.R.O., Ep.I/1/4–5.
3. C.R.O., Ep.I/1/1, f. 5; Ep.I/10/1, fos. 1–49.
4. Margaret E. Aston, *Thomas Arundel* (1967), 41, 53–68; R. W. Dunning, 'Wells Consistory Court in the Fifteenth Century', *Proceedings of the Somerset Archaeological and Natural History Society*, **106** (1962), 48, 50, 56–8; R. A. Marchant, *The Church under the Law* (1969), 60; C. Morris, 'A Consistory Court in the Middle Ages', *J.E.H.*, **14** (1963), 150–9; also probably true of Lichfield: L.J.R.O., B/C/1/1–2.
5. C.R.O., Ep.I/1/1, fos. 10, 12: sequestrators rather than commissaries were still acting in the late fourteenth century; C.R.O., Ep.I/1/1–6, but see below, p. 207–8.
6. C.R.O., Ep. I/10/1–2, 6–7; Ep. II/9/1.
7. C. Morris, 'The Commissary of the Bishop in the Diocese of Lincoln', *J.E.H.*, **10** (1959), 50–63; R. M. Haines, *The Administration of the Diocese of Worcester in the First Half of the Fourteenth Century* (1965), 116.
8. Morris, 'Commissary of the Bishop', 60–1; Aston, *op. cit.*, 53–68; cf. Haines, *op. cit.*, 40–4, 52–3.
9. C.R.O., Ep. I/1/4, f. 17; Ep. VI/4/1, fos. 5–72.
10. C.R.O., Ep. III/4/1; F. W. Steer and Isabel M. Kirby, *Diocese of Chichester: A Catalogue of the Records of the Bishop, Archdeacons and Former Exempt Jurisdictions* (1966), xxii–xxiii; C.R.O., Ep. IV/2/1–2; Ep. V/3/1.
11. Deedes, *Register of Rede*, II, 439–42; W. D. Peckham (ed.), *The Chartulary of the High Church of Chichester* (Sussex Record Society, **46**, 1946), nos. 274, 905; C.R.O., Ep. VI/1/3, f. 82; Ep. VI/1/4, fos. 199–200.
12. B. L. Woodcock, *Mediaeval Ecclesiastical Courts in the Diocese of Canterbury* (1952), 79.
13. C.R.O., Ep. III/4/1, fos. 97–119; Ep. I/10/1.
14. C.R.O., Ep. I/10/1, fos. 19, 21, 36–7, 40–2, 44–5, 63, 75, 78, 80, 90, 96–7, 102, 113.
15. C.R.O., I/1, f. 57; Ep. I/10/1, fos. 44, 46–7, 67.
16. L.P.L., Register Warham 2, f. 50; Ep. VI/4/1, fos. 8–9, 20–1.
17. B.M., Egerton MS. 2383(2); C.R.O., EP. I/1/5, f. 24; STC I/1 f. 1; cf. Morris, 'Commissary of the Bishop', 62–3.
18. Margaret Bowker (ed.), *An Episcopal Court Book for the Diocese of Lincoln, 1514–20* (Lincoln Record Society, **61**, 1967), 52; A. B. Emden, *A Biographical Register of the University of Oxford, 1501–40*

(1974), 638; F. G. Bennett *et al.* (eds), *Statutes and Constitutions of the Cathedral Church of Chichester* (1904), 60; C.R.O., Ep. I/1/5, fos. 29, 31–2; Ep. I/1/4, fos. 66–8, 70, 73; Cap. I/14/4a, fos. 11–19.

19. Emden, *op. cit.*, ii, 700–1; Bennett *et al.* (eds), *op. cit.*, 54–80; P.R.O., E. 135/8/34; C.R.O., Ep. I/1/5, fos. 43–5; M. E. C. Walcott, *The Early Statutes of the Cathedral Church of Chichester* (1877), 79; W. R. W. Stephens, *Memorials of the South Saxon See and Cathedral Church of Chichester* (1876), 127; Deedes, *Register of Rede*, I, 24; R. B. Manning, *Religion and Society in Elizabethan Sussex* (1969), 72–6; C.R.O., Ep. I/1/3, fos. 5–12; Ep. I/10/2, fos. 22, 41, 47, 69; Ep. I/10/3, fos. 6, 27; Ep. I/10/4, f. 7.

20. C.R.O., Cap. I/14/5, fos. 5–12; W. D. Peckham (ed.), *The Acts of the Dean and Chapter of the Cathedral Church of Chichester, 1472–1544* (Sussex Record Society, **52**, 1952), xxiv; Woodcock, *op. cit.*, 38–50.

21. C.R.O., Ep. I/1/5, fos. 3–142; Ep. I/1/4, fos. 46–111; Ep. I/10/2–7; Ep. I/18/2–3; Cap. I/14/1–3, 5; C. E. Welch, 'Bishop Sherburne of Chichester and His Donations', *Notes and Queries* (1954), 191–3.

22. C.R.O., Ep. I/10/2–3.

23. C.R.O., Ep. I/18/10, fos. 1–12: 1560, archdeacon of Chichester visited in person, but thereafter appointed the bishop's official to act for him – see STC III/4, 34, 41, 46, 50.

24. C.R.O., Cap. I/14/4a, f. 24; Ep. I/1/5, f. 28.

25. C.R.O., Ep. VI/4/1, fos. 8–9, 14–15, 27–8, 73–4.

26. C.R.O., Ep. I/10/2.

27. C.R.O., STC I/2, f. 38; Ep. I/10/5, f. 79: separate appointment as dean's official.

28. C.R.O., Cap. I/1/2, 87; EP. I/1/3, f. 76; Ep. III/4/1.

29. See below, p. 233.

30. C.R.O., Ep. I/10/2–5; STA I/1A, fos. 12, 24, 54, 76, 100; Ep. IV/2/1–2.

31. L.P.L., Register Warham 2, f. 349; Emden, *op. cit.*, ii, 1333; C.R.O., STA I/1A, fos. 49, 98–9, 100–3; *L.P.*, XIII(1), 1273.

32. C.R.O., Ep. I/10/1, fos. 14–33; Ep. I/10/2, fos. 2–128; Ep. I/10/3, fos. 2–35; no pre-1550 court books survive for the archdeaconry of Lewes.

33. C.R.O., Ep. I/10/1, fos. 1–29, 52–98; Ep. I/10/2, fos. 2–131.

34. C.R.O., Ep. I/10/3, 3a, 4.

35. C.R.O., Ep. I/10/1, fos. 33, 65, 69, 83, 102; Ep. I/10/2, fos. 5, 20, 64, 71–2, 93, 107–8, 117, 125; Ep. III/4/1, fos. 82–3; Ep. I/18/2, fos. 6–8.

36. Most faults discovered in 1520 had been repaired by summer 1521; see B.M., Add. MS. 34317, f. 63; C.R.O., Ep. I/10/4, fos. 5, 12, 15.

37. C.R.O., Cap. I/14/4a, f. 14; Ep. I/18/2, f. 25.

38. C.R.O., Ep. I/10/3a, f. 10; Ep. I/18/2, fos. 17, 20, 24, 29–32, 34; Ep. I/1/5; for incontinent priests see e.g. B.M., Add. MS. 34317, f. 52.

39. Examples: C.R.O., Ep. I/10/2, f. 26; Ep. I/10/3, fos. 31–2, 35–6,

38, 40; Ep. I/10/2, fos. 27–8, 31, 37. The vast majority of cases brought by incumbents to recover dues were won in the 1520s; this was not true at other times.

40. C.R.O., Ep. I/1/5, fos. 52–84, 88–9, 135–6; Ep. I/10/2, fos. 32, 32a, 105; Ep. I/10/3, f. 8; Ep. I/10/3a, fos. 7, 9.

41. See p. 228.

42. C.R.O., Ep. I/10/5, fos. 99–100, 104.

43. E.g. C. Hill, 'The Bawdy Courts', in *Society and Puritanism* (1964), 310.

44. C.R.O., Ep. I/10/1, fos. 8–32, 60–103; Ep. I/10/2.

45. C.R.O., Ep. I/10/1, f. 27; Ep. I/10/2, fos. 7, 22, 38, 41, 47, 69; Ep. I/10/3, fos. 6, 27; Ep. I/10/4, fos. 7, 26.

46. C.R.O., Ep. I/10/2, 3.

47. C.R.O., Ep. I/10/2, fos. 3, 8, 23, 34–5, 39, 60, 65, 70, 74, 95, 116, 126, 133.

48. E.g. C.R.O., Ep. I/1/5, fos. 109–14.

49. See p. 207; e.g., C.R.O., Ep. I/10/2, fos. 43–4, 98–100.

50. *S.R.*, 21 Henry VIII, c.5; J. C. K. Cornwall (ed.), *The Lay Subsidy Rolls for the County of Sussex, 1524–5* (Sussex Record Society, **56**, 1956), 13–28.

51. C.R.O., Ep. VI/1/4, fos. 6–7; M. Kelly, 'Canterbury Jurisdiction and Influence During the Episcopate of William Warham, 1503–32' (Ph.D. thesis, University of Cambridge, 1963), 55–93.

52. C.R.O., Cap. I/14/4a, fos. 14, 24; B.M., Add. MS. 34317, fos. 19, 24.

53. Kelly, *op. cit.*, 178–89; J. J. Scarisbrick, 'The Conservative Episcopate in England 1529–35' (Ph.D. thesis, University of Cambridge, 1956), 117–21; *idem*, 'The Pardon of the Clergy', *H.J.*, **12** (1956), 25–7; B.M., Add. MS. 34317, f. 33.

54. C.R.O., Ep. I/1/5, fos. 43–51, 136; Ep. I/1/4, fos. 75–9; Ep. I/10/5, fos. 9, 80–90.

55. B.M., Add. MS. 34317, fos. 28, 49; C.R.O., Ep. I/10/2, fos. 26, 43–4, 98–100; Cap. I/14/4a, f. 10.

56. C.R.O., Ep. I/10/3, f. 21; Cap. I/14/4a, f. 2.

57. M. Bowker, 'Some Archdeacons' Court Books and the "Commons" Supplication against the Ordinaries of 1532', in D. A. Bullough and R. L. Storey (eds), *The Study of Mediaeval Records: Essays in Honour of Kathleen Major* (1971), 282–316.

58. See S. E. Lehmberg, *The Reformation Parliament 1529–36* (1970), 81–104, 127–8; G. R. Elton, *Reform and Renewal* (1973), 130–5; for decline in court's activity see below, p. 231. probably the reform was being discussed in the summer and autumn of 1535: F. D. Logan, 'The Henrician Canons', *B.I.H.R.* **47** (1974), 99–103.

59. P.R.O., SP. 1/93, fos. 67, 71; SP. 1/79, f. 165a; SP. 1/83, p. 243; SP. 1/84, p. 119.

60. *L.P.*, IX, nos. 444, 509; B.M., Add. MS. 48022, f. 83; P.R.O., SP. 1/97, p. 93.

61. C.R.O., Ep. I/10/5, fos. 60, 62–3, 66–70, 72–3, 75; P.R.O., PROB 11/26, f. 77.
62. Lehmberg, *op. cit.*, 119, 128.
63. C.R.O., Ep. I/10/3, fos. 2–35; Ep. I/10/5, fos. 25–48, 84, 69–79, 91–105.
64. C.R.O., Ep. I/10/2; Ep. I/10/5, fos. 12–37, 84, 108–41; Ep. I/10/6, fos. 1–34; Ep. I/10/7, fos. 1–27; Ep. I/10/10, fos. 5–48.
65. *S.R.* 27, Henry VIII, c.20.
66. C.R.O., Ep. I/10/10, fos. 5–47: between October 1556 and October 1557, 317 appearances sought to deal with 122 office cases.
67. C.R.O., Ep. I/10/2, fos. 12, 34, 47, 60–1, 81, 89, 103; Ep. I/10/3, fos. 22, 25, 38; Ep. I/10/6, f. 24.
68. Manning, *op. cit.*, 27–31.
69. C.R.O., Ep. I/10/2; Ep. I/10/5, fos. 12–37, 108–41; Ep. I/10/6, fos. 1–34; Ep. I/10/7, fos. 1–27; Ep. I/10/10, fos. 5–48.
70. J. E. Ray (ed.), *Sussex Chantry Records* (Sussex Record Society, **36**, 1931), 50, 59; Le Neve, *op. cit.*, 71; Peckham, *Acts of the Dean and Chapter*, no. 449; C.R.O., Ep. I/1/6, fos. 65–8, 89–96; Cap. I/23/2, fos. 52–99; Cap. I/4/8/1.
71. C.R.O., STC I/8, f. 104; STC III/A, f. 1.
72. As the visitation returns show: C.R.O., Ep. I/18/4–8.
73. C.R.O., Ep. III/4/2, f. 2; STC I/8, fos. 109–10.
74. C.R.O., Ep. III/4/2, fos. 3–12.
75. C.R.O., Ep. I/10/10, fos. 29, 31, 34–5, 41, 45, 47–9; cf. F. D. Price, 'An Elizabethan Church Official: Thomas Powell, Chancellor of the Gloucester Diocese', *C.Q.R.*, **128** (1939), 94–112; F. D. Price, 'The Abuses of Excommunication and the Decline of Ecclesiastical Discipline under Queen Elizabeth', *E.H.R.*, **57** (1942), 106–15.
76. C.R.O., Ep. I/1/6; Ep. I/18/8–9; B.M., Harleian MS. 421, fos. 105–10; 425, fos. 102–5.
77. C.R.O., Ep. I/10/2, fos. 6–8; STC III/A, fos. 1–4; Ep. I/10/10, fos. 1–49.
78. C.R.O., STC III/A; Ep. I/18/11.
79. Manning, *op. cit.*, 29–30, 43, 131–3, 149.
80. See *ibid.*, 22; C.R.O., Ep. II/9/1, fos. 113–24; Ep. I/18/9, f. 47; Ep. I/1/7, f. 18; Ep. I/18/11, fos. 22–37, 54–66.
81. P. S. Allen and Helen M. Allen (eds), *The Letters of Richard Fox, 1486–1527* (1929), 146–51.
82. Woodcock, *op. cit.*, 84, 100; *V.C.H. Staffs.*, III (1970), 37; see p. 232 below.
83. P. Heath, 'Mediaeval Archdeaconry and Tudor Bishopric of Chester', *J.E.H.*, xx (1969), 243–52; C.C.R.O., EDC 1/3, fos. 18–27: I am grateful to Dr C. J. Haigh for drawing my attention to this phenomenon; Bowker, 'Some Archdeacons' Court Books', 286–316.
84. Bowker, *Episcopal Court Book, passim*; C. A. McLaren, 'An Early Sixteenth Century Act Book of the Diocese of London', *J.S.A.*,

**3** (7) (1968), 337–8; P. Heath (ed.), *Bishop Geoffrey Blythe's Visitations, c.1515–25* (Staffordshire Record Society, 1973), lviii–lix, xi–xiv; D. Knowles, *The Religious Orders in England*, III (1959), 70–3; A. Jessop (ed.), *Visitations of the Diocese of Norwich, 1492–1532* (Camden Society, N.S. XLIII, 1888), 65–319.

85. A. F. Pollard, *Wolsey* (1929), 193–202; Scarisbrick, thesis, 114–21; Allen and Allen (eds), *op. cit.*, 150–1; Kelly, *op. cit.*, 178.

86. J. Ridley, *Thomas Cranmer* (1962), 79–81.

87. C. J. Haigh, 'A Mid Tudor Ecclesiastical Official', *Transactions of the Historic Society of Lancashire and Cheshire, 122* (1970), 6, 17–18.

88. *V.C.H. Staffs.*, III, 47–9.

89. R. Peters, 'The Administration of the Archdeaconry of St. Albans, 1580–1625', *J.E.H.*, **13** (1962), 61–75; H. G. Owen, 'The Episcopal Visitation: Its Limits and Limitations in Elizabethan London', *J.E.H.*, **11** (1960), 179–85; Marchant, *op. cit.*, 204–35.

## 10. The decline of ecclesiastical jurisdiction under the Tudors

1. I have drawn heavily on B. L. Woodcock, *Medieval Ecclesiastical Courts in the Diocese of Canterbury* (1952), R. A. Marchant, *The Church under the Law* (1969), and R. Houlbrooke, 'Church Courts and the People in the Diocese of Norwich, 1519–70' (D.Phil. thesis, University of Oxford, 1970). All references to these dioceses come from the said works unless otherwise stated.

2. N. Adams, 'The Writ of Prohibition to Court Christian', *Minnesota Law Review*, *20* (1935–6); G. B. Flahiff, 'The Writ of Prohibition to Court Christian in the Thirteenth Century', *Medieval Studies*, **6** (1944).

3. E. Gibson, *Codex Iuris Ecclesiastici Anglicani*, II (1761), 1019.

4. D. Wilkins (ed.), *Concilia Magnae Britanniae et Hiberniae*, III (1737), 583; A. F. Pollard, *Wolsey* (1929), 167, 248.

5. A. F. Pollard, *Wolsey* (1929), 167, 248.

6. R. L. Storey, *Diocesan Administration in Fifteenth Century England* (St Anthony's Hall Paper, **16**, 2nd edn, 1972), 30; P.R.O., C. 1/142/9.

7. M. J. Kelly, 'Canterbury Jurisdiction and Influence during the Episcopate of William Warham, 1503–32' (Ph.D. thesis, University of Cambridge, 1963), 98–110.

8. P.R.O., S.C. 1/44, f. 83. I am grateful to Professor Storey for giving me a copy of this letter.

9. Simon Fish, *A Supplicacyon of the Beggars*, ed. F. J. Furnivall (Early English Texts Society, Extra Series, XIII, 1871), 8.

10. J. C. Cooper, 'Henry VII's Last Years Reconsidered', *H.J.*, **2** (1959), 110, 125.

11. W. A. Holdsworth, *History of English Law*, IV (1924), 234–8.

12. J. A. F. Thomson, *The Later Lollards, 1414–1520* (1965), 49, 135–7, 198–9, 237–8.

13. S. F. C. Milsom, 'Richard Hunne's *Praemunire*', *E.H.R.*, **76** (1961), 80–2; Thomson, *op. cit.*, 162–71; Pollard, *op. cit.*, 26–58.

14. J. J. Scarisbrick, 'The Pardon of the Clergy, 1531', *C.H.J.*, **12** (1956); S. E. Lehmberg, *The Reformation Parliament, 1529–36* (1970), 108, 118–20, 126–8; *S.R.*, 25 Henry VIII, c.19.

15. J. J. Scarisbrick, *Henry VIII* (1968), 330; E. Coke, *The Third Part of the Institutes of the Laws of England* (3rd edn, 1669), 122; J. A. Muller (ed.), *Letters of Stephen Gardiner* (1933), 369–73. For a request of the lower house of Convocation that *praemunire* be more closely defined, see E. Cardwell (ed.), *Synodalia*, II (1842), 436.

16. E. Gibson, *Codex Iuris*, II, 1019–20; C. St German, *Two Dialogues in English Between a Doctor of Divinity and a Student in the Laws of England* (1673 edn), 218.

17. M. Bowker, 'The Commons Supplication against the Ordinaries in the light of some Archidiaconal *Acta*' *T.R.H.S.*, 5 Ser., **21** (1971).

18. B.M., Cotton MS., Cleopatra F., II, fos. 250–4.

19. *L.P.*, IX, 119.

20. *Ibid.*, 1071; G. R. Elton, *Reform and Renewal* (1973), 134–5.

21. T. F. T. Plucknett, *A Concise History of the Common Law* (5th edn, 1956), 440–1.

22. *S.R.*, 37 Henry VIII, c.12.

23. F. D. Logan, 'The Henrician Canons', *B.I.H.R.*, **47** (1974).

24. S. E. Lehmberg, 'Supremacy and Vicegerency: A Re-examination', *E.H.R.*, **81** (1966); G. R. Elton, *Policy and Police* (1972), 247–8; C. J. Kitching, 'The Probate Jurisdiction of Thomas Cromwell as Vicegerent', *B.I.H.R.*, **46** (1973).

25. F. D. Price, 'The Abuses of Excommunication and the Decline of Ecclesiastical Discipline under Queen Elizabeth', *E.H.R.*, **57** (1942); C. Hill, *Society and Puritanism in Pre-Revolutionary England* (1964), 354–81.

26. See *S.R.*, 5 Elizabeth I, c.23, for attempt to improve procedure; see also F. D. Logan, *Excommunication and the Secular Arm in Medieval England* (Toronto, 1968), 66.

27. J. Strype, *The Life and Acts of . . . John Whitgift*, III (1822), 129–30.

28. K. V. Thomas, *Religion and the Decline of Magic* (1971), 312; Hampshire Record Office, C.B. 2, fos. 14v, 16v, 70v, 127; *S.R.*, 18 Elizabeth I, c.3.

29. *S.R.*, 27 Henry VIII, c.20; E. Coke, *The Second Part of the Institutes of the Laws of England* (1669), 648.

30. C. Hill, *Economic Problems of the Church* (1956), 91–9.

31. For an example in 1517 see Hampshire Record Office, Visitation Book 1, f. 14.

32. C.U.L., Ee.2.34, f. 189; Bodleian, Rawlinson MS. C 737, fos. 105v–6.

33. See p. 207; Bowker, *op. cit.*, 66–7.

34. W. Lyndwood, *Provinciale seu Constitutiones Angliae* (1679), 346–7.

35. W. H. Mildon, 'Puritanism in Hampshire and the Isle of Wight'

(Ph.D. thesis, University of London, 1934), 21; Thomas, *op. cit.*, 190–1; S. D'Ewes (ed.), *The Journals of all the Parliaments during the reign of Queen Elizabeth* (1682), 192–3.

36. C.U.L., Ee.2.34, f. 189.
37. P.R.O., E.135/25/31, f. 7.
38. B. P. Levack, *The Civil Lawyers in England*, 1603–41 (1973), 51.
39. T. F. Barton (ed.), *The Registrum Vagum of Anthony Harison*, I (Norfolk Record Society, **22**, 1963), 47.
40. P. Collinson, *The Elizabethan Puritan Movement* (1967), 181–3.
41. Storey, *op. cit.*, 18.
42. F. D. Price, 'Gloucester Diocese under Bishop Hooper', *Transactions of Bristol and Gloucester Archaeological Society*, **60** (1938), 71–83.
43. P.R.O., E. 135/25/31, f. 7.
44. See R. G. Usher, *The Rise and Fall of the High Commission* (1913), 99–100.
45. H. Robinson (ed.), *The Zurich Letters* (Parker Society, **51**, 1847), 358–62; 127–36; W. H. Frere and C. E. Douglas (eds), *An Admonition to the Parliament in Puritan Manifestoes* (1954), 15–18, 30–4; D'Ewes, *op. cit.*, 357–60; Collinson, *op. cit.*, 39–41.
46. Cardwell, *Synodalia*, I, 117–22, 130–1, 142–5, 152–9, 301–2, 305, 307–27.
47. Coke, *Second Part of the Institutes*, 644–5.
48. B. Levack, *op. cit.*, 76
49. N. Adams, 'The Judicial Conflict over Tithes', *E.H.R.*, **52** (1937).
50. St German, *op. cit.*, 362–6; R. G. Usher, *The Reconstruction of the English Church* (1910), 70; *S.R.*, 32 Henry VIII, c.7; Coke, *Second Part of the Institutes*, 648.
51. *S.R.*, 31 Henry VIII, c.14; 32 Henry VIII, c.7; 2 & 3 Edward VI, c.13; Coke, *Second Part of the Institutes*, 610–11.
52. *Ibid.*, 606, 611–12, 650–1; Hill, *Economic Problems*, 127, n.1.
53. *S.R.*, 32 Henry VIII, c.1.
54. W. Rastell, *A collection of entrees, of declaracions, barres, replicacions, reioinders, issues, verdits, etc.* (1596), 468. C. Viner, *A General Abridgement of Law and Equity*, XVII (1742–53), 562–3, esp. no. 32.
55. Coke, *Second Part of the Institutes*, 608, 613–14, 616.
56. W. J. Jones, *The Elizabethan Court of Chancery* (1967) 391.
57. Plucknett, *op. cit.*, 743.
58. R. G. Usher, *Rise and Fall of the High Commission*, 207–10; Levack, *op. cit.*, 79.
59. Usher, *Rise and Fall of the High Commission*, 321–2; Hill, *Economic Problems*, 285, 323–4, 330, 344; *Society and Puritanism*, 333–7.

# Index

Abbot, George, archbishop of Canterbury, 38–9, 143
Administrations, 201, 203, 211–13, 215
Admiralty, Court of, 201
Advocates, 201, 205, 210, 214, 248
Aldrich, Robert, bishop of Carlisle, 109
Alen, John, commissary of P.C.C., 196
Alley, William, bishop of Exeter, 116
Alvey, Yeldard, 46
Amberley, vicar of, 224
Amounderness deanery, 159–60
Andrewes, Lancelot, bishop of Winchester, 34, 38, 42, 45, 174
Anti-clericalism, 34, 40, 75, 229, 242–3
Apparitors, 203, 205–6, 221, 252–253
Aragon, Katharine of, 167
Archbold, registrar of Coventry and Lichfield, 90
Arches, the Court of, 18, 197, 201, 203–5
    Dean of, 200
Argall, Lawrence, registrar of P.C.C., 203–4, 209–11
Argall, Richard, registrar of P.C.C., 203
Argall, Thomas, registrar of P.C.C., 202, 205
Arminianism, 15, 28, 38–41, 45–6, 50, 52–3, 135, 140, 143, 185–186
    definition of, 54
Arminius, Jacobus, 54

Armitage, Staffs., 91
Atwater, William, bishop of Lincoln, 20, 23, 220, 236
Audience, Archbishop's Court of, 201, 203
Audience, episcopal courts of, 19, 24, 192
Augmentations, Court of, 111
Aycliffe, Durham, 140
Aylmer, John, bishop of London, 36, 117
Aysgarth, Yorks., 161

Backford rectory, Cheshire, 153
Bacon, Sir Nicholas, Lord Keeper, 172
Baddiley, Richard, secretary to Bishop Morton, 89
Bainbridge, Christopher, archbishop of York, 194
Baker, Edward, receiver of dean and chapter of Peterborough, 170, 182
Baker, Walter, 182
Baldock, Robert, 183
Bancroft, Richard, archbishop of Canterbury, 34, 36–8, 40, 45, 181
Bangor, bishops of, 120
Bangor deanery, 158–9
Bangor rectory, 156–7
Banwell, abbot of, 100
Barby rectory, Northants., 182
Barlow, Barnabus, 46
Barnes, Richard, bishop of Durham, 132–3, 135, 142, 144
Basire, Isaac, chaplain to Bishop Morton, 48

# Index

Bath and Wells, bishops of, 148, 165

Bath and Wells diocese, 108, 155, 171, 220

Battle Abbey, Sussex, 217

Baxter, Richard, 73

Bayley, William, archdeacon of Northants., 174

Beacon, John, chancellor of Coventry and Lichfield, 65

Bell, Richard, prior of Finchale, 131, 134, 138

Belley, Dr, chancellor of Lincoln, 83

Bellot, Hugh, bishop of Chester, 157

Bennet, Sir John, 191

Bentham, Thomas, bishop of Coventry and Lichfield, 26, 84, 237, 249

Best, John, bishop of Carlisle, 141

Bewit, Gabriel, vicar of Harrington, 81

Bible, the Great, 247

Bidston rectory, Cheshire, 151, 161

Bingnet, John, 82

Binsley, William, archdeacon of Northants., 177

Bird, John, bishop of Chester, 26, 147–54, 158, 165–6;
leases by, 149–51, 153–4;
debts, 154

Bishop Auckland, Durham, 133

Bishops, 15–16, 20, 24–6, 53, 193, 229–30, 241, 244, 247, 251–2, 256
as debtors to the crown, 108–9, 111, 115–17, 119, 154, 156
charitable works, 51
duties and role of, 33–4, 39, 43, 142, 215
*iure divino* status, 37–9, 54
and probate, 193–5, 207–8
and recruitment of the clergy, 57–63, 65–7, 74
as tax-collectors, 99–122 *passim*;

accountable for arrears, 100–101, 105–6, 109–11, 114
wealth, income, and economic problems, 35, 145–6, 168–9

Bishops' registers, 18, 78–9

Bishops' secretaries, 27, 89–90, 93, 250

Bishopthorpe, Yorks., 48

Blackburn deanery, 160

Blakiston, Marmaduke, prebendary of Durham, 143

Blakiston family, 136

Bodewell, Richard, dean of Court of Arches, 241

Bolton, William, proctor of Chichester consistory, 221

Bolton rectory, Lancs., 157

Bonner, Edmund, bishop of London, 149

*Book of Sports*, 44

Booth, Charles, bishop of Hereford, 236

Borough, Henry, deputy collector of Exeter, 116, 121

Bosham, Sussex, 215

Bowden rectory, 150, 153

Bowker, Margaret, 243

Brackenbury, Stephen, 140

Bradbridge, William, bishop of Exeter, 116, 121

Bradley rectory, Cheshire, 154

Brancepeth, Durham, 137

Brantingham, Yorks., 140

Breach of faith causes, 240–1

Brent, Sir Nathaniel, commissary of Canterbury, 47

Bridgeman, Dove, 160

Bridgeman, John, bishop of Chester, 150, 154, 157–60, 164–6
financial reforms, 160–4
leases and fines, 161–3

Brigham rectory, Yorks., 161

Brisley, Richard, chancellor of Chichester, 233–5

Bristol diocese, 34
collector of taxes in, 117

Brockholes rectory, Lancs., 170

288

# Index

Chadderton, William, bishop of
Chester and of Lincoln, 84, 150,
156–7, 159
Chamber, royal, 100–1
Chambers, John, bishop of Peter-
borough, 174–5
Chancellor, diocesan, 26, 82, 149,
158, 219–20, 248–9, 252
Chancery, Court of, 256
Charles I, 34, 39, 41, 50, 52, 162,
256–7
Cheney, Richard, bishop of
Gloucester, 116–17
Cheshire, 149–50
Chester, 146, 150
Chester, archdeacons of, 147, 154–
155, 159–60, 218–19
archdeaconry, 145, 147–8, 151,
159–60, 236–7
Chester, bishops of, 111, 146–66
*passim*, 169, authority, 150,
palace, 146, 152
Chester bishopric, endowment,
146–7, 152, 161, 163, 168,
income, 145–6, 152–3, 155, 160–
161, 163–6
Chester deanery, 158–9
Chester diocese, 22, 25, 49, 61, 67,
145–66 *passim*, 186, 236;
administration, 148, 158–60;
area and jurisdiction, 146–7;
chancellor, 149, 151, 154, 163–4
Chester nunnery, 151
Chester rural deans, 147–8, 158–9,
166, leases by, 158–9, organization, 159–60
Chichester, 215–18, 222, 233–4
All Saints in the Pallant, 217,
222
Cathedral Close, 217
Chichester, archdeacon of, 217–19
archdeaconry, 216–17, 219, 223,
233; commissary court, 216,
218–19, 221, 223, 225–6, 231–
234
Chichester, bishops of, 117, 168,
215–17, 233

Chichester Cathedral, 216, 220,
229
dean of, 217, 227, peculiar
court, 217–18, 222, 233
Chichester diocese, 18, 21, 24, 104,
171, 174, 186, 215–37 *passim*,
consistory court, 14, 216, 218,
222–6, 230–5, 237, jurisdiction,
215–18, 227
Childwall rectory, Lancs., 155, 157
Chipping, vicar of, 164
Chippingdale, John, 83
Church of England, wealth of, 34–
35, 37
economic problems, 25–6, 43,
57, 97–122 *passim*, 145–66
*passim*, 168–71
Church courts, 19–23, 78, 82–3,
174–6, 191–2, 215–16, 218,
229, 236–7, 243–8, 250–1,
253–7
fees, 196, 208–10, 213–14, 221,
234
jurisdiction, 18, 239–57 *passim*;
instance causes, 218, 223, 225–
226, 230–1, 237, 247–8; office
causes, 223–6, 229–32, 235,
237, 247, 251; proposed
limitation, 243
Puritan critique of, 251–2
reform of, 37, 251–2
Churches, maintenance of, 49,
223, 247
Civil lawyers, 47, 199–206, 241,
248–50
Clark, A., 71
Clarke, Gabriel, archdeacon of
Durham, 44–5
Clarke, Samuel, vicar of St Peter's,
Northants., 186
*Classes*, 175–6, 180, 182, 185
Clavering, Robert, bishop of
Peterborough, 175
Clennock, Maurice, commissary of
P.C.C., 200, 202
Clergy, education of, 20, 62–4, 69–
71, educational standards of,

Index

Jewel, John, bishop of Salisbury, 34
Jobson, Walter, 140
Jones, W. J., 256
Judges, ecclesiastical, 199–201, 227, 234, 241, 245–6, 248–9, 255
Judges, temporal, 240, 245, 250, 255–7
Juxon, William, bishop of London, 45, 51

Kautz, Arthur, 45
Kelly, Michael, 241
Kendal deanery, 148, 158
Kennall, John, deputy commissary of P.C.C., 198, 201
Kennedy, W. M., 14
Kent, 198
Kettering, Northants., 169, 176, 182
Ketton, Rutland, 87
Kidderminster, Richard, abbot of Winchcomb, 242
King's Bench, Court of, 129, 135, 240–2, 254, 256
King's Bromley, Staffs., 91
Kirkby chapel, tithes of, 162
Kirkby Ravensworth rectory, Yorks., 162, 164
Kitchin, William, 185
Kitching, Christopher, 17, 22, 79–80, 226
Knight, William, archdeacon of Chester, 147–8, 151
Knightley, Sir Richard, 172, 181, 184
Knowles, David, 127, 129–30, 138

Lambe, John, chancellor of Peterborough, 47, 176, 185–6
Lambeth Palace, 196
Lambeth Articles, 1595, 37
Lamont, William, 37
Lamplugh, Cumbs., 149
Lancashire, 136, 150, 154, 157
Lancaster, Duchy of, 161
Lance money, 119

Lander, Stephen, 20, 24
Laney, Benjamin, bishop of Ely, 46
Larke, Thomas, dean of Chichester, 220
Lathwett, Mr, vicar of Anderby, 88
Latimer, William, master of St Laurence Poultney, 100
Latimer, William, dean of Peterborough, 179
Laud, William, archbishop of Canterbury, 34, 39, 41, 45, 50, 63, 163–4, 174
Laudian movement, the, 29, 41–2, 51, 53, 185
Law, John, actuary of P.C.C., 205
Layburne, Sir James, 149
Layburne, Robert, commissary of Richmond, 149
Layton, Richard, 230
Leases, capitular, 139, 170, 175
Leases, episcopal, 37, 48, 107, 150–151, 161–3, 170, 175, fines taken on, 153, 161–3
Lee, Edward, archbishop of York, 104–5
Leicester archdeaconry, 83
commissary court, 83
Leigh, Thomas, auditor of First Fruits, 109
Leighton, Alexander, 41
Levack, Brian, 47
Lever, Ralph, prebendary of Durham, 132
Lever, Thomas, archdeacon of Coventry, 65, 137
plan for the reformation of the ministry, 65–6
Lewes, archdeacons of, 219, 227
archdeaconry, 216–17, 219, 227, commissary court, 216, 235
Lewin, William, commissary of P.C.C., 205
Leyland deanery, 160
Lichfield Cathedral, 141, 157, 219
Lichfield corporation, 90
Lincoln, archdeacon of, 216

295

Index

Rogers, Ezekial, 44
Rogers, John, rector of Chacombe, 183
Rogers, Richard, 38
Rogers, Simon, 182
Rokeby, John, chancellor of York, 26
Rothwell, Northants., 176
Russell family, 135, 139
Rustat, Robert, 81
Rutland, 167

Sacriston Hugh, Durham, 140
St Asaph, bishop of, 117
St Bee's, Cumbs., 155, 161
St David's, bishop of, 111
St German, Christopher, 243
St Ives, Hunts., 81
Salisbury Cathedral, 126, 141
Salisbury diocese, 35, 108
Sallow, prebend of, 91
Sampson, Richard, bishop of Chichester, 229, 233
Sampson, Thomas, prebendary of Durham, 137
Sandys, Edmund, archbishop of York, 63, 121, 193
Savage family, 149
Savile, Christian, 88
Scalby, John de, registrar of Lincoln, 77
Scambler, Edmund, bishop of Peterborough, 168–72, 176–8, 180, 186, exploitation of the see, 169–70, 175
Scambler, Edward, 175
Scarisbrick, J. J., 128
Schools, ecclesiastical control over, 72
   foundation of, 70–3
Scott, Cuthbert, bishop of Chester, 155
Scott, Gregory, prebendary of Carlisle, 140
Scottish Court, 134
Seath, Henry, deputy collector of Canterbury, 114

Sede vacante jurisdiction, 129
Selsey peninsula, Sussex, 218
Sequestration, for non-residence, 224
   for taxation arrears, 100, 119, 154
Seymour, Edward, duke of Somerset, 108–9, 127, 150
Sharpe, Henry, 178
Shawe, Alexander, vicar of Pagham, 222
Sheils, William, 24
Sheppard, Nicholas, archdeacon of Northants., 173, 186
Sherburne, Robert, bishop of Chichester, 20, 23–4, 102, 217–234, 236–7, and reform of the courts, 219–22, 227–8
Sherburne family, 163
Shoreham, peculiar court, 149
Shotwick rectory, Cheshire, 157
Shrewsbury School, 63, 72
Shropshire, 71
Simony, 182
Skinner, Ralph, dean of Durham, 134
Skynner, Richard, 60
Slingsby, Sir Henry, 42
Smart, Peter, prebendary of Durham, 132, 135, 143
Smith, Francis, 92
Smith, Gilbert, archdeacon of Northants., 173
Smith, Richard, official of archdeacon of Chester, 148
Smith, William, bishop of Lincoln, 20
Smith, William, vicar of All Saint's, Northants., 178–9, 182
Snell, George, archdeacon of Chester, 159–60
Somerby, Lincs., 86
Southam, Warwicks., 177
South Malling deanery, 217
Southwell, Notts., 48
Sowthorpe at Barnack, Northants., 168–9

# Index

Thirty-Nine Articles, the, 35–6
Thompson, A. H., 130, 143
Thornton College, 127
Thornton rectory, Lancs., 157
Thorpe, Lincs., 81
Thrapston, Northants., 176
Tithes, 224, 243–6, 254, increase in disputes, 245–6, inflation and, 246, prohibitions and, 254–5
Todd, William, prebendary of Durham, 130, 136
Toprat, Robert, 228
Topsell, Edward, 42
Tregonwell, John, advocate of P.C.C., 205
Tunstall, Cuthbert, bishop of Durham, 102, 112, 127–9, 133

United Provinces, the, 54
Uppingham, Rutland, 176
Upton, Northants., 179
Usher, Ronald, 14
Uthred of Boldon, 136

*Valor Ecclesiasticus*, 98, 104–5, 115, 119
Vaughan, Richard, bishop of Chester, 145, 156, 159, 163
Vescy, Henry, vicar of Thorp St Peter, 88
Vestiarian Controversy, 35
Villiers, George, duke of Buckingham, 38, 52
Visitation, 215, 221, 223, 234–5
Visitation, episcopal, of cathedrals, 132, of Peterborough, 180–1, of York, 49
metropolitical, 129, 229, 236
royal, 197–8, 230
Visitation articles, 251
Voysey, John, bishop of Exeter, 108–9, 236

Wake, Arthur, master of St John's Hospital, Notts., 178
Wales, 206

Walker, Walter, deputy registrar of Leicester, 83
Walker, William, deputy registrar of P.C.C., 202
Walsingham, Thomas, secretary of state, 156
Walton, Northants., 168
Walton, Brian, bishop of Chester, 163
War with France, 1542–6, 106
War with Spain, 1588ff., 113
Warham, William, archbishop of Canterbury, 101–2, 193–5, 204, 206, 212, 241
Warrington deanery, 160
Warwickshire, 71
Watson, Thomas, bishop of Lincoln, 134
Watts, Samuel, vicar of Great Dalby, 88
Waverton rectory, Cheshire, 157
Weaverham rectory, Cheshire, 150, 153
Weber, Max, 78, 93
Weemes, John, prebendary of Durham, 136
Wellingborough, Northants., 176
Wells, Humphrey, 91
Welsh dioceses, 17
Wentworth, Thomas, earl of Strafford, 133
Werrington, Northants., 168
Wessington, John, prior of Durham, 134, 136–7
West, Nicholas, bishop of Ely, 20, 102, 236
Westminster Abbey, deanery of, 40, 42, 48
Dean's Book of, 48
Westminster School, 48, 51
Weston, James, registrar of Coventry and Lichfield, 84, 90–91
Weston, James junior, 91
Weston, Robert, chancellor of Lichfield, 91
Weston, Simon, 91